T0330277

Merger and Acquisition Strategies

NEW PERSPECTIVES ON THE MODERN CORPORATION

Series Editor: Jonathan Michie, *Director, Department for Continuing Education and President, Kellogg College, University of Oxford, UK*

The modern corporation has far reaching influence on our lives in an increasingly globalised economy. This series will provide an invaluable forum for the publication of high quality works of scholarship covering the areas of:

- corporate governance and corporate responsibility, including environmental sustainability;
- human resource management and other management practices, and the relationship of these to organisational outcomes and corporate performance;
- industrial economics, organisational behaviour, innovation and competitiveness;
- outsourcing, offshoring, joint ventures and strategic alliances;
- different ownership forms, including social enterprise and employee ownership;
- intellectual property and the learning economy, including knowledge; and
- transfer and information exchange.

Titles in the series include:

Corporate Strategy and Firm Growth
Creating Value for Shareholders
Angelo Dringoli

The Internationalisation of Business R&D
Edited by Bernhard Dachs, Robert Stehrer and Georg Zahradnik

Corporate Governance, The Firm and Investor Capitalism
Legal-Political and Economic Views
Alexander Styhre

Merger and Acquisition Strategies
How to Create Value
Angelo Dringoli

Merger and Acquisition Strategies

How to Create Value

Angelo Dringoli

School of Economics and Management, University of Siena, Italy

NEW PERSPECTIVES ON THE MODERN CORPORATION

 Edward Elgar
PUBLISHING

Cheltenham, UK • Northampton, MA, USA

Published by
Edward Elgar Publishing Limited
The Lypiatts
15 Lansdown Road
Cheltenham
Glos GL50 2JA
UK

Edward Elgar Publishing, Inc.
William Pratt House
9 Dewey Court
Northampton
Massachusetts 01060
USA

A catalogue record for this book
is available from the British Library

Library of Congress Control Number: 2016942158

This book is available electronically in the **Elgar**online
Economics subject collection
DOI 10.4337/9781786430687

MIX
Paper from
responsible sources
FSC
www.fsc.org   FSC® C013056

ISBN 978 1 78643 067 0 (cased)
ISBN 978 1 78643 068 7 (eBook)

Printed and bound in Great Britain by TJ International Ltd, Padstow

Contents

Abbreviations

a	Expenses to increase resources
A	Depreciation and amortization
b	Rate at which the marginal labour hours decline as the cumulative number of units produced increases
βi	Beta of firm i
β_L	Beta of a levered firm
$\beta_L(C)$	Beta current of a levered firm
$B_L(P)$	Beta of a firm corresponding to a planned level of debt
β_U	Beta of an unlevered firm
C	Current operating costs
CFO	Cash flow from operations
cs	Credit spread
Cu	Unit cost of product
$D(0)$	Value of debt at initial date 0
$E(0)$	Value of equity at initial date 0
$EBIT$	Earnings before interest and taxes
$EBITDA$	Earnings before interest, taxes and depreciation
EBT	Taxable income
ER	Exchange ratio between shares of firm A and shares of firm T (number of shares of A for each share of T)
$FCFO(t)$	Free cash flow from operations in period t
g	Growth rate of cash flows
if	Return on free risk investment
INT	Interest expenses
kd	Cost of debt
ke	Cost of equity
m	Unit margin
N_A	Number of shares of firm A
NI	Net income
N_T	Number of shares of firm T
p	Product price in period t
P_T	Price of target firm T
Q	Quantity of product produced or sold

R	Revenues
R_j	Value of resource j
r_m	Return on the investment in a market share portfolio
S	Period up to the structural change (years)
t	Period of time (year)
T	Process or product lifetime (years)
$TC(Q)$	Total cost of producing quantities Q
TV	Terminal value of the firm
$V(0)$	Firm value at initial date 0
V_A	Value of acquiring firm A
V_{acq}	Value of acquisition
V_{AT}	Value of combined firm AT
V_{CC}	Value created or destroyed by change in WACC
V_M	Value created by the merger
V_{SA}	Value created for the shareholders of firm A
V_{SY}	Value of synergies
V_T	Value of target firm T
w_A	Value of a share of firm A
$WACC$	Weighted average cost of capital
w_{AT}	Value of a share of the combined firm AT
WC	Working capital (difference between current assets and current liabilities)
w_T	Value of a share of firm T
γ	Rate of decay in resource value
ΔI	Capital expenditures
ΔWC	Change in working capital
μ	Rate of accumulation in resource value
ρ	Weighted average cost of capital ($WACC$)
τ	Corporate tax rate

Preface

In the last decades, the volume of merger and acquisition activity has increased across the world, affecting virtually all industries, regardless of size and type of firm involved. Mergers and acquisitions occur in waves and represent a way to grow quickly, seizing the opportunities arising in certain industries. It also represents a way to easily overcome the barriers to entry, to profit from fiscal advantages, and to achieve a positive effect on the firm's image.

Through mergers and acquisitions, firms can seize the opportunities to grow and create new economic value, but, as a wide empirical evidence proves, they can also destroy value for shareholders.

This highlights that the decision to carry out an M&A is certainly a risky decision, because of the number of variables influencing the final performance, but it is also a decision frequently based on wrong objectives and an incorrect evaluation process. This firm belief led us to study in depth how this decision should be taken to increase shareholder value. For this to happen it is necessary that the value of the combined firms is greater than the sum of the values of the bidding and target firms, operating independently. But, for this to happen, it is also necessary for the estimated synergies to be well predicted, evaluated and carried out, appropriately managing the integration of companies.

With this as our starting point, the study aims at offering solutions for reducing the currently high percentage of M&A failures. To contribute to this result it is believed that the following is necessary:

- to acknowledge the creation of value for shareholders of the acquiring firm as the fundamental objective of an M&A;
- to define analytical models suitable for properly evaluating M&A;
- to design appropriate organizational structure and processes to implement M&As.

The approach of the book is normative; it uses a theoretical analysis to show what managers should do to increase shareholder value through M&A strategies and what the conditions are for favouring one or the other type of M&A. The perspective of the analysis is that of a company which considers the opportunity of acquiring another company for integrating its activities in a merger.

It is important also to specify that very often M&As are also motivated by the *value of control*, that is the value that occurs post deal when the target firm is managed more effectively by the new management. In this case an acquirer believes that incremental value can be created by running a target firm more efficiently.

In our analysis, we do not consider these types of M&As, but only M&As carried out to exploit the value of synergies, that is the value realized by combining the two different entities in an M&A deal. Even if it is difficult to separate the two values, it is necessary to clarify that synergies are obtained by combining the two different entities in an M&A deal, while the *value of control* does not require an analysis of the acquiring firm, because the value of control resides entirely in the target firm.

The order of presentation of the topics reflects the actual growth of many firms: expansion starts within a core industry and it is undertaken to enhance or protect a firm's position in that business (*horizontal expansion*). Then, a firm moves outside its initial industry integrating its activities or phases along its value chain (*vertical integration expansion*) until over the years it becomes increasingly more and more diversified, entering different related industries and finally unrelated industries (*product diversification expansion*).

Each M&A is viewed as an investment decision directed at creating value for shareholders, exploiting the various opportunities offered by the internal firm resources and the environment. Each M&A strategy implies different changes in the firm's system and causes different effects on the firm's long-term cash flows. Therefore, defining a growth strategy which creates value requires examining the internal conditions of the acquiring and the target firms, evaluating the dynamics of the external environment in which the firms operate and estimating the expected effects on the value of the combined company.

To evaluate whether or not an M&A strategy can create value, we present some analytical models capable of specifying the relevant conditions under which each type of strategy can create value and be suitable for practical use.

However, we know that, in order for a defined strategy to create value, it is also necessary to adapt the firm's organizational structure so as to effectively manage the increased complexity of the new business system. To reach this aim the organizational structures which can offer the best solution with respect to each growth strategy are analysed.

The book highlights the fact that growth through M&A does not necessarily produce an increase in the enterprise and in the shareholder value; that clearly results only under particular conditions. Thus, top managers must carefully evaluate every growth alternative.

The book contains 13 formal chapters.

Chapter 1 introduces a fundamental terminology and some basic concepts concerning M&A strategies, pointing out the principal patterns of firm development.

Chapter 2 examines the empirical evidence on M&A performance, according to a large and authoritative literature. The results of empirical studies indicate that a high percentage of M&As fail in terms of profits and value created for shareholders.

Chapter 3 provides the essential theory concerning the firm value and the evaluation of an M&A strategy.

Chapter 4 illustrates how to analyse in depth the structure of firms involved in an M&A, for discovering which activities and resources offer the best opportunities for producing synergies. Then, it illustrates how to analyse the industry structure and dynamics, to properly understand opportunities and risks in an M&A.

Chapter 5 examines the characteristics of horizontal M&As and the conditions under which they can create value. In particular, it examines the economic conditions from which synergies derive and proposes an analytical model that defines when an M&A can create value for the shareholders of the acquiring firm.

Chapter 6 addresses the economic rationale for vertical M&A strategies.

Chapter 7 shifts the focus onto product diversified M&As, examining the conditions for which they can create value.

Chapter 8 examines the alternatives for financing M&As and the effect on the merger value.

Chapter 9 examines the appropriate organizational models for managing M&A integration.

Chapter 10 presents a summary of results and the conclusions of the first part of the study.

In these chapters the theoretical exposition is often followed by numerical examples and simulations.

In Part II of the book some cases of successful M&As are presented. The purpose of these cases is to highlight how a firm chooses and implements a defined M&A strategy creating value. Chapters 11, 12 and 13 analyse three cases of successful M&A strategies: L'Oreal, Campari and Luxottica. These companies are all characterized by a long period of continuous growth mainly based on M&A strategies, accompanied by a systematic creation of value for shareholders. Each company is characterized by specific M&A strategies and reveals its own original pattern. At the same time, all three companies present a common behavioural pattern: each of them makes leverage on its specific resources and exploits its strategic assets to cope with industry dynamics and environmental changes. The direct analysis of these cases confirms that an M&A can be a fundamental instrument for growth, increasing competitive advantage and creating value for shareholders. Thus, the cases provide a link between theory and practice, making, we hope, the analysis more real and interesting.

The book is based on established traditions in strategic management research. In particular, a number of insights are drawn from three distinct bodies of research: the resource-based view of the firm; organizational economics − in particular transaction costs analysis − and the fundamentals of corporate finance. All these theoretical traditions made a substantial contribution to the arguments advanced here.

In particular, we believe that M&A strategies have to be based both on the existing firm's system characteristics, that is the firm's assets, resources and capabilities, and on the dynamics of industry structure. Heterogeneity of resources and firm-specific characteristics form the basis of diversity and the strategic variety of firms.

The book is mainly directed at researchers and students in economics and management. As it offers useful tools for managerial decisions, we think it is also of interest to managers and consultants.

This book is the result of some years of research developed at the School of Economics and Management at the University of Siena and at the LUISS University of Rome. Outside school I have learned a lot from my experience as a management consultant and as a member of the board of directors of some industrial companies and banks.

Prof. Angelo Dringoli

Siena, February 2016

To Simonetta and Tommaso

PART I

How to make M&As perform successfully:
rationales and models

1. Basic terminology, concepts and types of M&As

INTRODUCTION AND OBJECTIVES

In this chapter we summarize some basic terminology and concepts on M&As for developing further knowledge and understanding. We distinguish between different types of M&As, horizontal, vertical and diversified, from an economic point of view, focusing on the economic effects produced and the environmental conditions that favour a coherent and effective growth strategy. Then, we point out the differences between friendly and hostile acquisitions and the main defences used to stop the hostile takeovers. As the growth of a firm can also be carried out through internal development, a comparison between the advantages and disadvantages of M&A with internal development is presented at the end of the chapter.

MERGERS AND ACQUISITIONS: BASIC TERMINOLOGY AND CONCEPTS

M&A can be defined as a process in which two or more firms are combined to share their assets and resources and thus achieve common objectives, and in which the management of the two firms negotiate the terms of the deal which are then put in front of the shareholders for their approval.

M&A operations are ways of carrying out growth strategies through external operations. The terms "merger" and "acquisition" are often used as synonyms, even if they are different from a legal point of view. In particular, an acquisition is the buying of the totality or the majority or of a relevant percentage of a company's shares, sufficient for ruling the company if the propriety is spread among many shareholders. A merger, on the contrary, is an integration among companies with the annulment of the acquired firm, when this is incorporated by the acquirer (*merger by incorporation*), or the annulment of all firms when a new company is set up from the concentration of the companies in the merger transaction (*merger by union*).

More precisely, in the *merger by union*, a new legal entity is created from the participant companies, which lose their legal separate identities because of the merger. The entire capital of the merged companies is transferred to the new company, whose shareholders are all the shareholders of the merged companies.

On the contrary, in the *merger by incorporation*, one of the companies interested, the acquirer, incorporates the other company. Also in this case, the capital of the merger company is equal to the sum of the capital of the companies involved in the deal, but the legal identity of one of the companies in the merger transaction is preserved. Precisely, the acquiring company remains with its separate legal identity, while the other company goes out of existence.

The *merger by incorporation* is the most commonly used form because of its simplicity from a legal standpoint. In a *merger by incorporation*, three different cases are possible.

- The acquiring company does not own shares of the incorporated company. In this situation the acquiring company will pay cash for the shares of the incorporated company or it will exchange the new shares issued itself with the shares of the acquired company, according a well-defined exchange ratio. Then, the shares of the acquired firm will be annulled.
- The acquiring company already owns all the shares of the acquired company. In this situation, the merger will be carried out simply by the annulment of all the shares and the participation of the acquired firm.
- The acquiring company already owns a percentage of shares of the target firm. In this case, the holding company will increase its capital with the issue of new shares that will be exchanged with the shares of the acquired firm that it does not own yet. Then, all the shares of the target firm will be annulled by the merger firm.

Frequently, the term *merger* is simply used from an organizational standpoint, that is viewing the merger as a partial or a complete integration of the managerial functions in a single business structure, without a change in the legal profile of the companies involved, which remain separate legal entities.

Having made this clarification, we observe that in an M&A operation the participants have different objectives. The vendor aims to increase the selling price to the maximum level, while the acquirer wants to reduce it to the minimum level. To successfully close the deal, high competences are required, of financial, legal, organizational and strategic type. For this reason, in M&A operations some advisors are present for helping the vendor and the acquirer to correctly evaluate the companies, to verify if the operation is possible and to solve all technical issues.

Finally, we want to point out the difference between the M&A operations and the simple acquisitions of assets or business units of a company. In this case, the payment of the acquired assets is made directly to the vendor company, not to its shareholders. This form of acquisition, which is not examined in this study, can be advantageous in some situations, because it allows the selection of the activities to be bought, thereby avoiding the debts to be borne by the acquired firm. In some cases, the same purpose can be reached by transferring the required assets and activities to a new company, whose shares will then be acquired.

THE PROCESS OF ACQUISITION AND MERGER

In M&A operations the following key phases can be identified.

a) The evaluation of the target company. Once a company has been identified as a potential objective of the merger, it is necessary to evaluate if it has the required characteristics to create value for the acquirer.
b) The dealing and the agreement between the parties. The second phase is represented by the dealing between the parties to reach the planned objective in terms of price and method of payment.
c) Finally, the third phase is represented by the integration or consolidation of the companies interested in the merger. In particular, it is a matter of defining the organizational structure and the management procedures which are more suitable for reaching the planned target in terms of integration and performance.

TYPES OF M&As

M&As can be characterized by different growth patterns, according to the opportunities offered by the environment and the disposable resources the firm has.

Growth can be carried out through horizontal expansion processes in the business in which the firm is already operating. Moreover, growth can be accomplished through entrance into a different business, related or unrelated to the business in which a firm is already operating.

We will distinguish three different M&A strategies:[1]

- horizontal M&A;
- vertical M&A;
- product diversified M&A.

We refer to horizontal M&A when a firm carries out an M&A to expand its production and sales capacity in the existing market or in different local or international markets, continuing to operate in the same industry or business with the same basic product. The extension to different market segments through new types and models of the same basic product, is also considered as a horizontal expansion.

We refer to vertical M&A when a firm decides to acquire firms making operations or phases of activity located upstream or downstream with respect to the present activity or firms making components or services which before were acquired from other firms.

Finally, we refer to diversified M&A, when a firm acquires firms operating in different industries or businesses with substantially different products, related or unrelated to the existing ones. In this case we will distinguish between:

- related diversified M&As, when businesses are related either by markets or by product technologies;
- conglomerate diversified M&As, when businesses are not related either by markets or by product technologies.

In our view, the introduction of different models or types of a given basic product, directed at different market segments (for example a new type or model of sunglasses), does not constitute a diversified strategy, but a horizontal expansion strategy.

The proposed classification goes into less detail than those proposed by other authors (Ansoff, 1968; Rumelt, 1974; Rispoli, 1998), because it aims principally at emphasizing the fundamental difference between the structural firm changes required by M&A strategies involving entrance into different industries and those involving further expansion and penetration into the industry in which a firm is already operating.

In economic terms, a horizontal M&A determines an increase in the quantities produced and sold of a given product; a vertical integration strategy determines an increase in the added value of a firm; and a diversified strategy determines the production and sale of a different product (Table 1.1).

As will be clarified in the following chapters, each M&A strategy implies different changes in the combined firm structure and requires different resources for it to be successful. Also the environmental conditions favouring one or the other strategy are very different. Therefore, the analysis of the firm structure and the environmental conditions form the bases for a coherent formulation of an M&A strategy (Dringoli, 2011).

Table 1.1   M&A strategies and main economic effects

M&A strategies	Main economic effects
Horizontal expansion Expansion in domestic markets or entering different geographical markets, producing the same product or new types or models.	Increase in quantities produced and sold and consequent increase in revenues and costs.
Vertical integration Expansion along the value chain.	Increase in added value.
Product diversification Expansion entering different industries producing related or unrelated products.	Production and sale of a different product and consequent increase in revenues and costs.

FRIENDLY AND HOSTILE ACQUISITIONS

Acquisitions can be friendly or hostile. In the latter case, the target firm does not accept the takeover bid and adopts defensive actions to avoid it (Brealey and Myers, 1996; Weston et al., 2004; Sudarsanam, 2010). For example, it repurchases its shares or it looks for an available partner (a white knight) for accomplishing a friendly acquisition, or it tries to defend itself through poison pills, such as taking on a big new debt, or selling assets, or calling for Antitrust Authority intervention, etc. In Table 1.2 some defensive actions against a hostile acquisition are shown. Frequently, managers do not wait for a hostile bid before taking defensive action, but deter potential bidders by using poison pills that make their companies more expensive or more difficult to run.

Shareholders of the target firm can contest the takeover bid in order to extract a higher price from the acquirer; on the contrary, managers can contest the takeover because they believe their jobs may be at risk in the merged company. So they will try to stop the bid to save themeselves, not to obtain a higher price for shareholders.

Table 1.2 A summary of the main defences from hostile takeovers

Types of defence	Description
Extension of the board term	The term of the current board of directors is extended so that the bidder cannot gain control of the target immediately
Supermajority	A higher percentage of shares is needed to approve a merger, for example 80%
Fair price	Mergers are restricted unless a fair price is paid
Restricted voting rights	Shareholders who own more than a specified proportion of the shares of the target firm have no voting rights for the exceeding shares
Poison pills	Disinvest specific assets making the company unappetizing for the bidder
	Buy assets that the bidder does not want, and increase the company debt
	Buy assets that will create an antitrust problem for the bidder
	Issue shares to a friendly third party or increase the number of shareholders and the capital to be purchased
	Distribute reserve funds to shareholders as dividends, thereby reducing the company capital and increasing the leverage
White knight	Seeking a partner who is available for a friendly acquisition

COMPARING M&A WITH INTERNAL DEVELOPMENT

The choice of growing through acquisition instead of internal development requires comparing the advantages and disadvantages of the two alternatives (Table 1.3).

The advantages of internal development are the following:

- the investment can be defined precisely in relation to the actual needs and objectives of the firm;
- the investment can be made gradually in relation to the disposable resources.

The disadvantages of this alternative are the following:

- the investment determines an increase of production capacity in the industry with the risk of overcapacity if aggregate demand does not grow adequately; overcapacity in an industry can cause a price war among the competing firms with a consequent fall in margins and cash flows;
- the expansion of production can take a long time, as it requires building plants and obtaining the right machinery.

Table 1.3 Comparing M&A with internal development

	Internal development	M&A
Benefits	Right dimension of the investments Efficiency in investment location Use of new technologies Quick integration of the investments into the existing firm structure Simple and easy decisional processes	Objective rapidly reached Easily overcoming the barriers to entry Rapid increase in the market share Opening of strategic windows Positive effects on the firm image Exploiting fiscal advantages
Drawbacks	Increase in production capacity and negative effects on product prices	Difficulties in integrating firms Acquisition costs and uncertainty of firm value

Alternatively, growth through acquisition presents the following advantages:

- a greater rapidity in implementing the production expansion;
- a more rapid increase in customers' portfolio, sales and market share;
- an easier entry into a market or business;
- no increase in the aggregate supply of industry;
- the exploitation of synergies and new competences and know-how.

Conversely, growth through acquisitions has the following disadvantages:

- difficulty in correctly evaluating the target firm because of limited information;
- difficulty in estimating the integration time and costs of target firms.

Often, a firm decides to grow through acquisition when it can rapidly carry out a relevant increase in size, reducing the number of competitors and increasing its market share and thus its bargaining power.

However, management must not underestimate the costs of integrating different organizational structures. Empirical evidence shows that mergers and acquisitions frequently bring positive short-term return for shareholders of target firms, but more questionable long-term benefits to investors in acquiring firms.

Even though empirical studies highlight the wide variation in the results of acquisitions at the firm level, they show that, at the aggregate level, only 40–50% of acquirers do achieve positive returns in the two to three year period following acquisition (Kitching, 1974; Gregory, 1997; Agrawal and Jaffe, 2000; Capron and Pistre, 2002). This subject will be analysed in depth in Chapter 2.

NOTE

1. This classification of mergers and acquisitions is largely used in the literature. On this point see, for example: Porter (1985); Hitt et al. (1997); Weston et al. (2004); Gugler et al. (2003). A different classification is proposed by Bower (2001) who identifies five distinctive varieties of M&As on the basis of differing challenges the management want to face: overcapacity M&A, the geographic roll-up M&A, the product or market extension M&A, the M&A as R&D and the industry convergence M&A.

2. Data and empirical evidence on M&A performance

INTRODUCTION AND OBJECTIVES

In this chapter data on M&As is presented, with a particular focus on the period 2005–2012. Data points out that M&A is a very widespread strategy through which firms grow.

What about the real outcomes of M&As around the world? To answer this question we have analysed some significant empirical studies made in the last years. The results show that a large percentage of M&As reduce the value of the acquiring firm or do not produce significant increase in value. In other words, a large part of M&As do not produce the estimated synergies and the results expected by the shareholders of the acquiring firm.

All this stimulates the need to find solutions for reducing the percentage of M&A failures.

SOME DATA ON M&As

M&A is surely the most powerful way of growing used by firms in all industries and of all sizes. If well planned and correctly estimated, it can allow the firm to quickly increase its market position and become a more competitive organization.

M&As occur in waves (Brealey and Myers, 1996; Sudarsanam, 2010). In the last century, there have been at least five identified and clearly defined M&A waves. The first wave occurred between 1897 and 1904, after the "1883 Depression", that generated a subsequent period of economic growth. The second wave happened between 1916 and 1929 after the Clayton Act, enacted in the US to add substance to the US antitrust law regime. The third wave was identified between 1965 and 1969 during the "economic boom", a time of strong economic growth and technological development. The fourth wave occurred between 1981 and 1989 and it was characterized by "mega-M&A". The most recent is the fifth wave, which occurred in the USA and Europe and to some extent in Asia, between 1992 and 2002. It was particularly remarkable in terms of size and geographical distribution.

It is extremely interesting to examine the data of M&As over the world. In Table 2.1 we show the total deal volumes and the total number of deals in the period 2005–2012 together with other significant data. According to the Dealogic database (2013), during the period between 2005 and 2012, there were 394,132 M&As worldwide for a total deal value of $33,572 billion. The table summarizes the characteristics of completed M&As worldwide during this period. The value of M&A declined after 2007 as a consequence of the global financial crisis. However, also during the crisis, the percentage of cross-border M&As always increased.

We can observe that most M&As are carried out in the USA. Of 394,132 M&A deals completed across the world in this period, approximately 98,148 M&A deals were made in the USA, 20,990 in Canada, 32,262 in the United Kingdom, 76,464 in Continental Europe, 30,661 in Japan, 17,262 in Australasia and the remaining 118,345 in the rest of the world.

There are not relevant differences with the worldwide unit deal value. M&As made in the USA cover 33 percent of the worldwide deal value considering all types of M&A and also M&As with a value of less than one million dollars (Dealogic database).

Most deals are cross-border. Precisely, there are 252,988 deals for a value of 18,467 billion dollars against 141,134 domestic deals generating a worldwide domestic deal value of 15,105 billion dollars. We will learn from M&A literature that these types of M&As are more dangerous because two different cultures of two different countries often do not fit. Therefore there are numerous difficulties at synergy level and these deals have the highest failure rate. The reasons why the rate of cross-border deals has increased over recent years are principally two: globalization and the current economic recession. To be competitive in a globalized economy, it is necessary to consolidate one's own international market position. So, to increase the market share in the foreign markets quickly, often the simplest way is by acquiring a firm already operating in these countries. In this way a firm can quickly become operative in another country, often overcoming hard institutional barriers to entry. The recent economic crisis has pushed many firms to explore new markets.

From the Dealogic database it also results that public deals are bigger than private deals in terms of value, while the number of public M&As is smaller than the number of private deals. To be precise, the worldwide number of public deals is 48,665, while the number of private deals is 259,276, by using a database that covers also the M&As valued at less than one million dollars each. It is necessary to distinguish between the different results in the USA and in Continental Europe. In particular, the number of public deals is 66,080 in the USA and 7,264 in Continental Europe, while the number of private deals is 7,324 in the USA and 53,380 in Continental Europe.

Table 2.1 Worldwide merger deals, 2005–2012

	Deal value ($bn.)	N°total deals	Cross-border deals value ($bn)	N°cross-border deals	Domestic deals value ($bn)	N°domestic deals
2005	3,724	39,177	2,276	24,990	1,447	14,187
2006	5,047	45,604	3,010	29,511	2,036	16,093
2007	6,341	52,925	3,014	32,937	2,948	18,865
2008	4,217	52,024	2,148	31,740	2,069	20,284
2009	2,965	44,922	1,868	30,320	1,096	14,602
2010	3,732	51,219	1,940	33,213	1,602	18,006
2011	3,815	55,387	2,111	35,457	1,704	19,930
2012	3,729	52,874	2,007	34,830	1,722	18,044
Whole period	33,572	394,132	18,467	252,998	15,105	141,134
% (1)	0.15	34.9	-11.8	39.3	18.9	27.2

Note (1): % change in value or in number of deals.

Source: Our elaboration on Dealogic, 2013.

EMPIRICAL EVIDENCE ON M&As PERFORMANCE

Various methods are used to measure the outcomes of an M&A. The most common is comparing the short-term difference in stock performance and shareholder value before and after the deal, because, in an efficient capital market, stock price should quickly reflect all new information. Another method is comparing a firm's performance after the M&A to the performance of a firm similar in size and field of activity. Another way is measuring profitability, return on equity and cash flow of the merger and comparing them with those of companies before the merger. An alterative method is to estimate the change in market power (increased sales) of the acquiring firm before and after the M&A.

We believe that the success of an M&A can be correctly proved by the creation of value, that is the positive difference between the total value of the combined firm after the merger and the single values of the target and the acquiring firm before the M&A.

What are the real outcomes of M&As over the world? To answer this question we have analysed a series of empirical studies. The results of these studies, highlighting the date of the study, the type of sample and the outcomes, are summarized as follows.

A high percentage of failures

The majority of studies highlight a high percentage of failures in M&As: declines in profitability and in value after the merger for the combined firm.

In particular, Meek (1977), studying a sample of 233 large listed firms in the UK between 1964 and 1971, found a decline in profitability each year after the merger, with the combined profits exceeding the pre-merged profits only in the year of the takeover. For a seven-year period after the merger, profits were less than those the participants would have experienced if they had not merged. It is shown that post-M&A profitability declines as does efficiency. Young (1981) observed a rate of failure close to 50%. Also Ravenscraft and Scherer (1987), studying a sample of 471 M&As in the USA between 1950 and 1977 in manufacturing sectors, found a decline in the profitability of acquiring firms. This result is confirmed by a study of McKinsey & Co (1990) on a sample of 115 M&As in the USA and the UK. They found that 60% of M&As eroded firm value and only 23% earned more than the cost of capital. A subsequent study on a sample of 160 M&As across 11 industrial sectors between 1995 and 1996 showed that M&As did not accelerate revenue growth meaningfully over the subsequent three years and 42% of acquirers "lost ground".

Agrawal, Jaffe and Mandelker (1992), in a sample of 1,164 M&As from NYSE and AMEX in a period between 1955 and 1987, found that there was not a long-term increase in the firm's performance. They noted that the stockholders of acquiring firms suffered losses over the five years after the M&A and that performance did not increase, and also evidenced that after acquisition, performance was worse for mergers financed by equity rather than by cash, without specifying the difference. These results are confirmed by Chatterjee et al. (1992); studying a sample of 52 acquired firms, they found that M&As had eroded firm value.

On the contrary, Datta (1991), in a study on a sample of 173 domestic M&As in the manufacturing sector between 1980 and 1984 in USA, found that firms, that had paid a premium to acquire target firms, obtained significant positive returns. A significant increase in post M&A performance was also found by Healy et al. (1992), studying a sample of 50 large M&As between 1979 and 1984 in the USA. A positive relationship between M&As and value created for shareholders is observed by Lubatkin (1987) in a study on 1,031 large mergers. In particular, this author found that mergers led to permanent gains in stockholder value for both acquiring and acquired firms' stockholders. Different results in terms of profits and sales were observed by Gugler et al. (2003), studying a large sample of M&As, from Global Merger and Acquisition database of Thompson Financial Securities Data; they found that a majority of mergers led to higher profits than those predicted, but there was also a reduction in sales.

Other studies highlight the high percentage of failures. For example, KPMG International (1999), in a study on a sample of 700 M&As between 1966 and 1998, found that 53% destroyed value, 30% were neutral and only 17% created value. Also McKinsey & Company in a study on acquisitions in the US and the UK between 1972 and 1983 found a high percentage of failures. In particular ex post analysis indicated that 61% of the programmes evaluated ended in failure and only 23% in success; the results of the rest were not significant (1996). In another study on 5,000 non financial companies with sales exceeding $250 million, better results were found. Commenting on these studies, Copeland et al. (1995) annotated: "In sum, although the probability of success for the average buyer is only 50% at the best, these odds can be improved by having a strong core business, buying companies in related businesses where the chance of achieving real economic synergies is highest, and buying smaller businesses that can easily be integrated during the post acquisition phase of the program" (p. 435).

Agrawal and Jaffe (2000) in a comprehensive review of the literature suggested that the aggregate return to acquiring firms in the years following an acquisition was negative or, at best, not statistically different from zero. Sirower (1997) suggested a failure rate of 65%.

In a new recent research on 1,415 acquisitions from 1997 to 2009, McKinsey and Company found negative results on M&A performance: one third of M&As created value for the acquiring shareholders, one third did not, and for the final third the empirical results were inconclusive (Koller et al., 2010).

Also Moeller et al. (2003), studying a sample of 12.023 US M&As between 1980 and 2001, found large losses for the bidding firms' shareholders.

High percentage of failures have been confirmed by Conn et al. (2005) in a study on M&As in the UK, and by McDonald et al. (2005) in a study on M&As in Australia. In particular, these authors found that 34% of M&As increased firm value, 32% reduced firm value and 34% had no effects. More recent research shows that a high percentage of M&As fail. In particular, Cartwright and McCarthy (2005) and Harding and Rouse (2007) found that 83% of all deals fail to produce shareholder value and 53% actually destroyed value. This is also confirmed by Appelbaum et al. (2009) who announced that 83% of M&As failed, while Banal-Estañol and Seldeslachts (2011) concluded that more than 50% failed to benefit the acquiring companies.

In conclusion, even if the results of many studies have to be interpreted with caution, because of the different motivations explaining acquisitions, the majority of empirical studies highlight that M&As experience high failure rates. Frequently, in academic studies one finds that up to 50% of M&As fail (Shrivastava, 1986; Hunt, 1990; Cartwright, 1998; Hubbard 1999; Cartwright and Schoenberg, 2006). The same findings are shown by more practice oriented literature (Habeck et al., 2000; Paulter, 2003; Koller et al., 2010).

Failures due to the divergence between managerial and shareholder objectives

Often, the failure of M&As is explained as a consequence of the divergence between managerial and shareholder objectives. In fact, growth can be pursued by managers for their own objectives at the expense of shareholders, because it may provide increased career development opportunities and the pecuniary and non-pecuniary advantages of managing large firms.

In particular, Ravenscraft and Scherer (1987), studying a sample of 471 M&As in the USA between 1950 and 1977 in manufacturing sectors, showed that the profitability of acquiring firms declined after the M&A deal. They deem that diversified M&As in particular have been carried out by managerial "empire building" will, rather than by efficiency.

Seth et al. (2002) in a study on some cross-border acquisitions found that most M&As have been motived by value creation opportunities, but 23% of these by managerialism, with evidence of hubris.

Failures due to over-evaluated synergies

A large proportion of M&As failed because the acquiring firm over evaluated the expected synergies from the merger and paid too high a price for the target firm. In fact, a significant body of research has pointed out the different effects of the merger on the target and the acquiring firms. Frequently, the immediate impact of M&A is positive and very significant for the acquired firm, but it is negative for the acquiring firm. Precisely, while target firm shareholders enjoy positive results, shareholders of the acquiring firm frequently experience share price reductions in the months following acquisition, with negligible long-term gains (Agrawal and Jaffe, 2000).

Martynova and Renneboog (2011), studying a sample of 2,419 M&As of 28 European and UK countries in the last five waves, found that M&A share price increased at the announcement of M&A because the market expects to generate synergy value from the deal. Shareholders of the target firms captured this positive increase especially in cross-border and in diversifying M&As, even if there were negative revaluations of the share prices of the acquiring and target firms, following the announcement of the event day. Thus, the M&A wealth was only limited to "the bid announcement day". In particular, Kaplan and Weisbach (1992), in a study on a sample of large M&As completed between 1971 and 1982 in the USA, found that 44% of M&As had been disinvested by the acquiring firms, especially in diversifying M&As. This 44% of M&As disinvested because the target was overpaid or the combined firm did not fit.

Finally, empirical evidence shows that most target firms obtain the better results from the M&A (Moeller et al., 2004). This is confirmed by Andrade et al. (2001). They analysed a sample of M&A transactions between 1973 and 1998 and concluded that the target firms gained at the M&A announcement (+16%). On the contrary, also in the M&As, where synergies exist and create value, the shareholders of acquiring firms achieved only a smaller part of the benefits from synergies.

Looking at evidence, it is easy to understand why firm stockholders, especially those of the acquiring firm, often do not share the enthusiasm that managers have and they are sceptical about the perceived value of the M&A in a significant number of M&A deals. In fact, the results of empirical studies highlight that there is an important percentage of M&As where acquiring firms pay much more than the real value of synergy. These deals determine a loss in value of the acquiring firm shareholders. Often, the strong competition between the potential acquiring firms favours the over evaluation. An incorrect evaluation of the potential synergies is more frequent in cross-border M&As. A lot of empirical studies show differences in performance between cross-border and domestic M&As. For example, on a sample of 4,430 M&As between 1985 and 1995 in the USA, Moeller and Schlingemann (2004), find that the cross-border M&As result in being overpaid with respect to domestic M&As and that they produce lower stock prices and performance. They attribute this outcome to an incorrect evaluation of the potential synergies from an M&A deal. According to the authors this is more relevant in cross-border M&As and it derives from overestimating the value of synergies, or by underestimating the difficulty of achieving these synergies. Also Conn et al. (2005), in a study on M&As in the UK, point out that cross-border M&As present lower returns than domestic M&As. According to these authors in all cross-border M&As, cultural differences had a considerably negative impact. Differently, Teerikangas and Very (2006), examining 61 M&As, pointed out that there were no big differences between performance of cross-border and domestic M&As.

Failures due to mistakes in the integration process

Empirical studies highlight the importance of the integration process for the success of an M&A. In particular, Datta (1991), in a study on 173 domestic M&As in manufacturing sectors in the USA between 1980 and 1984, find that differences in top management styles of the M&A's firms have a negative impact on the performance of domestic acquisition in the USA. Chatterjee et al. (1992), studying a sample of 52 companies, observe that the gains in related M&As were associated with "acquired mergers' perceptions of cultural difference between their top management team and that of the acquiring firms". They find M&As eroded firm value where the two managements "are perceived to be incompatible".

On the other hand, Larsson and Finkelstein (1999), in a study on 61 cross-border and domestic M&As between 1960 and 1989, found that synergies were realized only with good employee integration.

More recently, Weber and Camerer (2003), examining some M&As, showed that cultural conflicts, in terms of language and problem solving, had led to a majority of corporate M&A failures.

Also Nguyen and Kleiner (2003) evidenced that most M&As failed during the process of integration. The authors identify different cultures, lack of communication, a lack of a clear vision of the business and the acquiring firm's inability to impose its own "leadership style" as the main reasons for M&A failure.

These results are confirmed by Homburg and Bucerius (2006), examining a sample of 232 horizontal M&As. In particular, they found that a high failure rate in M&As (between 60% and 80%) was determined by a slow integration process. Differently, Cartwright and Schoenberg (2006), in a study of M&As over the past 30 years, gave evidence that the failure rate remained incessantly very high, and they indicate that the motivations have to be researched in cultural and strategic fit during M&A processes. Also Appelbaum et al. (2009), in a study on 10 cases, show that 4 of 10 M&As failed due to a lack of cultural fit, communication, understanding of the new business and a quick leadership.

The importance of processes, used to put companies together, for a deal's success is confirmed by Marks and Mirvis (2010) on the basis of a 30-year research programme.

A way of proceeding to make M&As successful

The majority of empirical studies confirm the conventional belief that merger and acquisition experience high failure rates.[1] Empirical studies also shed light on the main causes of these failures. We believe these can be summarized as follows.[2]

First of all, failures are caused by a frequent divergence between managerial and shareholder objectives. In particular, a lot of M&As are pursued by managers at the shareholders' expense, for their own objectives such as advantages of managing larger firms. Second, failures often depend on over-evaluated synergies and on not appropriate measures of the effects of mergers. Third, failures frequently depend on the mistakes made in the integration process of firms involved in the merger.

As things stand, to increase the percentage of successful M&As, we believe the following are necessary:

- to assume the creation of value, for shareholders of the acquiring firm, as the final objective to be pursued through M&As;
- to define a complete analytical model capable of correctly evaluating all effects produced and the value created by an M&A;
- to design appropriate organizational structures and effective integration processes of firms and activities, for implementing M&As and reducing the divergence of interests between managers and shareholders.

In the following chapters, we will suggest a procedure and some analytical models to satisfy all these requirements.

NOTES

1. According to Risberg and Meglio (2010) the notion that mergers and acquisitions perform poorly is not a fact supported by *conclusive* empirical evidence. According to these authors, who analyse in depth some empirical studies, it is difficult compare results from different studies in M&As: samples are different, motives and objectives are different and variables used to explain or predict M&A performance are different. Without sharing their conclusions, we too believe that a clearer definition of the M&As performance and of boundaries of analysis could help scholars to better interpret findings and derive more effective managerial implications. We hope that our book offers useful insight and suggestions in this direction.

2. A similar conclusion has been drawn by Cartwright and Schoenberg (2006) on 30 years of mergers and acquisitions research. In particular, these authors advance three possible reasons for the lack of improvement in M&A performance over the years: "a) executives are undertaking acquisitions driven by non-value maximizing motives; b) the prescriptions from the academic research have not reached the practitioner community; c) the research to date is incomplete in some way" (p. 7).

3. Making M&As create value: an analytical model for evaluating M&As

INTRODUCTION AND OBJECTIVES

The high percentage of failures highlights the need to define more precisely the purpose of an M&A and use more effective models for evaluating and managing M&As.

To offer a contribution for reducing the percentage of failures in M&As, we believe it is necessary, first of all, to acknowledge that the ultimate aim of a corporation is to create value for its shareholders.

Then, it is necessary to define analytical models and procedures suitable for properly evaluating and implementing M&As to create value.

With this in mind, we will analyse the general conditions necessary for reaching this objective.

For this purpose, M&A strategies are conceived as investment decisions directed at modifying the firm's structure and reshaping the business system. Thus, the appraisal of the financial long-term effects of an M&A is necessary for evaluating if it is suitable for creating value for shareholders.

After a reminder of the general model of firm value and of the fundamental variables which it depends on, the effects of an M&A strategy are analysed, defining a quantitative model for evaluating the conditions for creating value for shareholders.

THE FUNDAMENTAL OBJECTIVE OF AN M&A: CREATING VALUE FOR SHAREHOLDERS

Regarding the objective of an M&A, we believe the increase of market share or simply the growth of the firm do not assure an efficient use of capital and are not sustainable over a long period of time.

In fact, frequently, M&As are carried out by managers only to favour a rapid growth of the firm, as if the increase of the firm size could also ensure the creation of value. Sometimes, the growth of the firm is pursued by managers only because it allows greater prestige and more power or higher wages for them. As highlighted in the literature, this particularly happens in large public companies where the prevalent power of top managers over shareholders often makes the manager's interest prevail over that of the shareholders. This consequently favours expansion strategies through M&As which were not coherent with the objective of creating value for shareholders (Marris, 1964). However, a growth strategy of the firm, which is not coherent with the creation of value, cannot be continued for a long time, but it will eventually come to an end, since the progressive reduction in incomes and cash flow will increase the leverage of the firm (that is the debt/equity ratio) to a level where the capacity for further funding the investments will be severely reduced and eventually cancelled. In other cases the progressive reduction in incomes and the increase of debt caused by the M&A can even threaten the survival of the firm. Moreover, the negative performance in terms of profits of the merger will determine a progressive fall in the value of shares until a takeover of the firm is launched by new acquirers. So, if the capital markets are efficient, the growth itself cannot continue for a long period of time. Even the existing managers will not be able to maintain their position; they will be removed and replaced by managers capable of developing strategies which create value for shareholders.

In order to evaluate an M&A strategy, it is necessary to define a choice criterion which can generally be accepted and suitable. We assume an M&A is evaluated on the basis of effects produced on shareholders' equity value. On the basis of the Anglo-Saxon capitalism, this is the ultimate aim of the modern corporation on which the world's legal systems converge. More precisely, an M&A will be profitable only if it increases the equity value of a firm's shareholders.

On this subject, it is necessary to briefly recall the difference between the value of equity (E), that is the market value of shareholders' capital, the enterprise value (V), that is the market value of total assets, and the book value of assets (A), that is the value of assets as shown on the balance sheet. While the market value of assets will depend on the present value of expected operating cash flows, the book value of assets is simply the sum of the value of a firm's assets according to accountancy principles.

The following relation is valid:

$$E = V - D \tag{3.1}$$

where D is the value of debt.

Having said that, it is necessary to clarify that an M&A always implies, for the acquiring firm, an increase in total assets, as well as the book value, and at the same time it also determines an increase in liabilities or in equity, for the financing of the new assets. But it does not necessarily imply an increase in shareholder value, because this depends on the incremental operating cash flows, the investment and the cost of capital.

In the following chapters this subject will be analysed carefully, defining the specific conditions for how each M&A strategy creates value for shareholders.

OVERCOMING THE DIVERGENCE BETWEEN MANAGERIAL AND SHAREHOLDERS' OBJECTIVES

Growth through M&A can also be pursued by managers for their own objective at the shareholders' expense, because it may provide increased career development opportunities and the pecuniary and non-pecuniary advantages of managing large firms.[1] In particular, growth through M&A can progressively reduce the enterprise value and the shareholders value, when it is unprofitable and inefficient (Marris, 1964). Therefore, shareholders have a clear interest in reducing the divergence between their own interests and management interests and in limiting the chance of managers to succeed with decisions which pursue their own interests rather than those of shareholders.

A means for reducing the interest divergence with managers is represented by a management compensation structure as well as incentives capable of promoting management motivation to work for enhancing shareholders' wealth, so supporting both managerial and shareholders' goals.

In addition, as the probability of managers pursuing their own interests rather than those of shareholders is higher in an environment where incomplete and imperfect information exists, shareholders have to monitor management performance carefully and continuously verify the value of growth strategies. But shareholders must also create the conditions for vigorously replacing managers who operate to protect and expand their personal empires at the expense of shareholders. We will return to these topics in Chapter 9.

DETERMINING THE VALUE OF THE FIRM: THE BASIC MODEL

Corporate finance literature has emphasized that the value of a firm is obtained by discounting expected free cash flows from operations $FCFO(t)$, achieved in the lifetime of a business, at the weighted average cost of capital ρ (Levy and Sarnat, 1986; Copeland and Weston, 1988; Copeland et al., 1995; Brealey and Myers, 1996; Ross et al., 1999).

Considering an unlimited lifetime period, the value of the firm $V(0)$ can be expressed as follows:

$$V(0) = \sum_{t=1}^{\infty} \frac{FCFO(t)}{(1+\rho)^t} \tag{3.2}$$

with $FCFO(t)$ being free cash flows from operations in period t (year), equal to cash flows from operations $CFO(t)$ minus working capital change $\Delta WC(t)$ and the capital expenditures $\Delta I(t)$ necessary for maintaining the efficiency of the firm and favouring the operating cash flows; and ρ the weighted average cost of capital, that is the cost of the different components of financing used by the firm, weighted by their market value proportions ($WACC$).

In practice, for determining the value of a firm, some assumptions must be introduced regarding the dynamics of $FCFO(t)$ and this means setting out a credible scenario about future environmental conditions and a firm's competitive advantage.

We can assume that the existing firm positioning can be maintained over time and the free cash flow from operations, ($FCFO$), as an average value of flows obtained over a defined period of time, can be maintained constant for an unlimited period of time, by sustaining a flow of investments $\Delta I(t)$ (steady state hypothesis). In this case, the value of the firm will be:

$$V(0) = \frac{FCFO}{\rho} \tag{3.3}$$

In the case of a more favourable scenario, represented for example by a sustained growth of the economy or of the industry, we can assume that the $FCFO(t)$ will increase at a constant rate g, for an unlimited period of time, by sustaining a flow of increasing investment $\Delta I(t)$. Such being the case, the value of the firm will be:

$$V(0) = \frac{FCFO\ (1)}{\rho - g} \tag{3.4}$$

where $FCFO(1)$ is the free operating cash flow at the end of the first year.

Finally, the value of a firm can be determined by analytically estimating the $FCFO(t)$ that a firm will gain according to a defined business plan over a credible time horizon S, say three to five years (short-term cash flows), and by assuming that the free cash flows of the following periods (long-term cash flows) remain constant and equal to an average value $FCFO$ for an unlimited period of time. This can be a credible scenario if a firm can maintain the competitive position obtained at the end of the plan horizon S.

In this case we will have:

$$V(0) = \sum_{t=1}^{S} \frac{FCFO(t)}{(1+\rho)^t} + \left[\frac{FCFO}{\rho} \frac{1}{(1+\rho)^S} \right] \qquad (3.5)$$

If $FCFO(t)$, after the first period S, grows at a constant rate g for an unlimited period of time, the value of the firm will be:

$$V(0) = \sum_{t=1}^{S} \frac{FCFO(t)}{(1+\rho)^t} + \left[\frac{FCFO(S+1)}{(\rho-g)} \frac{1}{(1+\rho)^S} \right] \qquad (3.6)$$

Instead of making long-term forecasts on the $FCFO$, it is possible to assume the terminal value $TV_S(T)$ to be equal to the liquidation value of assets. That can be justified as a precaution or as a way of avoiding the pitfalls of observing too long a period. Accurate accounting or market measure of assets can be more robust and reliable over a limited period of say three or five years rather than an infinitely discounted series of future cash flows.[2] In the case where the terminal value is expressed by the liquidation value of all assets that characterize the expansion, we will have:

$$TV_S(T) = \sum_{j=1}^{n} \frac{ASSETS_j(T)}{(1+\rho)^T} \qquad (3.7)$$

Note that the equity value E is equal to the difference between the value of the firm V, that is the value of all of activities, and the value of financial debts D:

$$E(0) = V(0) - D(0) \qquad (3.8)$$

The choice of one or the other model depends on the different credible scenarios for the firm and on the purpose of valuation.

THE COST OF CAPITAL

The cost of capital (ρ or $WACC$) depends on the unit cost of debt and the unit cost of equity, as well as the capital structure, that is the proportion of debt and the equity used by the firm. As for the cost of capital ($WACC$), we use the general formula for estimating:

$$\rho = WACC = kd\,\frac{D}{V} + ke\,\frac{E}{V} \qquad (3.9)$$

where *kd* is the cost of debt and *ke* the cost of equity, *D* the value of debt and *E* the value of equity.

As for as the *cost of debt* (*kd*), this will depend on the condition of financial markets and the risk of financial distress of the firm. In particular, a rising debt leverage will cause a deterioration in firm rating and an increase in the cost of debt.

If i_f is the yield of risk free bonds, such as 10-year Treasury Bonds, the required yield from a firm's bonds will be equal to the return on the risk free bonds plus a credit spread (*cs*) to cover the risk of financial distress of the firm. This is mainly determined by the variability of its operating income and the financial leverage, that is the ratio between debt and equity (*D/E*). Precisely it will be:

$$kd = i_f + cs \qquad\qquad (3.10)$$

where:

$$cs = f(D/E) \qquad\qquad (3.11)$$

Statistical data prove that, as the leverage ratios increase, in association with lower fixed-charge coverage ratios or financial coverage ratios[3], bond rating will decline and debt costs will increase. On this point, see the data of Table 3.1 taken from Weston et al. (2004). It clearly highlights the relationship between the leverage ratio, the Ebit/Fixed charges ratio, the bond rating and the cost of debt. In particular, Table 3.1 shows that AAA bonds, with a leverage ratio less than 25% yield 7.2% with a differential of 220 basis points over the promised yield on 10-year US Treasuries, equal to 5%.[4] Differently bonds with a BBB rating and a leverage ratio from 67% to 90% require yields of about 8% (80 basis points higher than AAAs) and BB bonds carrying leverage ratio from 90% to 233% require a yield of about 13.6% (560 basis points higher than BBBs).

Other authors, such as Damodaran (2006) highlight the relationship between interest coverage ratio and default spread.

Therefore, on the basis of financial market conditions, it is a matter of estimating the cost of debt of a firm, according to its rating, depending on the financial leverage and interest coverage ratio.

In addition, for calculating the real cost of debt, we have to consider that financing by debt, instead of by equity, produces an increase in net operating cash flow, and thus in free cash flow from operations, due to the interest exemption from income tax and thus in net cash flow from operations. Precisely, the increase in cash flow from operations, net of tax (CFO_D) will be [5]:

$$\Delta CFO_D = kd\, D\, \tau = INT\, \tau \qquad (3.12)$$

It is well known that, rather than considering the fiscal benefits directly on *FCFO*, for evaluating a firm, it is possible to disregard them directly on the cost of debt by tax rate, τ, as a large part of the literature does (Copeland et al., 1995; Brealey and Myers, 1996). In this way, the real cost of debt for a firm will be simply:

$$\text{Cost of debt} = kd\,(1-\tau) \qquad (3.13)$$

As far as the cost of equity, *ke,* is concerned, it can be calculated applying the CAPM theory (Sharpe, 1964; Lintner, 1965; Fama, 1968; Copeland and Weston, 1988; Brealey and Myers, 1996); thus, the cost of equity can be expressed as follows:

$$k_{e,i} = i_f + (r_m - i_f)\,\beta_i \qquad (3.14)$$

where i_f is the return on free risk investment, r_m the return on the investment in a market share portfolio and βi the beta of the firm *i*. This is an index expressing the relative risk of firm i with respect to the risk on the market share portfolio, considered equal to 1.

In the expression (3.18), $(r_m - i_f)$ is the premium required for investing in a market portfolio because of higher risk. So, the second addend indicates the premium required to invest in the firm *i* over the return on the risk-free investment i_f.

Table 3.1 Leverage, Ratings and Debt Costs (2003)

D/E	Ebit/Fixed charges	Bond rating	Debt costs	Spread
25% or less	>7 x	AAA	7.2 %	2.2%
25% to 43%	4x to 8x	AA	7.3%	2.3%
43% to 67%	3x to 5x	A	7.6%	2.6%
67% to 90%	1.75x to 2.5x	BBB	8.0%	3.0%
90% to 233%	1x to 2x	BB	13.6%	8.6%
233% and above	0.75 to 1.25x	B	16.0%	11.0%

Source: Weston, Mitchell and Mulherin (2004).

The beta of a firm *i* (βi) is influenced by the type of business in which a firm *i* operates, by its operating leverage and its financial leverage. In particular, we can consider that, other things remaining unchanged, an increase in financial leverage will proportionally increase the equity Beta of the firm. In fact, intuitively the compulsory payments on debt increase the variance in net income, because a higher leverage increases income during good times but decreases income during bad times (Damodaran, 1994 p. 31). If all of the firm's risk is borne by the stock holders (i.e. the beta of debt is zero) and debt has a tax benefit for the firm, it results that [6]:

$$\beta_L = \beta_U [1 + (1 - \tau) D/E] \qquad (3.15)$$

where: β_L is the beta for the levered firm; β_U the unlevered beta of the firm (i.e. the beta of the firm without any debt); τ the corporate tax rate and D/E the debt to equity ratio (*financial leverage*).

The unlevered beta of a firm is determined by the type of the business in which it operates and by its operating leverage. In practice, statistical data on returns on shares allow us to calculate r_m, k_e and the *leveraged beta* value of every company (for those listed on the official market and then approximately for the others which are comparable). So, from this empirical data, it is possible to derive the value of beta for the same firm, considered unlevered. Then, we can calculate the new beta corresponding to a *new planned level of financial leverage*, according to a simple and intuitive function. In particular, we know that, other things remaining unchanged, an increase in financial leverage will increase the equity beta of the firm.

Therefore, from the expression (3.18), knowing the current beta of the firm i, $\beta_L(C)$, it is possible to derive the beta unlevered β_U of the same firm, as follows:

$$B_U = \beta_L(C) / [1 + (1 - \tau) D/E] \qquad (3.16)$$

And then we can calculate the new beta levered $\beta_L(P)$ corresponding to the planned level of financial leverage $(D + \Delta D)/E$, as the consequence of financing the firm by a larger debt. It will be:

$$\beta_L(P) = \beta_U [1 + (1 - \tau) (D + \Delta D)/E] \qquad (3.17)$$

Thus, we will obtain the new value of k_e (P):

$$k_e(P) = i_f + (r_m - i_f) \beta_L(P) \qquad (3.18)$$

In other words, knowing the beta of the firm in correspondence of a given value of leverage (current value), we can find the value of $k_e(U)$, that is the value of the cost of equity for the firm without any debt, and then calculate the new level of $k_e(P)$ in correspondence of the planned level of debt, according to the formula. Finally, we can recalculate the *WACC*, as being:

$$WACC = \rho_M(D) = K_e(P)\,E/V + K_d(P)\,(1-\tau)\,(D+\varDelta D)/V \qquad (3.19)$$

In conclusion, the increase of debt will require a higher cost of debt and a higher cost of equity because of the higher risk of financial distress of the firm. In particular, the weighted average cost of capital will reduce as the debt/equity ratio increase moderately up to a given level and the debt rating remains at AAA. As the leverage ratio continues to rise beyond that point, the average cost first increases moderately but then it rises sharply, when the leverage ratio reaches below-investment-grade status. At some point, the WACC curve rises because the increased costs of debt and equity offset the bigger debt proportion. Because the WACC curve falls and then rises, it must have some low point: this identifies the optimum capital structure. In practice, this is an optimum capital structure range.

Figure 3.1 shows the relationship between the leverage measured by D/E and the costs of debt, equity and the resulting *WACC* or ρ. With no debt, the unlevered firm's cost of equity and *WACC* would be *ku*. As shown in Table 3.1, for a debt ratio of up to 25% equity, the debt rating remains at AAA. As the leverage ratio begins to rise beyond that point, its cost of debt increases moderately until it reaches below-investment-grade status, when it increases sharply. The cost of the equity rises even faster.

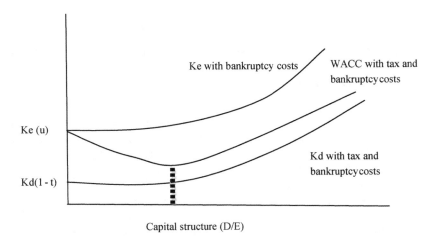

Figure 3.1 Effects of bankruptcy costs and income tax on the cost of capital

DETERMINANTS OF THE FREE CASH FLOWS FROM OPERATIONS

The following description shows the determinants of free cash flows from operations, *FCFO*, in each period *t*:

+	Revenues	*R*
−	Current operating expenses	*C*
=	Earnings before interest, taxes and depreciation	*EBITDA*
−	Depreciation and amortization	*A*
=	Earnings before interest and taxes	*EBIT*
−	Interest expenses	*INT*
=	Taxable income	*EBT*
−	Taxes	*EBT tc*
=	Net income	*NI*
+	Interest expenses	*INT*
+	Depreciation and amortization	*A*
=	Cash flow from operations	*CFO*
−	Working capital change	ΔWC
−	Capital expenditures	ΔI
=	Free cash flow from operations	*FCFO*

where τ is the tax rate on taxable income (corporate profit). That is:

$$FCFO = (EBITDA - A - INT)(1-\tau) + INT + A - \Delta WC - \Delta I \qquad (3.20)$$

$$FCFO = EBITDA(1-\tau) + A\tau + INT\tau - \Delta WC - \Delta I \qquad (3.21)$$

Note that $A\tau$ are the lower taxes due to the application of corporate tax on earning after depreciation and amortization. Also note that in a leveraged firm the *FCFO* is increased by the tax benefit ($INT\tau$) deriving from the application of corporate tax to earnings after interest. Finally, note that the capital expenditure ΔI affects the *FCFO*. In fact, in a finite-lived asset, the capital expenditure ΔI is the investment needed to maintain the asset's cash flows until the end of its lifetime, while in an infinite-lived asset, capital expenditure is the investment needed to maintain cash flows for ever. Therefore, to maintain a given *FCFO* over time it is necessary that a flow of capital expenditure for the firm structure remains efficient; as a consequence the higher the projected future growth of cash flows (*g*), the higher the rate of increase in capital expenditure, ΔI (Damodaran, 1994).

THE VALUE OF THE FIRM AS A FUNCTION OF MANAGERIAL ECONOMIC VARIABLES

In order to determine the value of the firm,[7] as the majority of financial literature does (see, for example, Copeland and Weston, 1988; Copeland et al., 1995; Brealey and Myers 1996), we prefer to disregard the financial tax benefits (*INT* τ), by reducing the cost of debt in the expression of weighted average cost of capital (*WACC*) by tax rate, that is $k_d (1 - \tau)$.

In this way, we will use the following expressions for calculating the *FCFO* and the WACC:

$$FCFO(t) = EBITDA(t)\,(1-\tau) + A(t)\,\tau - \Delta WC - \Delta I(t) \tag{3.22}$$

$$WACC = \rho = kd\,(1-\tau)\frac{D}{V} + ke\frac{E}{V} \tag{3.23}$$

The *WACC* will depend on the cost of debt, *kd*, the tax rate τ, the cost of equity, *ke* and the capital structure of the firm (*D/V* and *E/V*).

The *EBITDA(t)* mainly depends on the quantities of product sold $Q_v(t)$, the sale price *p(t)* and the current unit operating expenses *Cu(t)*. Therefore, we will simply express *EBITDA(t)* as:

$$EBITDA(t) = [P(t) - Cu(t)]\,Q(t) \tag{3.24}$$

and thus:

$$FCFO(t) = [P(t) - Cu(t)]\,Q(t)\,(1-\tau) + A(t)\,\tau - \Delta WC(t) - \Delta I(t) \tag{3.25}$$

This solution is very useful, because it enables the representation of the *FCFO* (and consequently of the firm value) as a function of the most relevant economic variables of the business management: the product price *P(t)*, the operating costs *C(t)*, the quantities sold *Q(t)* and the capital expenditure $\Delta I(t)$. These are the variables under the evaluation and control of the management (Dringoli, 2011).[8]

Figure 3.2 shows the determinants of value: price, costs and volumes (number of units sold). Volumes (*Q*) and price (*p*) depend basically on the differential benefits provided to consumers and the competitive position of the firm in the industry. Costs (*C*) depend on the firm operating structure.

Within the industry, the firm may create value in many different ways in relation to the importance given to each of the four value determinants: product benefits, organization costs, unit margin and sales volumes. Each strategy tends to leverage on one of these factors (Porter, 1980).

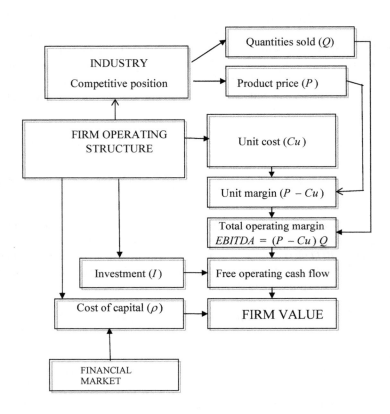

Figure 3.2   Framework for the analysis of firm value

ACQUISITIONS, SYNERGIES AND THE VALUE CREATED BY THE MERGER

As the interest of the shareholders is considered to prevail over all other interests, the creation of value for shareholders must be the primary objective of an M&A operation. Other possible objectives, such as the acquisition of a higher competitive advantage or a better positioning in respect of the competitors, or more market power, or a reduction in costs, are to be considered subordinate objectives and evaluated on the basis of their effects in terms of value creation for shareholders.

On this subject, the expression "creation of value" means the ability to obtain from the capital invested in the M&A a yield larger than the cost of capital, so that the present value of discounted cash flows produced by the merger is larger than the required investment. In general terms, there are two main factors which are capable of generating value through the M&A operations: the economies of scale and the economies of scope. In effect, in many industries, the increase in the scale of activity favours the reduction in unit operating cost, so that an M&A operation can be a good solution for quickly increasing the size of activity and thereby exploiting economies of scale, made possible by technological progress.

The other main factor that favours the creation of value through M&A operations is represented by the economies of scope. As we will see in more detail in the next chapters, these are economies deriving from exploiting idle resources, already present in the acquiring company, by the acquisition of firms with complementary products and services.

In synthesis, the value created (additional value) by an M&A mainly derives from increasing cash flows that the merger produces with respect to the cash flows of the companies standing alone. This incremental effect is called "synergy" and it is well represented by the expression $2 + 2 = 5$, where the additional one point is exactly the synergy effect, that is the effect of the integration of the companies in the merger. These incremental cash flows can be classified as follows.

Cost synergies

Cost synergies can derive from reduction in costs, mainly due both to economies of scale in production and distribution of products and to economies of scope, by exploiting idle resources and activities shared or transferred to new businesses (diversified M&A). These economies can derive, for example, from the exploiting of immaterial assets, such as the product brand, the marketing organization, the proprietary technologies and the so-called human capital. Cost synergies can also originate from an integrated running of technical and distribution activities of the consolidated firm. On this subject, we can distinguish between hard or tangible synergies and soft or intangible synergies.

Revenue synergies

Revenue synergies can derive from advantages in product differentiation and the consequent increase in the sale price of products, as well as from a wider range of products and services offered by the merger, with the consequent increase in quantities sold. Incremental revenues can also derive from collusive activity. These are benefits obtained by a reduction in competition, due to the reduction in the number of competitors and the consequent increase of the market power of the acquiring company. These synergies can be obtained mainly through horizontal M&As.

In general, synergies are benefits that are difficult to evaluate with precision and to clearly prove. The uncertainty of the estimated values also derives from the uncertain effectiveness of the organizational changes necessary for completing the integration of the companies. For example, it is common knowledge that some M&As, which look good on paper, have been unsuccessful, because of the difficulties in integrating different business cultures.

Cost and revenue synergies will determine an increase in net operating cash flows and therefore in the value of the combined firm. We call this incremental value the value of synergies. This is the first component of the value created by the merger.

Synergies in capital expenditure and working capital

Increases in *FCFO* can also derive from saving in working capital and in capital expenditures, by optimizing and reducing redundancies in investments from the combined firm.

Financial synergies from diversification?

In our analysis we do not consider the financial synergies, that is the potential benefits deriving from the reduction of the variability in cash flows by diversifying into other industries.

First of all, because these potential benefits are negligible in related diversified M&As, that are the object of our study. Then, because the benefits of diversification are not obvious, also in unrelated diversified M&As. In fact, it is true that the variance in cash flows of the combined firm should be significantly lower than the variance in cash flows of the individual firms operating independently, if the cash flows of the two firms involved in the merger are not highly correlated. But this reduction in cash flow variance will have no impact on merger value, because it is firm-specific risk, which is assumed to have no effect on expected returns. More precisely, the Betas of firms, which are measures of market risk, are always value-weighted averages of the two merging firms. In fact, the shareholders can accomplish the same diversification at a much lower cost, without paying the acquisition premium that firms pay (Damodaran, 1994). Therefore, a diversified M&A, without operating synergies, will have no effect on the value of the combined firm.

Value created or destroyed by the change in the cost of capital for the combined firm

In addition to the effects on the net operating cash flows, it is necessary to consider the effect the merger will produce on the average cost of capital of the combined firm, as a consequence of changes in operating risk and in financial risk.

In effect, the cost of capital of the combined firm can be lower or higher than the cost of capital of the companies involved in the merger, because of the difference in operating risk, due to the changes both in firm operating structure and in business dynamics. This will determine a further increase or decrease in the value of the merger.

Besides, the cost of capital for the combined firm can increase or decrease with respect to that of the acquiring firm, because of the effect of changes in the capital structure of the merger, due to the way the acquisition is financed and the consequent variation of financial leverage.

In conclusion, evaluating an M&A requires not only estimating the value of the target firm standing alone, but overall estimating the incremental value the merger can produce *by the integration* of the acquired company. The incremental cash flows are the consequence of the integration in production processes and products, and the disinvestment of assets and so on. Therefore, a fair evaluation of an acquisition also requires correctly estimating the costs in implementing the merger, that is the costs necessary for integrating the companies, so that synergies are produced.

Finally, it is necessary to estimate the possible effects on the value of the combined firm, deriving from the change in the average cost of capital.

DISTINGUISHING CONTROL VALUE FROM SYNERGY VALUE

It is important to remember that M&As are also motivated by *the value of control*. According to Damodaran (2005), we can define the value of gain control as "the incremental value that an acquirer believes can be created by running a target firm *more efficiently*".

If the value of gaining control is one of the principal reasons for some M&As, we think it is better not to mix value of control with the value of synergies, since they do not have the same meaning. It is necessary to clarify that the value of *synergies* is achieved by *combining* two different entities in an M&A deal, while the *value of control* occurs after the deal, when the target firm is managed more effectively by the new management. It does not require an analysis of the effects deriving from combining the acquiring firm with the target, *because the value of control resides entirely in the target firm*.

Therefore, it is true that companies can also pursue profitably non-synergistic M&As, buying firms at a low price and then selling them at a high price, often using high financial leverage. However, M&As only driven by the *value of control*, such as those made by private equity investors, focused on industrial turnaround, are not included in our analysis.

AN ANALYTICAL MODEL FOR EVALUATING M&As

Acquisition as an investment: the basic model for evaluating M&As

The analytical models explained above allow clarification of the fundamental variables that influence the firm value and offer practical frameworks for evaluating acquisition strategies.

As a defined M&A will produce relevant discontinuities in incomes and operating cash flows, it is necessary to evaluate in detail the effects of this strategy on the acquiring firm value, in order to verify if it creates value for shareholders. With this aim in mind, we will consider an acquisition as an investment and we will determine its value through the discounted cash flow method (DCF), that is by estimating the present value of the *incremental net operating cash flows* produced over time and the capital required.[9]

The proposed method has the merit of being easily usable and providing practical help to managers, focusing the analysis on the fundamental variables that influence the value of an M&A strategy: investments, prices, quantities and costs.

On the contrary, we express some doubts on the possibility of using, in M&A evaluation, the more complex methodology of *real options*[10] (Dixit and Pyndick, 1994; Dixit, 1995; Copeland et al., 1995; Hull, 1997; Amram and Kulatilaka, 1999; Kogut and Kulatilaka, 2006). These doubts arise from the difficulties in this practical application. In any case, an M&A can be considered a valuable real option only under particular circumstances. To be precise, this is true only if it offers a chance to carry out a further expansion investment in the business, paying a price for it (*strike price*) that is lower than the expected value of this at the future date.

In more detail, the model we propose for evaluating M&As assumes that the average increase in operating cash flows, produced by the investment (the acquisition of the target firm), can be maintained *constant* for an undetermined period of time. We consider it prudent to assume a synergy growth equal to zero, as a small change in expected growth can have a dramatic effect on the value of the synergies and would be sufficient to justify a high premium for the target. In addition, this choice can be more easily shared by the two parties involved in the deal.

Obviously, it is possible to adopt a more risky perspective. In this case, it is a matter of considering synergies to grow at a given rate *g*, using a growth model for valuation, like that presented in the previous paragraphs.

However, we believe that our simpler model, based on constant synergies over time, allows a more prudent evaluation to be made and thus it is able to offer a quantitative framework suitable for guiding correct managerial decisions, in a context that suffers the problems of horizon, uncertainty and complexity.

To reduce the complexity of analytical representation, we also assume that both the acquiring firm and the target firm are in a steady state, with a growth rate (*g*) of the estimated *FOCF* equal to zero. Therefore, the values of firms standing alone can be simply calculated by using the following expressions[11]:

$$V_A(0) = \frac{FCFO_A}{\rho_A} \; ; \; V_T(0) = \frac{FCFO_T}{\rho_T} \qquad (3.26)$$

where ρ_A and ρ_T are the cost of capital of the acquiring and the target firms. This solution allows us to concentrate on the main variables influencing the value of the merger, avoiding the dramatic effects on the value that also small differences in expected growth rates can have. However, to consider different growth rates of firms involved in the merger, it is a matter of applying the evaluation model represented by the expression (3.9).

Under these hypotheses, the net value created by the merger, $V_M(0)$, will be given by the difference between the value of acquisition (V_{acq}) and the capital invested in the M&A (I_M) :

$$V_M(0) = \frac{(FCFO_T + \Delta FCFO)}{\rho_M} - I_M \qquad (3.27)$$

where: $FCFO_T$ is the free operating cash flow of the target firm standing alone (assumed constant over time); $\Delta FCFO$ is the *incremental free operating cash flows determined by the synergies in costs and revenues*, ρ_M is the cost of capital for the combined firm (that will be equal to the cost of capital of firm A or to a weighted average of the cost of capital of the two firms A and T) and $I_M(0)$ is the total capital invested in the merger, which mainly includes the price paid for the target firm (PT).

The first term of the expression (3.27) is the value of the acquisition (Vacq); precisely it is:

$$V_{ACQ}(0) = \frac{(FCFO_T + \Delta FCFO)}{\rho_M} \qquad (3.28)$$

of which: $V_T(0)$ is the value of the target firm T, standing alone:

$$V_T(0) = \frac{FCFO_T}{\rho_T} \qquad (3.29)$$

and $V_{SY}(0)$ is the value of synergies:

$$V_{SY}(0) = \frac{\Delta FCFO}{\rho_M} \qquad (3.30)$$

In other words, we consider that the combined firm will become more profitable, because of the existence of synergies, but that it will not grow after the merger faster than firms operating separately. This also means that the combined firm, after the investment, remain in a stationary state for an unlimited period of time.

In spite of the limits of the proposed model, we believe nevertheless that they can be accepted, because of the magnitude of the inevitable imprecision in strategy valuation.

As we have explained above, we can write:

$$\Delta FCFO = \Delta EBITDA \, (1 - \tau) + A \, \tau - \Delta WC - \Delta I \qquad (3.31)$$

where, the incremental operating cash flow will mainly depend on the product unit margin and the incremental quantities sold, in accordance with the expression (3.25).

Therefore, an M&A will create value only if the value of the acquisition is greater than the required investment for the programmed M&A, however it is financed (acquisition and other investment required).

In conclusion, we will evaluate an M&A as a complex one-stage investment, which can be accepted or rejected according to its contribution to value creation for shareholders. For an acquisition to create value for the shareholders of the acquiring firm, it is necessary that the increase in value of the combined firm, with respect to the value of the acquiring firm before the acquisition, is larger than the negotiated value (price) for the acquired firm (the investment). In other words, the acquisition will create value for shareholders of firm A if:

$$(V_{AT} - V_A) - P_T > 0 \qquad (3.32)$$

where $(V_{AT} - V_A)$ is the value of acquisition, $(Vacq)$; V_A and V_T are respectively the market value of firm A (the acquiring firm) and the market value of target firm T, when they operate independently; V_{AT} is the value of the combined firm after the acquisition and P_T the negotiated value (price) for firm T, that is the investment made by firm A for acquiring the assets of T.

We remember that the value of the acquisition of T can be expressed by the sum of the value of the firm T standing alone plus the value of synergies. That is:

$$V_{acq} = V_T + V_{SY} \qquad (3.33)$$

In addition, we have to consider the possible change in the operating risk of the combined firm, and the effect on the average cost of capital. The effect on the value of the combined firm can be calculated as follows:

$$V_{CC} = \frac{(FCFO_A + FCFO_T)}{\rho_M} - [\frac{FCFO_A}{\rho_A} + \frac{FCFO_T}{\rho_T}] \qquad (3.34)$$

where ρ_M is the cost of capital of the combined firm, due to the change in operating risk and ρ_A and ρ_T the cost of capital of firms A and T before the merger.

Obviously, the effect on the merger value can be either positive or negative, according to the value of the cost of capital for the merger (ρ_M) and the cost of capital of the firm A (ρ_A) and the firm T (ρ_T) standing alone.

Therefore, all this considered, the total value created by the merger, V_M, both considering the effects of synergies and that of the change in cost of capital, will be:

$$V_M = \frac{\Delta FCFO}{\rho_M} + \frac{(FCFO_A + FCFO_T)}{\rho_M} - [\frac{FCFO_A}{\rho_A} + \frac{FCFO_T}{\rho_T}] \qquad (3.35)$$

We remember that the value of acquisition V_{acq} is the value of the firm T standing alone plus the total value created by the merger (V_M), that is :

$$V_{acq} = V_T + V_M \qquad (3.36)$$

The value created (or destroyed) for the shareholder of the firm A (V_{SA}) will be given by the following expression:

$$V_{SA} = (V_T + V_M) - P_T \qquad (3.37)$$

where P_T is the price paid for the target firm by the acquiring firm A (that is the investment).

Note that, in order for the acquisition to be profitable for the shareholders of firm A, it is not sufficient that the value created by the merger, V_M , is larger than zero. It is necessary for at least a part of this value to remain with the shareholders of the acquiring firm. For this to happen, the value created by the acquisition must not be entirely distributed to the shareholders of firm T. In other words, the price for the firm T must be lower than the value of acquisition:

$$P_T < V_{acq} \qquad (3.38)$$

That is:

$$P_T < V_T + V_M \qquad (3.39)$$

The price paid for the target firm defines the sharing of synergy benefits. In effect, when it is a matter of acquiring a firm, the problem is who gets the benefits of the synergies: the shareholders of firm A or the shareholders of firm T, or both of them? That will depend on the price paid for the target firm T. Since the acquiring firm and the target firm are contributors to the creation of synergies, the sharing of the benefits of synergies among the two firms will depend on the possibility that the bidding firm can be replaced by other firms. Generally, if there are multiple bidders interested in the acquisition, the shareholders of the target firm will get the majority of synergy gains.

It is useful to point out that the acquisition price of target firm T, P_T, is the value contractually defined by parties for firm T, as the value of its operating assets on the basis of asset side valuation method. Therefore, the resulting value of shares of firm T, E_T , will be:

$$E_T = P_T - D_T \qquad\qquad (3.40)$$

Obviously, the premium obtained over the market value of firm T before acquisition will be gained by the shareholders of T.

While we propose analytical models for estimating the value created by growth strategies, we are also aware of their limits, principally deriving from the difficulties in correctly evaluating risk and the terminal value of the M&A. However, we believe that these difficulties are inherent to the object of analysis, rather than the proposed methodology. Obviously, the models must be used with great care considering that the evaluation regards firms and not simply a project and also taking into consideration the sensitivity of firm values to different values of variables.

However, we believe that the advantages of the methodology proposed are relevant with respect to other traditional methods of valuation, such as return on investment (*ROI*), payback period, etc., based on accounting variables.[12] In fact, the proposed methodology forces managers to consider the true determinants of economic value and their relationships, helping them to come back to fundamentals of investment decisions.

In the following chapters we will examine analytically the specific sources of value in the different M&A strategies taken into consideration.

THE ROLE OF "MULTIPLE METHOD" IN EVALUATING M&As

The multiple (or comparable firms) method of evaluation

An alternative method to evaluate a firm is the one based on how similar firms are currently priced by the market.[13]

In practice, we often value an asset on the basis of how similar assets are priced in the market; for example when we decide to buy a house we look at the prices paid for similar houses in the same town and in the neighbourhood. So, on the basis of a significant parameter, for example the price per square metre, we determine the value of our prospective house, multiplying this parameter by the number of square metres of our prospective house.

In the same way, we can evaluate a firm or shareholder capital. Therefore, to use this method it is necessary, first of all, to find *comparable* firms already priced by the market and then to choose a relevant common parameter to refer the price to. For example, this relevant common parameter can be *EBITDA*, *earnings*, *revenues*, *book value of equity*, etc.

Therefore, if the parameter used is *EBITDA*, the firm value of our firm will be determined considering the *Price/EBITDA* ratio characterizing similar firms (comparables), and then applying the relative value, or *multiple,* to the *EBITDA* of our firm. In other words, if the market has priced x times the *EBITDA* of comparable firms, we will determine the potential price of our firm by multiplying the *EBITDA* of our firm x times.

As we can see, in this way a firm is evaluated on a *relative* basis and not on the specific cash flows produced over time and on the cost of capital, as in DCF valuation. The limit of this method is evident from a theoretical point of view. In addition, its weakness depends on the difficulty of finding really comparable firms, in terms of markets, technology and resources. Finally, as multiples reflect the market mood, using the relative valuation determines values that are too high, when the market is overvaluing comparable firms, or too low when it is undervaluing these firms.

However, the practical advantages of this method are important. They can be summarized as follows:

- it requires less time, information and resources than the DCF;
- it is easy and intuitive and it is easier to justify the valuation to clients and other analysts;
- it is based on market prices and therefore reflects the mood of the market.

All this explains why this method of relative valuation is so widespread in practice.

We think *relative valuation* or *multiple method* has an important role in firm evaluation, that is separate and different from DCF valuation. Its role is to check the result of DCF method, and to ensure that DCF is correctly used.

In any case, in M&A evaluation the *multiple* method should be used only for determining the stand-alone values of the firms involved in the merger. But, to determine the value created by the merger, it is necessary to estimate specifically the incremental cash flows produced by the merger and the change in the cost of capital of the combined firm, as a consequence of the way the merger is financed.

On the contrary, the use of the multiple *Price/EBITDA* method can produce dangerous mistakes in evaluating the merger, as we will show in the following point.

Pitfalls in the multiple method: the "bootstrapping" effect

The so-called "bootstrapping" effect can be produced when the values of firms are determined by using the *Price/EBITDA* multiple (or even the Price/Earning multiple with the necessary differences) and the acquiring firm presents a *Price/EBITDA* ratio larger than that of the target firms (Brealey and Meyers, 1996). In this case, if the acquiring firm incorporates companies that have a lower *Price/EBITDA* ratio and the market continues to evaluate the *EBITDA* of the merger using the larger multiple of the acquiring firm, instead of a mean value, a continuous increase in the value of the acquiring firm will be produced.

For a numerical example see Table 3.2. In other words, if these expectancies continue, that is if the market continues to evaluate the *EBITDA* of the merger at a multiple larger than that of the target firms, (for example, because the investors anticipate a more rapid growth in future earnings), a continuous process of acquisitions will determine a continuous increase in the value of the merger.

It would be an easy way to create value! In effect, in this way you would achieve a growth in value not by product improvement or by increasing operating efficiency, but simply by the merger of slow-growing firms with low *Price/EBITDA* ratios. Obviously, this positive effect cannot last forever. A merger can even transform iron into gold by exploiting synergies between companies, but surely this result cannot continue indefinitely! In effect, increasing complexity in integration, increasing costs of coordination and increasing risks will put an end to easy success and luck. So, if investors are not foolish, the growth of value will stop because the rate of expansion of cash flows will slow down and consequently the multiple for determining the share price will decrease. Inexorably, the house of cards will fall. This, in fact, is what the empirical evidence confirms, as we have seen in Chapter 2.

Table 3.2 Bootstrapping effect

	Firm A	Firm T	Merger 1 Average multiple	Merger 2 Acquiring multiple
Total *EBITDA* (€000)	100	50	150	150
Price/EBITDA	10	5	8.33	10
Firm Value (€000)	1,000	250	1,250	1,500

We observe that assuming the merger will produce no economic benefit, the combined firm should be worth exactly the same as the firms involved were, when apart. The market value of the merger should be equal to the sum of the separate values of the two firms (merger 1). On the contrary, if the market evaluates the total *EBITDA* of the merger at the highest multiple of the acquirer (10), that really produces earnings with a faster growth, the market value of the combined firm will increase (merger 2). Thus, we see how to play the bootstrap game: it is sufficient to continue expanding through the merger of companies with lower *Price/EBITDA* multiples.

NOTES

1. On this subject see: Ansoff (1968, 1988); Porter (1985, 1987); Campbell and Sommers Luchs (1998).
2. See Johnson (2006). In order to determine the terminal value, this author suggests searching for a value that likely investors will attribute to the company, given the performance trajectory of the company over the last years. According to Johnson, if the accounting is done on the basis of market prices and accurate replacement values, accounting measures can be robust and reliable. He calls this alternative approach scenario-based retrospective valuation or alternatively the CV view of valuation (p. 190).
3. Precisely, interest coverage ratio = (Operating income + Lease expense) / (Interest expense + Lease expense); Fixed charges coverage = *EBIT* / Fixed charges.
4. Bonds rating are related to leverage ratios and pre-tax fixed charge coverage. Other factors include firm size, competitive factors in the industry and prospective growth rates.
5. In fact, financing a firm entirely by equity, the operating cash flow (CFO_E) will be:
$$CFO_E = (EBITDA - A)\,(1 - \tau) + A = EBITDA(1 - \tau) + A\,\tau$$
    where A is the depreciation and amortization and τ the tax rate on income. Differently, financing by debt, we have:
$$CFO_D = (EBITDA - A - kd\,D)\,(1 - \tau) + A + kd\,D =$$
$$= EBITDA\,(1 - \tau) + A\,\tau + kd\,D\,\tau$$
    Therefore, the *CFO*, net of tax, increases by the fiscal benefit $kd\,D\,\tau$, because of debt financing.
6. The expression (3.19) can be derived considering that the return on equity after taxes *ROE* is expressed by the following:
$$ROE = (RO - kd\,D)\,(1 - \tau)\,/\,CN \qquad (1)$$
    where *RO* is the operating profit, *kd* the cost of debt, τ the tax rate on income and *CN* the net capital. Calling *ROI* the return on the invested capital *Ci*, that is:
$$ROI = RO\,/\,Ci = RO\,/\,(CN + D) \qquad (2)$$
    being the invested capital equal to the sum of debt and the net capital, we can write the return on equity after taxes as follows:
$$ROE = [(ROI\,Ci) - kd\,D]\,(1 - \tau)\,/\,CN =$$

$$= ROI\,(1-\tau) + ROI\,(1-\tau)\,D/CN - kd\,(1-\tau)\,D/CN \qquad (3)$$

This formula indicates the way the *ROE* varies according to the variations of financial leverage *D/CN*.

Note that if $D/CN = 0$, we have $ROE = ROI\,(1-\tau)$. Therefore this expression is the return of the unlevered firm. On the basis of the expression (3), the beta of a firm is assumed to vary, with respect to the financial leverage, in the same way (that is proportionally), according the following expression:

$$\beta_L = \beta_U + \beta_U\,(1-\tau)\,D/E - \beta_D\,(1-\tau)\,D/E$$

If $\beta_D = 0$ we have simply:

$$\beta_L = \beta_U + \beta_U\,(1-\tau)\,D/E = \beta_U[1 + (1-\tau)\,D/E\,]$$

From this expression, it is possible to derive, given the current beta of a leveraged firm β_L, the beta unlevered, as follows:

$$\beta_U = \frac{\beta_L}{1+(1-\tau)D/E}$$

Thus, from this general expression, it is possible to calculate the new value of the Beta of a firm, $\beta_L\,(P)$, corresponding to the planned level of its debt $D(P)$ and financial leverage. It will be:

$$\beta_L\,(P) = \beta_U[1 + (1-\tau)\,D(P)/E\,]$$

7. On the value of the firm see also the preceding work of Rappaport (1986). This author introduces drastic simplifications into his model: a constant unit operative margin (the ratio between the operating income and the sales), a constant rate of sales growth, etc.

8. Many authors underline the opportunity, from a practical point of view, to simply express cash flow on the basis of the most relevant economic variables used in the operating management of the firm. See, for example, Rappaport, (1986); Copeland et al. (1995); Grant (1998).

9. On the analytical methods for evaluating strategies see, in particular: Rappaport (1986); Day (1990); Johnson (2006).

10. In synthesis, by an acquisition a firm can acquire a real option, that is an opportunity to further expand the investment or to postpone it over time, when the scenario is more definite, thereby reducing the risk. This flexibility has a value that can be determined. Following the methodology developed for financial options, the acquisition of a firm can be considered the price of an option, the further investment - required to capitalize the new opportunities - is the exercise price of the option (strike) and the present value of expected cash flows is the market value of this future investment. So, the value of this option, at expiration, will be positive if the value of the expected cash flows rises above the exercise price and it will be precisely equal to the value of investment minus the exercise price. Conversely, if the value of the future investment is less than the exercise price, at point of expiration, the option value will be equal to zero. Because of uncertainty in cash flow trajectories, the option is valuable as the

buyer (investor) can wait for a favourable scenario to happen before making his subsequent investment. As the option theory proves, options are valuable where uncertainty is high and the expiration time for decision is located in the distant future. For more in-depth study, see Dixit and Pyndick (1994); Amram and Kulatilaka (1999).

11. In case the firms involved in the merger are characterized by significant rates of growth (*g*), the value of the firms can be calculated using the following expression:

$$V = \frac{FCFO}{\rho - g}$$

according what was observed on page 24.

12. For a systemic review of the impact of accounting policy, see Edwards et al. (1987).

13. The multiple method and other valuation methods and procedures to determine the value for mergers and acquisitions are also described by Mellen and Evans (2010) and by Petitt and Ferris (2013).

4. Identifying the opportunities for successful M&As

INTRODUCTION AND OBJECTIVES

Growth through M&A can assume different patterns according to the direction of the expansion to be carried out: horizontal, vertical or diversified.

The specific growth pattern that a firm should follow, in order to create value, depends on the characteristics of its business system and the external environment, in particular the structure of the industry and its dynamics.

Therefore, it is necessary, on one hand, to analyse in depth the structure of firms involved in the merger, for discovering which activities and resources can offer the best opportunities for successful M&As. On the other hand, it is very important to analyse the structure and the dynamics of the industry where the firm wants to expand its activities, so as to properly understand opportunities and risks.

These investigations will allow us to identify the type of M&A which is more capable of creating value for shareholders. The chapter analyses how strategic assets and resources, as well as the opportunities and the threats of industry dynamics, can be identified and valued for the choice of an M&A strategy that creates value.

CHOICE OF THE M&A STRATEGY

M&A strategies are differently characterized according to the direction of the expansion and their economic effects: they have been distinguished in horizontal, vertical and diversified M&As. Each M&A strategy determines different changes in the *structure* of a firm, that is in the fundamental characteristics of the business system (production and distribution capacities, logistic system, organizational structure, etc.). These changes are not reversible in the short-term, because they modify some distinguishing and specific features of a firm (tangible and intangible assets) (Dringoli, 2000; 2006). These changes also produce different outcomes according to the dynamics of the external environment.

Consequently, an M&A must be undertaken after evaluating the specific structural characteristics of the firm and the long-term dynamics of demand

and competitive forces. In other words, it is the irreversibility of structural changes that makes it necessary to look at the long-term future.

In particular, an M&A strategy must be defined correctly by considering not only the internal characteristics of the firm's business system, but also the dynamics of the external environment and particularly of the industry. In fact, it is customers' behaviour and competitors' reactions that can prevent the acquiring firm from reaching the planned objectives, as happens in a competitive game.

In other words, for an M&A strategy to be reliable, it has to be consistent with the environment trends and with the firm's structure and its distinguishing resources.[1] In synthesis, management must choose a strategy which exploits the firm's specific culture and exclusive know-how. That will allow the firm to reduce its operating costs and increase its revenues, thereby obtaining a competitive advantage over its competitors.

The in-depth knowledge of a firm's structure and its distinguishing resources also means correctly understanding the actual limits to the firm's growth. This allows the opportunities to be clearly defined, as well as the new resources to be acquired, in order for the growth to be sustainable.

ANALYSIS OF THE FIRM STRUCTURE: ACTIVITIES, ASSETS AND RESOURCES AS FUNDAMENTAL BASES FOR M&A VALUE

A firm as a chain of activities: identifying the strategic assets for successful M&As

As the creation of value through an M&A mainly depends on savings in costs and increases in revenues that a merger determines, it is necessary to analyse in depth the structure of the firms involved in the merger, to discover which activities can offer these opportunities and which M&A strategy has to be undertaken to exploit them.

For this purpose, it is useful to employ the *value chain model* proposed by Porter (1985). Following this author, we will distinguish between *primary* and *support activities* in the firm system. Among the *primary activities* there are: inbound logistics, operations, marketing and sales, outbound logistics and after-sales service. Among the *support activities* there is: a firm's infrastructure (e.g. finance, accounting, etc.), human resource management, technology development and procurement (Figure 4.1).

SUPPORT ACTIVITIES	FIRM INFRASTRUCTURE					
	HUMAN RESOURCE MANAGEMENT					
	TECHNOLOGY DEVELOPMENT					
	PROCUREMENT					
PRIMARY ACTIVITIES	INBOUND LOGISTICS	OPERATIONS	MARKETING & SALES	OUTBOUND LOGISTICS	SERVICE	

Note: The value chain depicts the firm as a collection of value-creating activities.

Figure 4.1 Michael Porter's value chain (1985)

As far as the *primary activities* are concerned, there are five generic categories of activities; each of them is dividable into a number of distinct activities that depend on the particular industry and the firm strategy.

1. *Inbound logistics*. These are activities associated with receiving and storing product inputs, such as buying, material handling, inventory control, etc.
2. *Operations*. These are activities concerning the transformation of inputs into the final product, such as machinery, assembly, packaging, equipment maintenance, etc.
3. *Marketing and sales*. These are activities associated with promoting and selling products.
4. *Outbound logistics*. These are activities concerning storing finished products, order processing and physically distributing the product to buyers.
5. *Service*. These are activities associated with providing after-sale service to clients to enhance or maintain the value of the product such as installation, repair, part supply, etc.

Support activities can be divided into four generic categories, as shown in Figure 4.1, each of which is dividable into a number of distinct activities that are specific to a given industry.

1. *Procurement*. These are activities associated with the function of purchasing inputs used in the production and selling of products. Purchased inputs include raw materials, energy and other supplies

associated not only with primary activity but also with other support activities, as well as services.

2. *Technology development.* These are a range of activities that are directed at improving the product and the process; they take many forms, from basic research and product design to process equipment design, media research and servicing procedures.

3. *Human resource management.* These are activities that consist of recruiting, hiring, training, development and compensation of all types of personnel.

4. *Firm infrastructure.* These are a range of different activities including general management, planning, finance, accounting, legal, government affairs and quality management.

In using this representation it is possible to identify in detail, with reference to each different activity, which of them present *tangible or intangible assets* capable of determining economies of scale and/or economies of scope through an M&A. In particular, *strategic assets* are those favouring the reaching of a competitive advantage for their rarity.

A firm as a set of resources: identifying the distinctive and critical resources for successful M&As

A complementary way to represent the firm structure is to view it as a set of *resources.*[1] Precisely, according to the resource-based theory (Hofer and Schendel, 1978; Barney, 1988, 1991 and 1996; Wernerfelt, 1984; Grant, 1991; Peteraf, 1993; Collis and Montgomery, 2005) we can consider the firm as an organized set of resources (tangible and intangible), through which specific activities and processes are carried out so as to obtain products or services for markets.[2]

A firm's resources can be classified into three categories: tangible, intangible and organizational capabilities (Grant, 1998; Collis and Montgomery, 2005). Tangible resources are assets that can be seen and quantified. They are indicated in a firm's balance sheet and include production facilities, real estate, plant, etc. Intangible assets include brands, company reputation, technological knowledge, patents and trademarks.

Organizational capabilities represent the firm's capacity to deploy resources; they include the set of abilities incorporated in a firm's activities and processes from product development to manufacturing and to marketing. They are the result of the quality of people employed and their experience and accumulation of learning over time. The primary bases for the firm's capabilities are the skills and knowledge of its employees (the value of human capital).

The stock of resources a firm possesses at a certain date, especially intangible resources and capabilities, is a sedimentation of activities and processes carried out from period to period that slowly accumulate over time, according to rates specific to the type of resource. Think, for example, of a firm's reputation, brand image, brand loyalty or marketing expertise or R&D know-how, distribution network, etc. Like the assets of the firm, the existing stock of resources depreciates over time, due to environmental changes and competition from rival firms, so it is necessary to plan appropriate expenditure flows for maintaining or increasing the stock level, also for externally acquiring the desired resources in a market transaction, for example purchasing an entire company or business unit.

A firm's resources are the fundamental basis of actual competitive advantage at the business unit level and thus at the level of income and cash flow. In fact, they are the durable stocks of resources that characterize the product being offered, the level of product differentiation and the costs of organization (Nelson, 1994). Moreover, resources are the fundamental basis of growth strategies, because they determine *what a firm can do in the future*. More precisely, resources define the acceptable domain of strategies a firm can pursue for creating value within the actual business and for entering into new businesses (Nelson and Winter, 1982; Wernerfelt, 1984; Winter, 1987; Hamel and Prahalad, 1994; Nelson, 1995; Collis and Montgomery, 2005).

In fact, as many of a firm's resources cannot be produced instantaneously, because they are the result of a cumulative process demanding time, the opportunities for growth are limited by the current resource stock and by the speed at which a firm can produce and accumulate new resources.[3]

Roughly speaking, we can express the growth of a firm as a function of its specific stock of resources, considering a given industry structure and dynamics. Therefore, if all firms in an industry cope with the same external variable, they nevertheless have different growth responses because each of them has a unique, specific set of resources.

In this context, the value of resources, such as firm reputation, research and development (R&D) capabilities, advertising goodwill, etc., should be viewed as a capital good that has been accumulated over time through an appropriate flow of expenses adding increments to an existing value, according to the efficiency of these expenses. But the asset value depreciates over time and needs maintenance. Thus, for example, advertising goodwill depreciates over time because consumers tend to forget brands and competitors operate to affirm their brands. Therefore, continuous advertising is needed to maintain a constant level of goodwill and a given rate of sales.[4]

Similarly, the stock of knowledge depreciates over time and it is necessary to have a flow of internal R&D investments to maintain a firm's stock of knowledge.

In conclusion, the stock of resources of a firm and its knowledge, competences and capacities are the results of its history and they condition its planning and strategic capacity (Nelson, 1995). The heterogeneity of its resources and the consequent firm-specific characteristics are thus the basis of diversity and strategic variety of a firm, together with chance factors.

However, if the opportunities for growth are limited by the current resource stock and by the speed at which a firm can internally develop new resources, a firm can overcome this limit, through M&As. This strategy allows the acquiring firm to increase new pools of resources and its knowledge base externally, so enlarging the acceptable domain of its opportunities to innovate and create value (Capron and Pistre, 2002; Collis and Montgomery, 2005). In this context, an M&A strategy can be useful, in particular, for obtaining technological know-how and developing new technical capability (Hitt et al., 1997; Chakrabarti et al., 1994; Ahuja and Katila, 2001).

Therefore, M&As not only allow the existing resources to be more exploited, but they also allow new complementary resources to be added and developed, favouring new patterns of growth, removing boundaries and creating new value (Fig. 4.2). In fact, when purchasing an entire company, it is possible to acquire the desired resources in a market transaction externally, so to exploit the existing one, but at the same time quickly develop new ones.[5]

In this context, for defining a successful M&A strategy it is of fundamental importance to understand which resources are critical for growth and value, and which can be developed through acquisitions.[6]

Schemes for identifying strategic assets and resources to be exploited through M&As

The value chain model can be used for identifying firm strategic assets and resources capable of being exploited in an M&A.[7] It is a matter of comparing the chain value of the companies involved in the potential merger, so as to identify which assets and resources are complementary and which are similar. *Complementary* assets and resources are those that round out each other; *similar* are those that the target and the acquirer firms have alike prior to the acquisition.

To this aim, we will consider, in particular, tangible and intangible assets and firm capabilities in all support and primary activities (Dringoli, 2011). This analysis will be completed by the evaluation of revenue and cost structures as well as of asset and liability structures of firms interested in the merger. Schemes for identifying strategic assets and resources and for analysing cost and revenue structures are shown in the Tables 4.1; 4.2; 4.3 and 4.4.

The analysis of assets and resources of the acquiring (*A*) and the target (*T*) firms allows the identification of those which can be exploited in different geographical markets or in different market segments and the evaluation of the effects in terms of incremental revenues or cost savings for the combined firm.

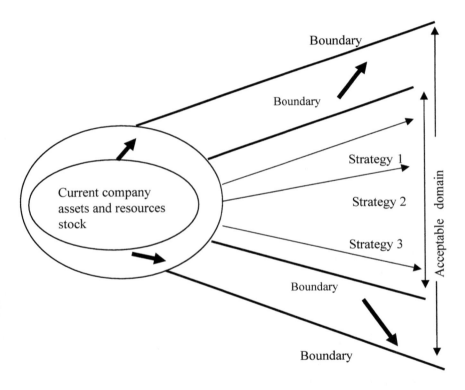

Figure 4.2   Enlarging the acceptable domain of firm development through M&As

Table 4.1　　*A scheme for identifying strategic assets and resources for M&As: support activities*

Support Activities	Assets and resources for M&As	Firm A	Firm T
Firm infrastructure	*Tangible assets* Information system and technology platform; financial resources; etc. *Intangible assets* Know-how in planning, finance, accounting, legal, government affairs and quality management. *Capabilities:* General management, etc.		
Human resource management	*Intangible assets* Firm reputation with employees and the community; Educational, technical and professional qualifications of employees; the commitment and loyalty of employees; motivating empowering and retaining employees. *Capabilities*: HR management expertise; general management skills.		
Technology development	*Tangible assets* R&D laboratories; research facilities, etc. *Intangible assets* Reputation in R&D activities; stock of technology: patents, trademarks, copyrights and trade secrets. *Capabilities*: R&D know-how, personnel expertise, etc.		
Procurement	*Tangible assets* Access to raw materials. *Intangible* Firm reputation with suppliers. *Capabilities*: Buying expertise.		

Table 4.2 A scheme for identifying strategic assets and resources for M&As: primary activities

Primary activities	Assets and resources for M&As	Firm A	Firm T
Inbound logistics	*Tangible assets* Logistic machinery and plants. *Capabilities*: Inbound logistic expertise		
Operations	*Tangible asset* Location and alternative uses for land and buildings; general and specialist machinery; plant capacity. *Intangible assets* Technological knowledge; product and process patents; proprietary technology, copyrights, etc. *Capabilities*: Manufacturing expertise.		
Marketing and sales	*Tangible assets* Directed operating stores and franchising stores *Intangible assets*: Company and products brands; wholesalers and retailers network; Sales organization; established relations; reputation for quality and reliability, etc. *Capabilities*: Marketing and selling expertise; effective brand management and brand promotion		
Outbound logistics	*Tangible assets* Central and local stores. *Intangible Assets* Level of service reputation. *Capabilities*: Logistic management expertise; efficiency and speed of distribution; effective use of logistic management techniques.		
Service	*Intangible Assets* Friendly service management. *Capabilities*: Quality and effectiveness of customer service		

Table 4.3. A scheme for the analysis of cost and cash flow structures of the firms interested in the merger

			Firm A	Firm T
+	Revenues	R		
−	Current operating expenses	C		
	Raw material costs			
	Production labour cost			
	Production service costs			
	Selling and marketing costs			
	R&D costs			
	Administrative costs			
=	Earnings before interest, tax, depreciation and amortization	$EBITDA$ A		
=	Earnings before interest and taxes	$EBIT$		
−	Interest expenses	INT		
=	Taxable income	EBT		
−	Taxes	$EBT\ tc$		
=	Net income	NI		
+	Interest expenses	INT		
+	Depreciation and amortization	A		
=	Cash flow from operations	CFO		
−	Working capital change	ΔWC		
−	Capital expenditures	ΔI		
=	Free cash flow from operations	$FCFO$		
	Other relevant data:			
	Quantity Produced	Q_p		
	Number of clients	N_C		
	Unit Cost of Product	Cu		
	N° Employees	N_e		
	Labour productivity = Quantity produced/N°employees	Π_L		

Table 4.4   *A scheme for the analysis of Asset and Liability structure of the firms interested in the merger (industrial firms)*

ASSETS

Liquidity		*Li*	%
Current assets		A_C	%
Trade debtors	*Cc*		
Other credits	*Cd*		
Inventories	*Inv*		
Fixed assets		A_F	%
Industrial and office building	*Ib*		
Plant and equipment	*P*		
Other machinery	*M*		
TOTAL ASSETS		*CI*	100
DEBT AND EQUITY		*D*	%
Debt			
Trade creditors	D_T		
Bank creditors	D_B		
Long-term debt	D_{LT}		
Common Capital	*CN*		
TOTAL FINANCINGS		*F*	100
Other relevant data			
Debt/Common capital		*D/CN*	%
Current assets/Short-term debt		A_C/D_C	%

A list of resources and capabilities that are generally critical for M&A strategies is shown in Table 4.5.

Table 4.5 Critical assets and resources for successful M&A strategies

Types of resources	Resources for growth
Tangible assets	Plant production capacity
	Plant productivity and flexibility
	Distribution network
	Procurement logistic system
	Centralized R&D laboratory
	Administrative and support system
Intangible assets	Brand reputation
	Brand loyalty
	Patents
Core capabilities and competences	Production distinctive know-how
	Marketing and communication expertise
	R&D competences
	Coordination and control competences

Source: Dringoli (2011).

OPPORTUNITIES AND THREATS FROM INDUSTRY STRUCTURE AND DYNAMICS

After the internal analysis of firms involved in the merger, the analysis of industry dynamics will complete the information necessary for the choice of the most appropriate M&A strategy, for example preferring a horizontal M&A to a vertical or a diversified one.

The analysis of the industry structure, where the firm operates and where it wants to expand (horizontal M&As) or where the firm is interested in entering (vertical or diversified M&As), is the second foundation for a careful choice of an M&A strategy capable of creating value.

This analysis must discover if the industry offers the conditions and opportunities for an M&A to be successful. In this respect, the analysis of the most relevant competitive forces operating in the industry, where it already operates, or where it wants to enter, is of fundamental importance.

These competitive forces are the following (Porter 1985):

- the current competitors;
- the suppliers;
- the clients;
- the firms producing substitute products;
- the potential entrants.

Therefore, the analysis has to focus on these forces, to discover the threats they represent to the firm value and if these offer the opportunity for M&A strategies to create value.

The current competitors in the industry

The number of competitors and the concentration rate deeply affect the level of sale prices and therefore the profits in the industry. On this subject, remember that the continuum of competitive situations can be divided into four broad categories: perfect competition, imperfect or monopolistic competition, oligopoly and monopoly. To each of these a different intensity of price competition is related. Generally in perfect competition markets, the concentration[8] is low and the intensity of price competition is fierce; in monopolistic competition, concentration is low and the intensity of price competition may be fierce or weak, depending on product differentiation. In oligopoly, concentration is high and price competition may be fierce or weak depending on rivalry between different firms. Finally in monopoly, concentration is very high and the intensity of price competition is generally weak, unless there is the threat of new entrants (Besanko et al., 1996).

Obviously, these frameworks provide only some schemes of reference, which are not to be generalized. For example, sometimes there are cases of high competition in the presence of only two competitors or cases of low competition in markets characterized by multiple firms with differentiated products or by firms with a strong dissuasive power of the possible reaction to price competition of other incumbent firms. This will depend on the amount of financial resources available and the ability of possible competitors to retaliate with relevant effects in the markets.

However, in general, rivalry is high among competitors and price levels shrink when the industry presents the following characteristics:

- the number of competitors is large and they are more similar in terms of size and capability;
- the industry conditions, for example the unemployed capacity, spur competitors to decrease prices or to use other competitive weapons in order to increase sales volumes;

- the switching from one brand to another is easy and not expensive.

When an industry presents these characteristics, a horizontal M&A strategy can offer the opportunity to the acquiring firm to modify the market structure of the industry, reducing price competition with significant revenue synergies.

On the contrary, an M&A strategy directed at diversifying in a similar industry will expose the acquiring firm to strong competition and low prices and thus to a poor performance.

Suppliers with high bargaining power

Suppliers in an industry may be a competitive force, since their bargaining power may increase the costs of raw materials, components and services, and reduce the margins and earnings of the buyer firm. In other words, suppliers, using their dealing power, may require changes in some elements of the supply relationship that are favourable to them: price increases, standardization of the products provided, reduction of product variables, lengthening of delivery time, increase of the minimum order, reduction of assistance or design support, etc. Conditions favouring a high bargaining power of suppliers and high price of factors are (Hax and Majluf, 1984; Grant, 1998):

- supply markets containing few firms and which are more concentrated than the industries of the buyer firms;
- a limited availability of substitute products for those of the suppliers;
- the significant contribution of the supplier's products to the quality of products of the buyer firm or to the efficiency of the production process;
- the high differentiation of the supplier's products and/or high re-conversion costs for the acquiring firm;
- the capability of suppliers to integrate downstream.

In an industry characterized by suppliers with a strong bargaining power, a vertical upstream M&A can offer the acquiring firm the opportunity to reduce the bargaining power of some suppliers and obtain relevant cost synergies. On the contrary, a diversified M&A in a similar industry will expose the firm to a poor performance, because of the bargaining power of suppliers.

Clients with high bargaining power

Clients may be an important competitive force in the industry, since through their bargaining power they are able to compel the firm to lower prices, in this way gaining a part of the value created by it. In effect, very often, small and medium-sized manufacturers operating with a large client suffer from the bargaining power of the client and accept lower prices. In general, conditions increasing the bargaining power of clients are the following (Grant, 1998):

- the market is concentrated: there are few big clients;
- margins of clients are high;
- clients can integrate upstream;
- final customers are strongly linked to clients.

In these cases, a downstream vertical M&A, by the integration of wholesale or retailing networks, can offer the acquiring firm important synergies in revenues and costs, as we will see in Chapter 6. On the contrary, a diversified M&A in a similar industry will be risky, unless the acquiring firm can obtain relevant competitive advantages from economies of scope.

Manufacturers of substitute products

Manufacturers of effective substitute products may represent a further important competitive force, capable of affecting the prices and profits in the industry. Beyond certain price levels, in fact, the demand will move towards substitute products, causing a reduction of the firm's profit in the medium term. So, the existence of substitute products increases the price elasticity of the demand, since clients may move their demand towards substitute products each time the product price exceeds what they are likely to pay. For example, producers of artificial sweeteners threaten sugar manufacturers; producers of glass bottles compete against manufacturers of plastic, paper, cardboard and aluminium containers; producers of artificial fibres for the textile industry compete against producers of natural fibres, and so on. Obviously, if substitute products are not perfect, thanks to the product differentiation, the firm will have greater running control in prices and will be able to stably maintain higher profits.

When manufacturers of substitute products represent an important competitive force in the industry, a diversified M&A can allow the acquiring firm to reduce the competive pressure on the base industry, by controlling the product price and so maintaining high profits. On the contrary, a horizontal espansion in an industry, characterized by perfect substitute products, will further expose the firm to possible pressures on prices and thus on profits.

The potential entrants and the barriers to entry

Potential entrants can represent a strong threat to the level of profits in an industry. In fact, the entry of new competitors will increase the supply in the industry and will push down the price of products and as a consequence also the revenues and cash flows of the incumbent firms.

Therefore, there are no lasting advantages in making M&As by entering industries with low barriers, because the current favourable conditions can be rapidly reversed by the entry of potential rivals.

On the contrary, an industry with high barriers to entry can offer interesting opportunities for successful diversified M&As. These can allow the acquiring firms to quickly enter the industry and exploit the existing assets and resources, drawing profit from economies of scope, without sustaining the costs of entry through internal development and the negative effects of the consequent increase in the total supply of the industry.

It is common knowledge (Bain, 1956; Modigliani, 1958; Sylos Labini, 1964) that the entry barriers in an industry are determined by:

- scale economies;
- product differentiation;
- cost advantages, independent of scale, for incumbents.

Scale economies cause entry barriers because they compel the new competitor to enter the business with a high scale of production, and therefore with a significant supply, such as to determine a considerable post-entry price decrease. The entry of new firms, by adding new production capacity, would trigger a price reduction and therefore decrease the profits of all firms over a long period. Post-entry price conditions can therefore diverge significantly from pre-entries and cause the annulment of extra profits before entry. So, scale economies tend to discourage potential rivals, creating a condition which is favourable to the incumbent firms and thus to a higher level of price and profits in the industry (Besanko et al., 1996).

Product differentiation determines another entry barrier because it is not sufficient for the entrant to build the production capacity and offer the product to acquiring market share. It is necessary to differentiate the product significantly, in order to modify already consolidated preferences. In addition, product differentiation is not easy to achieve: it requires investments, sometimes extremely high ones, the results of which are by nature very uncertain.

Finally, cost advantages, not depending on scale, are the advantages the incumbent firms have independently of their size. They are related to different factors, among which are control over scarce resources in the procurement (natural resources, raw materials) or sales markets (long-term or exclusive relationships with suppliers or customers), the availability of patents or owned technologies, non-replicable production and distribution locations, the experience and availability of a qualified labour force, any other market imperfection, or the amount and the cost of capital of new entrants compared to firms already operating in the industry.

As things stand, industries with high entry barriers can be actractive for M&A deals, because they favour the sustainability of high prices and consequently of profits. In particular, these conditions will favour horizontal M&As, directed at increasing the market power of an incumbent firm and at further reducing competition in the industry. Besides, they will favour diversified M&As, because these represent a simple and fast way to diversify, drawing advantage from the economies of scope, whereas it would be difficult and risky to enter a similar industry through internal development.

Further characteristics of the industry influencing M&As performance

Other structural characteristics of the industry that can influence the success of an M&A are the following: a) economies of scale; b) the growth of demand; and c) the dynamics of technological progress.

Economies of scale

The presence of economies of scale will favour a successful M&A. In fact, the larger size of the combined firm will allow this firm to adopt a larger scale of activity, so obtaining a cost advantage over the other incumbent firms.

The growth of aggregate demand

The performance of an M&A will be significantly affected by the growth of the aggregate demand of products and services. Businesses characterized by a low growth rate usually show a greater rivalry among competitors and lower profitability in the long run. The opposite considerations count in sectors that are characterized by high growth rates (Thompson and Strickland, 1998). In fact, these dynamics can have a determining effect on product prices and sales, determining the success of a diversified strategy. In particular, a rapid growth in aggregate demand can favour the reaching of planned sales and the increase in product price; conversely, a small growth with a large increase in product supply can produce in-excess product capacity, thereby causing a fall in product price and destructive retaliation from rival firms.

The dynamics of technical progress

The dynamics of technical progress has to be carefully evaluated before making an M&A. In fact, it can change the competitive conditions in the industry, rapidly destroying the competitive advantage, as well as distinctive competences created through the M&A.

IS THERE A WINNING M&A STRATEGY?

What the theory suggests

From a theoretical point of view is there a type of M&A to prefer as the best performing and is there an optimal pattern of growth that a firm should follow over time in order to create value (that is an optimal sequence of M&As)?

The structural theory and the resource-based theory, which we have mentioned before, suggests that an M&A strategy for being successful should be based on the firm's specific assets and resources and tuned with the external conditions of industry demand and competition. Therefore, each M&A strategy has to make leverage on firm-specific resources and favourable external conditions: scale economies, transaction costs, economies of scope, learning economies, and so on.

All this suggests that each firm has its specific successful pattern of growth, according to the existing assets and stock of resources and the ability to acquire and develop new resources (Norman, 1977; Teece, 1987, 2007; Teece et al., 1997).

However, considering the entire life cycle of a firm, a *horizontal M&A* should generally be the way that initially allows a firm to better make leverage on its initial specialist resources and develop those of the acquired firm.

This first growth phase should be followed, if necessary, by a vertical M&A, either in manufacturing or in distribution activities, to improve efficiency and market power.

Finally, further expansion should be based mainly on a related diversified M&A, so as to exploit the accumulated set of multipurpose-excess resources. Unrelated diversification should not be accomplished because it does not produce synergies; in addition it is not an efficient strategy because uninformed central managers cannot run R&D and investment-intense divisions, especially in a highly competitive environment.

What empirical research highlights

As for the patterns of firm growth, what does the empirical evidence tell us? Examining the long period of history of the largest American corporations from the 1880s to the 1930s, Chandler (1962 and 1990) found that horizontal, vertical and diversified processes generally took place one after the other, during the life of corporations, both in relation to the firm's internal resources and the environmental conditions. The first two strategies were carried out in the initial phases of the growth of firms, in order to penetrate and consolidate their position on the existing markets, whereas diversification strategies were implemented in the subsequent phases of the firm's life, so as to better exploit the organizational capacities, as well as the accumulated know-how especially in marketing, distribution and R&D activities (Chandler, 1962).

However, while diversification strategies permitted the continuing and expanding use of a firm's resources, they did not assure their efficient employment. In fact, expanding through diversification enlarged the range, number and complexity of entrepreneurial activities required of the senior executives, making it more and more difficult to efficiently administer different products and markets. For this reason, structural reorganization became necessary for rationalizing the use of expanding resources.

So, for Chandler, the chapters in the collective history of the American industrial enterprises were characterized by phases in which resources were accumulated, then rationalized, then expanded and then once again rationalized. After the Second World War the expansion of companies was characterized by the same model. In the 1960s the dominant trend was diversification and conglomeration (Shleifer and Vishny, 1994). In America and Europe the large enterprises progressively moved into other industries that appeared to have greater profit potential, even though their existing resources gave them little or no competitive advantage. Many firms entered distant or unrelated businesses by acquiring other firms already operating there (conglomerate diversification). This process continued in the 1960s and 1970s and it was characterized by waves of acquisitions and mergers. For the period 1973–1977 half of all assets acquired through merger and acquisition were in unrelated industries.

In the 1980s takeovers, in contrast, reversed this process and brought American corporations back to greater specialization (Shleifer and Vishny, 1994). These takeovers were followed by sell-offs of a substantial fraction of the target's assets to other firms. Restructuring was a major activity in American and European industry: the reduction in unrelated diversification was directed at recovering the efficiency necessary for sustaining continuing increasing competition (Hill and Hoskisson, 1987; Ravenscraft and Scherer, 1987; Shleifer and Vishny, 1994; Johnson et al., 1993).

Thus, a phase characterized by a re-focusing of activities on the firm's core business historically followed after a strong unrelated diversified growth, generally accomplished by a high number of M&A operations. This refocusing strategy became necessary in order to arrest the fall in efficiency of the organizational structure, often caused by over-diversified expansion that increased the firm size but reduced performance and destroyed value.

In many cases a rapid expansion into distant or unrelated businesses had put an enormous strain on firm structure and reduced performance (Grant et al., 1988). The increase in the number of divisions administered and the wide variety of businesses in which some firms operated, created increasing difficulties in managing the firm because of a lack of information, a reduction in its quality and the inability of senior managers to evaluate it. In other cases too much diversification created significant problems because over time the firm produced less innovation.

The resulting weakness in performance led firms to sell off many of their divisions and to concentrate on products and processes in which they had their strongest production, marketing and research capabilities for creating value. In the 1990s and the 2000s restructuring strategies were successfully carried out with strong reductions in the level of unrelated diversified activities by many enterprises.

The following conclusions can be drawn from empirical research.

1. There is a basic pattern of growth over time, characterized by an initial phase of horizontal expansion in local and international markets, sometimes accompanied by vertical integration expansion up and down the value chain, followed by a phase of product-related diversification and sometimes a subsequent phase of unrelated diversification.

2. The last phase of unrelated diversification is generally followed by a phase of restructuring, with strong reductions in the level of unrelated diversification and the return to core business activities where a firm's distinctive resources can be more efficiently exploited. Therefore, empirical evidence confirms that a growth

strategy destroying value can be pursued, but it cannot be sustained over time; such a growth can be carried out in the short-term, but it is not sustainable in the long-term.

3. The external conditions, especially the environmental and the industrial ones, are of fundamental importance in differentiating growth patterns.

4. The model of growth remains unique for each firm and depends on the firm's specific resources, in addition to the dynamics of industry structure. For each individual firm the various phases in the growth pattern vary in length, importance and impact and the different types of M&As have a very different relevance on growth and firm value. The cases presented in the second part of this book represent emblematic examples of different successful M&As. These successful companies belong to different industries and are not homogeneous regarding their initial firm structure and distinctive resources.

In the following chapters we start by examining the horizontal M&A strategy, this being the most frequent way for external growth; then we will continue with the analysis of vertical and diversified M&As.

NOTES

1. We use the term resource in its broad sense (Barney, 1991) and hence it includes activities, capabilities, etc. which allow the firm to generate rents.

2. Hofer and Schendel (1978) consider five types of resources and competences at a business unit level: 1) financial resources; 2) material resources (such as plant, machinery, stores, inventories, etc.); 3) human resources; 4) organizational resources (quality control systems, financial control methods, etc.); 5) technological capabilities (high quality products, low cost production, high brand loyalty, etc.).

3. From a conceptual point of view, a firm's resources can be considered as state or level variables according to the concept of state used in system dynamics theory. A state or level variable is an accumulation, or integration over time, of flows or changes that come into and go out of the level. Conversely, a rate variable is a flow, decision, action or behaviour that changes over time as a function of influences acting upon it. The state or level variables characterize a system at a certain date and influence the way the system works. Also the firm system can be represented by a set of state variables, according to the principle of system dynamics. For example, a firm's image is a state variable as it represents the

customers' accumulation of intangible impressions stemming from information flows over an extended duration. Similarly, scientific knowledge is an information level variable and in a similar way so are a firm's employees, plants, and so on. On these topics, see the relevant theoretical contribution of Winter (1987). On the representation of the firm as a dynamic system, see: Forrester (1961); Simon (1981); Roberts (1999); Ceccanti (1996); Dringoli (2000 and 2006).

4.   On this subject we refer to the classical papers on optimal advertising policy of Telser (1962) and Nerlove and Arrow (1962). On the process of resource accumulation and decay see also Dierickx and Cool (1989).

5.   On the importance of developing existing resources and also acquiring them when it is necessary in order to sustain the growth, see the classic study of Norman (1977). The capacity of a firm to create, extend or modify its resource base for sustaining the growth and creating value in a rapidly changing environment is what recent literature calls dynamic capabilities (Helfat et al., 2007). On the studies for investigating dynamic capabilities see: Teece, et al., (1997); Eisenhardt and Martin (2000); Zollo and Winter (2002); Winter (2003); Helfat and Peteraf (2003); Teece (2007); Ambrosini et al., (2009); Easterby-Smith et al. (2009).

6.   According to Wernerfelt (1984) this analysis can be conducted through what is called a resource-product matrix in which the checked entries indicate the importance of a resource in a product and vice versa. In this context, a firm acquisition can be seen as a purchase of rare resources in a highly imperfect market.

7.   Also Collis and Montgomery (2005) propose the value chain for identifying the key success factors for a strategy. Barney (2001) suggests using the value chain to identify the firm's resources. This author proposes a model of analysis of resources named VRIO (value, rarity, imitative and organization of resources) useful for defining the strengths and weaknesses of a firm.

     According to Barney, resources have to be valued on the basis of their value with respect to the environmental opportunities and threats; of their rarity, that favours the reaching of a competitive advantage, of facilities to be imitated and of firm organization capability in exploiting them. On the basis of the application of the VRIO framework it is possible to identify the key resources which make a firm a winner. In this context, Barney also presents an interesting application of the VRIO framework.

     Previously, Ansoff (1968 and 1988) had proposed organizing resources and skills along the major functional areas: research and development, operations, marketing, general management and finance. Within each of these functional areas he recognizes four categories of skills and resources: 1) facilities and equipment; 2) personnel skills; 3) organizational capabilities; and 4) management capabilities. In any case, it is a matter of analysing the organized set of activities and processes that are carried out by personnel application in order to obtain products or services for markets, identifying the relevant firm's resources.

8. Concentration in an industry can be measured by the Herfindahl–Hirshman index; it equals the sum of the squared market shares of all firms in the market. For its mathematical structure the HH index represents a more informative measure than the traditional N-firm concentration ratio.

5. Horizontal M&As

INTRODUCTION AND OBJECTIVES

A horizontal M&A strategy is a course of action directed at increasing production capacity and sales, while continuing to produce the same basic product. The target firm can operate in the existing market of the acquiring firm or in different geographical markets as well as in markets characterized by different types and models of the same products. Horizontal M&As differ according to the objectives pursued and the different size of the capacity jumps.

In this chapter we will analyse the conditions necessary for a horizontal M&A strategy to create value; the relevant variables are also analysed in their fundamental relations through a quantitative model, in order to offer a useful guide for decision making.

Stable or growing aggregate demand and economies of scale result as being the most important external conditions necessary for horizontal M&As to create value. Conversely, capabilities in exploiting similar and complementary assets and resources, as well as in increasing market power, emerge as being the most important internal factors for a successful M&A.

RATIONALES FOR HORIZONTAL M&As

The levers for creating value through horizontal M&As can be summarized as follows:

- the reduction in costs by integrating similar activities and resources, and by removing excess capacity in support and primary activities;
- the reduction in costs, by exploiting economies of scale both in support and primary activities;
- the increase in revenues by exploiting complementary assets and resources for selling different types of products in geographically different markets;
- the increase in revenues due to a bigger bargaining power with respect to customers and the consequent increase in product price, because of a larger market share;

- the reduction in costs because of *economies of experience*, or learning economies, made possible by a larger cumulative production;
- the reduction in capital expenditure and in working capital made possible by the integration of companies.

Reduction in costs by integrating similar assets and resources and by removing excess capacity in support and primary activities

Horizontal M&As offer good opportunities for improving efficiency, because firms have similar activities and resources with common customers, common markets, directly competing products, etc. So, the merger favours a reorganization of similar assets and resources and higher efficiency. To carry this out is a matter of removing redundant assets and resources along the existing value chains and of exploiting tangible and intangible assets and resources capable of creating value.

In particular, a horizontal expansion is favoured by the similarity of the value chains of firms involved, because of the similarity of types and models of a basic product. That allows a reduction in product costs of the combined firm, by sharing some technical and marketing activities and resources. However, as some assets are redundant, post-acquisition asset divestiture is necessary.[1] Therefore, to obtain an effective reduction in costs, the acquiring firm has to develop a dynamic process of resource redeployment and asset divestiture, after the acquisition. In other words, the acquiring firm has to reconfigure the structure of its assets and resources, and asset divestiture can be a way of achieving the process of activity reconfiguration. In particular, it is a matter of selling a part of physical and organizational assets, reducing labour forces, shutting facilities and factories, etc. This asset divestiture can apply to both target and acquirer business units (Porter, 1987; Ravenscraft and Scherer, 1987; Weston, 1994; Capron et al., 2001). Through divestiture the combined firm will gain efficiency and reduce the unit cost of products.

Obviously, the additional costs of integrating assets and resources and redesigning the organizational structure of the combined firm, as well as the costs of asset divestitures, have to be considered together with the positive effects expected by the acquisition.

Reduction in costs due to a larger scale of activity (*economies of scale*)

A horizontal expansion strategy can also create value, in the presence of stable aggregate demand, for exploiting *economies of scale*.

It is common knowledge that economies of scale occur when the unit cost of a product decreases as the activity scale for that unit increases (Pratten, 1971; Scherer et al., 1975; Norman, 1979; Hay and Morris, 1979; Bellandi, 1995; Besanko et al., 1996). Generally, the scale of production units is measured by the rate of output per unit period. More precisely, "economies of scale are said to exist with respect to a particular input, or to all total inputs, when the appropriate elasticity of the cost (production) function, evaluated at constant relative factor prices and incorporating a given technology, is less than the unity over some or all of the range of attainable scales" (Norman, 1979). This definition makes no presumption that the elasticity of the cost function will be constant with scale.

We can have economies of scale with respect to a plant, an establishment (which may be made up of a group of contiguous plants) and a firm which can be reported as an organizational unit containing a number of establishments. In particular, there are technological economies of scale when the cost per unit of production decreases with the increasing scale of production.

Economies of scale can occur in other areas of a firm's activities, for example in distribution, marketing or R&D activities (we call them managing scale economies). In this case the economies of scale occur when the unit cost of distribution or R&D activities decreases with the increasing scale of the activity. In the pharmaceutical industry, for example, there are high economies of scale in R&D activity.

Economies of scale can occur also in capital funding and in raw material procurement. In this case, the lower unit cost comes from ordering and delivering larger quantities of raw materials and product components.

Technological economies of scale are present especially in industries where the technology allows the firms adopting the larger plants to carry out production processes in a more efficient way, with a production cost per unit decreasing with the scale of plant production.[2]

When economies of scale can be obtained in primary or support activities, an M&A can allow the acquiring firm to expand activity, making it profitable to invest in a larger scale plant or other operating structures, (distribution network or R&D activity). This will allow a competitive advantage in costs with respect to rivals to be obtained.[3] This cost advantage can also make it convenient for the combined firm to reduce the price of the product, thereby damaging the rival firms to the extent of provoking the exit of the weakest competitors from the market. This will happen if the economies of scale can give a substantial advantage in costs to the firm expanding its scale of production.

However, as the attack on the market share of the competing firms will cause reactions, this strategy must be undertaken only after correctly evaluating the advantages that can be obtained compared to the costs deriving from the possible reactions of the rival firms.

Examples of aggressive expansion strategies can be found in the oil-refining industry, as well as in the chemical and pharmaceutical industries.

In synthesis, as we said before, economies of scale are not only present in production activity, but also in other activities of the firm, such as logistics, marketing and R&D activities. The increasing relevance of economies of scale has changed the competitive balance in many industries, to the advantage of those firms that carried out horizontal expansion processes more rapidly. Among these are the automobile, chemical, steel and cement sectors.

Increase in sales and revenues by exploiting complementary and polyvalent assets and resources

A horizontal M&A can also create value by exploiting complementary and polyvalent assets as well as resources between the acquiring and the target firm (Figure 5.1).

This is especially true in cases of different distribution networks from the acquiring and the target firm that can be used for the expansion of the sale of different types and models of the product offered by the firms involved in the merger.

In other cases, the quality of some assets and resources, such as sales force, the know-how in manufacturing and the expertise gained in managing marketing activities, can be used to increase sales and revenues of the acquiring or the target firm's types of products.

Other relevant opportunities can derive from a wider portfolio of products, from sharing logistics, machinery, quality control activities, as well as from know-how about product management, expertise in operations and distribution, brands, etc. More revenues can also derive from exploiting marketing activities (promotion, advertising, distribution channels and after-sales network), procurement activities (raw materials and financial resources) and infrastructure activities (planning and control system, finance, etc.). In particular, a horizontal M&A can enable sales and revenues to increase in geographically different markets, for example foreign markets, by sharing market expertise, brand image, technical know-how, etc.

In addition, the acquisition can allow the acquiring firm to use resources from the target firm for changing its resource profile, modifying competences and redeploying resources, thereby gaining revenue synergies (Karim and Mitchell, 2000).

Strategic assets and resources in primary activities of the acquiring firm	Sales of different product types and models of the target firm
Inbound Logistics: logistic machinery and plants *Operations*: machinery and plants *Marketing & Sales*: direct operating stores; wholesalers and retailers network *Outbound Logistics*: central and local stores *After-sale service*: reputation and service network	

Figure 5.1   Using polyvalent assets and complementary resources for promoting sales of different types of products in a horizontal M&A

Increase in product price through higher market power in industry

A horizontal M&A can create value through the increase in bargaining power towards customers, as a consequence of a higher market share. As economic theory shows, a concentration in industry favours collusive price policies with favourable effects on profits of the incumbent firms.

Reduction in unit production cost through economies of experience

Economies of experience or learning economies can be another relevant factor favouring horizontal M&A strategy. Economies of experience represent the lower costs deriving from an increase in the cumulative production of a firm. These economies derive from learning processes in operations, developing as long as the production cycles are repeated with the increase of cumulative production (Abell and Hammond, 1979; Spence, 1981; Baden Fuller, 1983; Lieberman, 1984; Adler and Clark, 1991; Besanko et al., 1996; Dringoli, 2011).

The learning processes, especially in product manufacturing, determine a reduction in the quantities of factors necessary for operations, thereby reducing the unit cost of the product. These economies mainly depend on greater labour efficiency due to labour specialization, and the improvement in operations activities, working techniques and methods, by virtue of the increase in cumulative production. In fact, this phenomenon occurs as the effect of repeating the same operation or the same sequence of operations, that is as the effect of the number of times one operation or a sequence of operations is repeated. It is really this repetition of activities which produces learning, favouring organizational solutions that reduce the time of operations and thus the unit cost per product.

Through a horizontal M&A a firm anticipates the increase of its cumulative production, thus expanding its capacity. So, it would also anticipate the learning effect, reducing the unit cost of a product and gaining a competitive advantage over its rivals (Saloner et al., 2001). In other words, because learning economies are a result of cumulative production and not simply of the period of time the firm has made a product, a firm growing more rapidly than the others can benefit from the experience effect earlier. Therefore, the presence of high learning economies drives a firm to accelerate its growth, in order to obtain a cost advantage over the competing firms (Ghemawat, 1985).

The intensity of learning economies differs from one industry to another, according to the complexity of operations. In fact, the learning economies are above all present in labour-intensive production. According to the Boston Consulting Group (1972), in a large number of industries the learning economies are expressed by a rate of reduction of costs from 20% to 30% each time cumulative production is doubled. For example, in the aeronautical sector, where these studies were first developed, the learning process was considerably relevant, with a reduction in costs of approximately 30% at each doubling of production. That was due to the high specialization of the labour-intensive activities and the introduction of process standardization for many components, made possible by the increase of cumulative production.

In the microprocessors industry these economies have been higher than the mean for industries, with a rate of cost reduction from 40% to 50% at each doubling of cumulative production, while in the automobile industry this rate has been estimated as being approximately equal to 12%.[4]

Reduction in capital expenditures and working capital

A merger of companies operating in the same industry can allow significant reductions in working capital, because of the opportunity of sharing stocks of common raw materials, components and final products. Similarly, a horizontal merger can offer great opportunities to reduce capital expenditure both for the economies due to a larger scale of investment, and for the savings deriving from sharing new infrastructures, plants and machinery.

Furthermore, relevant reductions in capital expenditure can be carried out in R&D investments for new products or processes, by avoiding the duplication of projects and structures. Recent M&As in pharmaceutical and automotive industries have been mainly driven by this type of merger synergies.

ADDITIONAL COSTS IN HORIZONTAL M&As

When a firm decides to grow through a horizontal M&A, it is also necessary to consider the additional costs of integrating and reorganizing activities. These costs can reduce the advantages obtained through the merger. In particular, the major sources of horizontal integration costs are the following:

- costs in reorganizing primary and support activities and removing redundant assets and resources;
- costs in integrating different firm cultures, especially in production and marketing activities;
- costs in coordinating and controlling a more complex organization.

To increase efficiency in primary and supporting activities it is often necessary to restructure the organization, with the assignment of new positions of responsibility. There is the need to develop new knowledge and to motivate employees, etc.

Horizontal strategies are more frequently adopted by firms operating in the development and in maturity phases of an industry. This happens because in the development phase of an industry, firms have advantages in exploiting scale economies; in mature phases they have advantages in increasing the market share for acquiring more market power. A summary of the benefits and costs of horizontal acquisitions is shown in Table 5.1.

THE ADVANTAGES OF HORIZONTAL ACQUISITIONS WITH RESPECT TO INTERNAL EXPANSION

A horizontal expansion can be obtained, rather than through M&As, throu internal development, that is increasing a firm's capacity with direct investmen These investments can take the form of new production lines or departments, well as expansion of the existing plant or even the building of a new plant. T internal development may also require investments in new stores, commerc branches and offices and marketing activities.

Table 5.1 A summary of benefits and costs of horizontal M&As

Potential benefits	Potential costs
Reduction in operating costs by reorganizing assets and resources and removing the redundant ones	Cost of resource redeployment and assets divestiture
Reduction in operating costs by exploiting economies of scale	Cost of coordinating and integrating new activities
Revenue synergies through increased market power and the consequent increase in product price	
Revenue synergies through exploiting complementary and polyvalent assets and resources	
Reduction in working capital investment and in capital expenditures	

Generally, internal expansion requires a long period of time from the date when the decision is taken to the date when the investments are completed. The disadvantages of an expansion carried out through internal development are the risks of delaying the increase of production with respect to a faster growth of demand and a faster growth of competitors. The advantages of internal expansion are the possibilities of exploiting all the know-how the firm has accumulated in different business areas and of being able to monitor directly the entire expansion process. In addition, when carrying out an internal development, a firm can apply those technologies and organizational solutions which better fit the existing firm structure (Dringoli, 2011).

Conversely, the growth through M&A provides the advantage of a faster increase in production capacity and market share. In addition, the acquiring firm can rapidly increase the number of customers and sales and also exploit the technical and organizational know-how and other complementary assets and resources of the purchased firm. However, a horizontal expansion through M&A often involves high costs for integrating the different production processes and different firm culture and management systems, as can be seen in Chapter 9. Furthermore, a growth through M&A also requires evaluating assets and resources in a condition of limited information, with the risk of overvaluing the target firm.

TYPES OF HORIZONTAL M&As AND SYNERGIES

Bearing in mind the rationales for horizontal M&As, we may now specify the expected synergies that an M&A can produce, according to the goals the management want to obtain through the expansion strategy. On this point, we distinguish the following types of horizontal M&As:

- *Market share increase M&As*; we refer to M&As for increasing market share through the acquisition of companies operating with similar products in the same market for increasing volumes of sales and market share;
- *Geographical market coverage M&As*; we refer to M&As for extending market coverage through the acquisition of companies operating with similar products in different geographic markets, including foreign markets;
- *Product line extension M&As*; we refer to M&As for market penetration through the acquisition of companies producing different types or models in the same geographical market;
- *Product and market extension M&As;* we refer to M&As for extending market cover and penetration through the acquisition of companies operating in different geographical markets with different types of products.

With reference to different types of horizontal M&As, it is a matter of evaluating the reduction in costs and the increase in revenues that an M&A can favour. To reach this aim, it is necessary to compare the value chains of firms involved in the merger, for evaluating which activities are to be integrated, exploited or removed and the expected effects in terms of costs and revenues.

The schemes shown in Chapter 4 can offer a useful basis for this. It also allows planning the new value chain of the merger and the expected effects in terms of cost and revenue synergies.

Horizontal M&A strategies have been adopted by successful firms in many industries, from the automotive to the banking one. In the second part of this study two emblematic cases of successful horizontal M&A strategies are analysed: L'Oreal (see Chapter 11) and Luxottica (see Chapter 13).

Market share increase M&As

Through the acquisition of companies dealing with similar products in the same geographical market, an acquiring firm rapidly expands sales of a given basic product, adding the sales of the target firm to its own sales. Generally, in this case both support and primary activities of firms are *similar* and that favours a wide reorganization of assets and resources in all the activities of the value chain, by eliminating excess capacity, removing the less efficient assets and exploiting the most efficient ones. That will boost a reduction in costs, especially if economies of scale are available. Often, these are relevant in production and logistic activities, but also in some support activities, such as technological development and firm infrastructure. In addition, this M&A strategy allows a rapid increase in market share and consequently of market power. The stronger competitive position of the combined firm will favour a higher level in product price, thus increasing revenues and cash flows.

Geographical market coverage M&As

Through the acquisition of companies dealing with similar products in different geographic markets, especially foreign markets, an acquiring firm extends its activity (for a given basic product) to other different geographical markets, either domestic or foreign. In this case, not only are the support activities similar but so is a part of primary activities, especially inbound logistics, operations, etc. Therefore, the merger offers good opportunities for a reorganization of assets and resources of firms, removing those which are less efficient. In addition, the increase in the volume of activities may favour exploitation of economies of scale in some primary and support activities. All this can boost a relevant reduction in costs. In particular, when a horizontal expansion strategy is implemented through cross-border M&As, the positive effects can derive from activities which are bigger in size, while operating units remain local.

Product line extension M&As

Through the acquisition of companies dealing with different types or models of the same basic product in the same geographical market, an acquiring firm extends a company's product line, penetrating the market of a given basic product with different types and models directed to different groups of customers. In this case, because of the different types and models of a product, only part of the support and primary activities of firms is similar. That reduces the opportunities for reorganization by the removal of less efficient assets and resources. For this reason, the integration does not favour a widespread reduction in costs, as a differentiation in products requires different production and marketing activities, with different brands and distribution networks.

On the contrary, some support and primary activities will be common to all firms involved in the merger and will offer the opportunity for reductions in costs, by the removal of less efficient assets and resources. In particular, information system and technological platforms, financial resources and competences, know-how in planning and accounting, HR management expertise, access to raw materials, service management and others may offer interesting opportunities for integration.

In addition, some assets and resources in support activities – especially intangibles such as know-how in management, firm reputation, etc. – will favour an increase in revenues of all types and models of a product.

Product and market extension M&As

Through the acquisition of companies dealing with different types of products in different geographical markets, an acquiring firm exploits complementary assets and resources to favour the sale of different products in different geographical markets, so as to penetrate these markets and to reach different groups of customers. In this case, part of the assets and resources of the target firm will be *complementary* to those of the acquiring firm in operating and supporting activities. All this will favour an increase in revenues due to *cross selling* of products in the markets involved.

This type of merger is also used to quickly build a market position in different geographical markets and in different products, by acquiring companies with strong functional activities (primary or support activities), strategic assets and distinctive resources, such as distribution networks, brands, technological know-how. Sometimes this M&A can also allow relevant barriers to entry in an industry or in a country to be overcome.

HORIZONTAL CROSS-BORDER M&As

M&A strategies require particular attention when they regard the acquisition of foreign firms. In addition to what we have already explained, some specific internal and external factors have to be considered. They are:

- national resources;
- specificity of competitive advantage of local companies;
- difficulty in exporting products.

With regard to the first factor, relevant cost synergies can derive from a foreign country's disposable resources, for example labour, energy and raw materials. Secondly, a foreign company can quickly produce some types or models of products in a country where its internal resources can be better exploited. Finally, a cross-border M&A may allow the location of a production capacity in a foreign country, avoiding the high costs of transporting products, and drawing advantage from the customers' preference for local firms and products and overcoming the high barriers, set by the local public authorities (import duty, customs duty, tax, etc.).

An alternative way to acquisitions, especially in international markets, is setting up a joint venture with a local firm. It may be preferred to the complete acquisition of foreign companies, for entering into a foreign market (Harrigan, 1986; Pisano et al., 1988). In fact, this solution allows a firm to overcome the existing barriers to entry into an industry or a country and to reduce both the cost of the necessary investment and the risk. This solution also allows the firm to exploit its knowledge of and relationships with local firms already operating in the target market. This, for example, has been the method adopted by international car companies for entering the Chinese automobile market in the last decade.

The disadvantages of this solution are the difficulties for the entrant firm in managing the business with local producers or distributors who over time can develop divergent objectives, and also become competitors.

In short, entry into a foreign market through an M&A requires a more complex valuation of the sources of competitive advantage and synergies.[5] However, a cross-border horizontal M&A can also allow the acquiring firm to obtain new significant resources to exploit, for a competitive advantage both in local and foreign markets.

Generally, a horizontal cross-border M&A represents the final phase of the international expansion of a firm. In fact, when analysing the history of large corporations, it emerges that overseas development over time generally follows a model characterized by three typical phases. The first phase is characterized by the indirect export of products, mainly using local distributors; the second phase by the consolidation of a presence abroad through the substitution of local import firms with a direct distribution network and sales force; the third phase by the investment in production capacity, in order to better adapt the product to the local customers' needs and to exploit local production advantages (Hitt et al., 1997). The organization of a direct network or a production facility can be speeded up through M&A operations.

RISKS IN HORIZONTAL M&As

Risks arising from industry dynamics

First of all, the failure of a horizontal M&A can be caused by a change in the external scenario and particularly in the industry by:

- reduction in the aggregate demand;
- the expansion policies of rival firms and the consequent overcapacity in the industry;
- limits to economies of scale;
- an unexpected evolution of technological progress and the accelerated obsolescence of plants and machinery.

First, a reduction in the aggregate demand of the industry can cause a structural imbalance between demand and supply with a consequent reduction in prices and in the profits of the firms operating in the industry. This situation can go on for a long time, especially when there are high exit barriers in the industry, which make it convenient for even the less efficient firms to remain in the industry.

It is well known that the risk of overcapacity and structural imbalance between demand and supply is particularly high in commodity industries, as all products are homogeneous.

Second, a critical variable for the success of an expansion strategy through M&A is represented by the competitors' behaviour. If they too adopt an expansion strategy through M&A, the level of concentration in the industry will further increase. In this situation, the risk of triggering a price war with negative effects for all the competitors is especially high in oligopolistic markets, because of the interdependence of the decisions among the incumbent firms.

Limits to economies of scale can cause a failure of a horizontal M&A strategy. They can derive from production technologies that do not produce further reduction in costs, as long as the size increases. In addition, they can arise from the increasing organizational costs for managing and controlling an activity which become more and more complex (Pratten, 1971; Scherer and Ross, 1980).

Finally, a rapid evolution in technologies, following expansion, can cause failure of this strategy because of the reductions in margins for all firms operating with old technologies and the consequent necessity for renewing the existing plant before the planned date.

Risks arising from the inadequacy of firm resources and capabilities

Even if the external conditions studied above are the main causes of failure of a horizontal M&A, sometimes the failure is due to internal causes, either to insufficient resources and capabilities of the acquiring firms or to erroneous estimates of cost and revenue synergies, especially in cross-border M&As. It is a fact that especially the inadequacy of managerial resources and organizational capabilities result in being the cause of failure of M&A strategies, even when the external scenario has been correctly forecast. This is due to the increasing complexity of managing a larger-sized firm, adapting marketing and distribution processes to different markets and sometimes monitoring functions and activities developed in foreign countries.

In the case of a failure of a horizontal M&A it will be necessary to adopt a downsizing strategy, that is a strategy for reducing production capacity, by a decrease in the number of operating units and in the number of employees, in order to meet the new conditions of aggregate and specific demand. This strategy will allow the firm to concentrate its resources on the most profitable market segments and geographical areas.

A MODEL FOR DETERMINING THE VALUE CREATED BY HORIZONTAL M&As

For determining the value created by a horizontal M&A, it is necessary, first of all, to correctly estimate the synergy gains obtained by a horizontal M&A.

Cost synergies mainly derive from savings in costs obtained by exploiting interrelationships among activities and by exploiting economies of scale by virtue of a reconfiguration of activities and resources.

Revenue synergies derive from the cross selling of products and from the higher bargaining power of the acquiring firm over the competitive forces, due to the firm's larger size and the larger market share. This allows the firm to charge higher prices for its products, in particular, when only a few firms remain operating in the industry, thereby making it easier to maintain collusive behaviour over time.

To sum up, the combined firm will obtain, as a consequence of the acquisition, an increase in its operating cash flows, with respect to the sum of operating cash flows of firms standing alone, by virtue of:

- an increase in revenues (ΔR_{SY}), mainly due to an increase in price of product (p) and an increase in gross margin (ΔM_{SY}) due to the cross selling of products;
- a reduction in total operating costs (ΔC_{SY}) due to a reduction in the unit operation cost of product (C_U);
- an increase in operating costs due to the integration process (ΔC_O) (coordination costs).

The synergy gains can be directly estimated considering that revenue synergies, ΔR_{SY}, and cost synergies, ΔC_{SY}, are: [6]

$$\Delta R_{SY} = \Delta p\,(Q_A + Q_T) \qquad (5.1)$$

$$\Delta C_{SY} = \Delta Cu\,(Q_A + Q_T) \qquad (5.2)$$

where: Q_A and Q_T are respectively the sales of firms A and T; Δp and ΔCu are the increase in market price of product and the reduction in weighted average unit cost of firm A and firm T.

We can generalize this model also considering that sales in quantities of products increase as a consequence of the cross selling of products of the companies involved in the merger. In this case a larger volume of sales ΔQ will produce an increase in revenues equal to:

$$\Delta R = \Delta Q_{SY}\,(p + \Delta p) \qquad (5.3)$$

And an increase in costs equal to:

$$\Delta C = \Delta Q_{SY}\,(C_U + \Delta C_U) \qquad (5.4)$$

where (C_U) is the unit operation cost of product.

Consequently, the combined firm will also obtain an increase in the gross margin equal to:

$$\Delta M_{SY} = \Delta Q_{SY} [(p + \Delta p) - (C_U + \Delta C_U)] \tag{5.5}$$

Therefore, the total increase in operating cash flows, determined by the merger, will be

$$\Delta EBITDA = \Delta R_{SY} + \Delta C_{SY} + \Delta M_{SY} + \Delta C_O \tag{5.6}$$

ΔC_O being a negative value.

Taking into consideration also the possible reductions in working capital (ΔWC) and in capital expenditures ($\Delta Capex$), the additional free cash flows from operations will be given by the following general expression:

$$\Delta FCFO = (\Delta R_{SY} + \Delta C_{SY} + \Delta M_{SY} + \Delta C_O)(1-\tau) + \Delta WC + \Delta Capex \tag{5.7}$$

Consequently, according to the model proposed in Chapter 3, the net value created by synergies will be:

$$V_{SY} = \frac{\Delta FCFO}{\rho_M} \tag{5.8}$$

Considering also the effect of changes in the cost of capital, the value created by the M&A will be:

$$V_M = \frac{(FCFO_A + FCFO_T)}{\rho_M} - [\frac{FCFO_A}{\rho_A} + \frac{FCFO_T}{\rho_T}] + \frac{\Delta FCFO}{\rho_M} \tag{5.9}$$

Finally, on the basis of the price paid for the target firm (P_T), we can calculate the value created for the shareholders of the acquiring firm. Precisely it will be:

$$V_{SA} = (V_T + V_M) - P_T \tag{5.10}$$

where ($V_T + V_M$) is the value of the acquisition V_{Acq}.

DETERMINING THE VALUE CREATED BY A HORIZONTAL M&A: AN EXAMPLE

From a practical point of view, for determining the value of a horizontal M&A, first of all we have to evaluate the firms involved in the merger standing alone, by discounting the expected free cash flows of each firm at the cost of capital (ρ).

Then we will determine the value of the combined firm, according to the above presented model.

For this purpose, consider two firms A and T operating independently in the same industry and having the financial characteristics indicated in Table 5.2.

The values of these firms are estimated respectively at €10,000,000 and €3,000,000 and the total value of them standing alone is €13 million.

Let us assume that firm A evaluates the opportunity to buy a firm T at a price $P_T = 6,000,000$. The management of firm A estimates that, as a consequence of the merger, the combined firm will increase its market power and product price by 5%, whereas the cost of goods sold will be reduced by 10%. No synergies in working capital and capital expenses are expected. We also assume that the cost of capital does not change.

In this case, applying the analytical model shown above, the value of the combined firm will result in being equal to €23,050,000; the value of acquisition will be €13,050,000 and the total value of synergies will be €10,050,000 of which €4,050,000 is the value of revenue synergies, deriving from a higher market power, and €6,000,000 the value of cost synergies (Table 5.2).

In fact, according to the expression (5.8), it will be:

$$V_{SY} = \frac{\Delta FCFO}{\rho_M} = \frac{(\Delta R + \Delta C)\,(1-\tau)}{\rho_M} =$$

$$= 4,050,000 + 6,000,000 = 10,050,000 \qquad (5.11)$$

Note that as the cost of capital does not change, the value created by the merger is equal to the value of synergies.

On the contrary, if the cost of capital of the combined firm is lower than the cost of the acquiring firm, because of the reduction in operating risk, due to the larger size of the merger and the bigger market power, it is necessary also to calculate the effect of this change on the value created by the merger. As we have have just explained, the increase in value of the merger is given by the following:

$$V_{CC} = \frac{(FCFO_A + FCFO_T)}{\rho_M} - [\frac{FCFO_A}{\rho_A} + \frac{FCFO_T}{\rho_T}] \qquad (5.12)$$

Table 5.2 Horizontal M&As: the value of merger

Economic variables (€)	Firm A	Firm B	Firm AB combined	Firm AB – Firm A	Synergy
Total assets	5,000,000	3,000,000	8,000,000		
Fixed capital	3,600,000	1,600,000	5,200,000		
Price	60	60	63		
Sales (tons)	100,000	80,000	180,000	80,000	
Revenues	6,000,000	4,800,000	11,340,000	5,340,000	540,000
Cost x unit	40	50	40		10
Total costs	4,000.000	4,000,000	7,200,000	3,200,000	800,000
EBITDA	2,000,000	800,000	4,140,000	2,140,000	1,340,000
Tax rate (%)	25	25	25	25	25
EBITDA $(1 - t^*)$	1,500,000	600,000	3,105,000	1,605,000	1,005,000
DA (Depr. & Amm.)	360,000	160,000	520,000	160,000	
DA t	90,000	40,000	130,000	40,000	
ΔWC (Working Cap.)	50,000	20,000	70,000	20,000	
Capital expenditures	540,000	320,000	860,000	320,000	
FCFO	1,000,000	300,000	2,305,000	1,305,000	1,005,000
Cost of capital (%)	10	10	10	10	10
Value of synergies					10,050,000
Value of firm	10,000,000	3,000,000	23,050,000		
Value of acquisition			13,050,000		
Value of merger (1)			10,050,000		
Value of merger (2)			15,812,000		

Note: The firm value is calculated by using the following model: $V = FCFO^*/\rho$.

For example, if the cost of capital of the combined firm drops from 10% to 8%, because of a reduction in operating risk, we will obtain different values of synergies and of the merger. Precisely, the value of synergy will be:

$$Vsy = €1,005,000/0.08 = €12,562,000.$$

In turn, the value created by the reduction in the *WACC* will be:

$$V_{CC} = €1,300,000/0.08 - (1,000,000/0.10 + 300,000/0.10) = €3,250,000$$

Therefore, the total value created by the merger will be:

$$V_M = V_{CC} + Vsy = €3,250,000 + 12,562,000 = €15,812,000$$

The value of acquisition being $Vacq = V_T + V_M = €18,812,000$, the value created for the shareholders of the firm A will be:

$$V_{SA} = €18,812,000 - 6,000,000 = €12,812,000.$$

Therefore, with respect to the previous case, the reduction in *WACC* increases the value created by the merger by €5,762,000 (15,812,000 − 10,050,000).

NOTES

1. On the restructuring strategies see: Baden-Fuller and Stopford (1992); Gouillart and Kelly (1995); Hitt et al. (1997); Collis and Montgomery (2005).
2. According to the economic literature (Pratten, 1971; Scherer et al., 1975; Norman, 1979; Hay and Morris, 1979; Bellandi, 1995; Besanko et al., 1996), one of the principal factors of economies of scale is represented by the technical relationship between the input and the output of a product. Precisely, there are some inputs where an increase determines a more than proportional increase of output, thus causing higher productivity. Another important factor of economies of scale is the indivisibility of some inputs. To be more precise, some inputs are not disposable in small quantities or, in any case, in quantities which are continuously variable and thus the indivisibility of these inputs favours a larger size, because it offers the possibility of dividing the cost of input, which remains substantially constant, on a larger quantity of products. Let us consider, for example, inputs such as plants or machinery, which cannot be reproduced in units having a production which is smaller than a certain capacity (for example presses, furnaces, etc.). Similar situations also occur in R&D activity. In fact, in

many cases, it is not possible to successfully carry out these activities under a certain structural or organizational dimension. A threshold of specialized persons is necessary, as is a minimum amount of laboratory machinery and a support structure, all of which constitute the minimum dimension in order for this activity to be successful. This is an extreme example of indivisibility factors, because smaller R&D structures determine insignificant output. The third factor of economies of scale is specialization. In many cases, the use of a larger quantity of inputs makes it possible to develop more effective specialization processes, which conversely would not be possible when the size of the activity is small. These scale economies, linked to specialization, are typical of mass production processes, characterized by the continuous production of the same product or the same combination of products over time.

3. The concept of economies of scale can be further clarified in analytical terms. In this context, we can definitely say that economies of scale are present where the total cost of producing a given quantity $nq1$ with one plant having a production scale equal to $nq1$ is lower than the total cost of producing the same quantity $nq1$ with n plant, each of scale equal to $q1$. That is:

$$C(nq1) < nC(q1)$$

where: $nC(q1)$ is the total cost of producing the quantities $nq1$ with n plants, each of scale or capacity $q1$, and $C(nq1)$ is the total production cost for producing $nq1$ quantities with one plant with a scale (capacity) equal to $nq1$. The preceding expression indicates that increasing n times the scale of production of a plant ($nq1$), the firm obtains a unit cost lower than the cost the firm will bear obtaining the same total production, but with n plants each having a scale of production equal to $q1$. Economies of scale can include labour input (the relationship between plant scale and labour costs), the capital cost for plants (the relationship between plant scale and capital cost) and materials and energy inputs. A function of total long period production cost that exhibits economies of scale is offered, for example, by the following:

$$C = k q a$$

where: C is the total production costs, k is a parameter; q is the production scale, the exponent a is a constant (with $a < 1$).

For example, assuming $k = \$10,500$ and $a = 0.6$ we obtain the following unit production cost function:

$$C/q = 10,500 \, q \, 0.6$$

Over the range of plants from 10,000 tons of scale to 40,000 tons, the unit cost of production decreases from about \$264 to \$151.

4. Learning by doing has been documented in many studies concerning air-frames industry (Alchian, 1963), automobiles assembly (Baloff, 1971), chemicals (Pisano, 1994) and semiconductors (Bohn, 1995; Gruber, 1992; Hatch and Mowery, 1998; Hatch and Dyer, 2004) industries.

5.   The decision for entering into a foreign market can be also analysed by using the theory of transaction costs. Barriers to entry can be considered as transaction costs, as well as the cost regarding the business deal and the monitoring of the agreement in licensing contracts and in joint ventures with local firms. Therefore, according to this theory, the direct investment is preferable when there are high transaction costs, because of the inefficiency of foreign markets and the high specificity of the relevant resources. On the theory of transaction costs see Chapter 6.

6.   In fact the variations in revenues and in operating costs of the combining firm with respect to the values of the firms standing alone are the following:

$$\Delta R_{SY} = (p(0) + \Delta p(Q_A + Q_T) - p(0)(Q_A + Q_T) = \Delta p(Q_A + Q_T)$$
$$\Delta C_{SY} = Cu(0)(Q_A + Q_T) - Cu(1)(Q_A + Q_T) = \Delta Cu(Q_A + Q_T)$$

Therefore, the synergy gains expressed in increment of *EBITDA* are:

$$\Delta p(Q_A + Q_T) + \Delta Cu(Q_A + Q_T).$$

Note that $p(0)$ is the market price of product and $Cu(0)$ is the weighted average unit cost of firms A and B standing alone, while $p(1) = p(0) + \Delta p$ and $Cu(1) = Cu(0) - \Delta Cu$ are respectively the price and the average unit cost after the merger.

6. Vertical M&As

INTRODUCTION AND OBJECTIVES

In this chapter we examine the different types of vertical M&As and the conditions favouring these strategies. The analysis follows the lines already discussed in the previous chapter with particular focus on transaction costs as a relevant and specific factor of vertical M&As.

After the analysis of advantages and drawbacks in vertical M&A, the conditions for a vertical M&A which creates value are defined through an analytical model. The analysis highlights that high transaction costs and efficiency in intermediate product markets are the most important external conditions for vertical M&As to create value. Conversely, capabilities in increasing efficiency by integrating processes and by exploiting asset and resource relationships result as being the most important internal factors for successful vertical M&As.

RATIONALES FOR VERTICAL M&As

Through vertical M&As a firm decides to extend its activity, directly producing raw materials, components or services for its product, instead of buying them from other firms. Thus, it is a matter of directly carrying out operations or phases in the production cycle which before were carried out by external firms. In this way a firm moves its activities upstream or downstream in the product cycle.

The levers for creating value through vertical M&As are the following.

- Reduction in total costs by joining different phases of the operating cycle of a product;
- Reduction in capital expenditure by exploiting assets and resources of specialized firms;
- Reduction in costs of raw materials and components by exploiting economies of scale;
- Reduction in transaction costs of raw materials, components and services;
- Increase in margins by integration of wholesaler and retailer activities;
- Reduction in costs of raw materials and components by a stronger competition with the other suppliers;

- Increase in product price as a consequence of an increased control of value chain.

Reduction in total costs by joining different phases of the operating cycle of a product

A vertical M&A can favour a reduction in costs by integrating the activities concerning semi-manufactured items, products and services. These cost advantages can be relevant especially when technological interdependences are present in different phases of the operating cycle of a product, as happens for example in the steel, paper and chemical industries. They mainly reflect differences in technical efficiency, when producing items through an integrated structure. This especially happens with goods requiring high asset specificity, so implying specialized uses for inputs, determining fewer outlets for an outside supplier.

Reduction in capital expenditure

Acquisitions can offer the opportunity to reduce capital expenditures, exploiting the technical advantage of highly specialized target firms. For example, the acquisition of firms specialized in R&D activities can allow the acquiring firm to save a massive amount of money for maintaining competitive products in technical markets. M&As, driven by savings in capital expenditure, often occurred in pharmaceutical and in high technology industries. Emblematic cases have been offered by Microsoft and Cisco acquisitions in the software industry and by Novartis acquisitions in the pharmaceutical industry.

Reduction in costs by exploiting economies of scale

An M&A can also offer the opportunity of expanding the volume of activity of the target firm, producing a larger quantity of raw materials, components or intermediate products, so as to exploit economies of scale. This mainly occurs when the industry of raw materials and intermediate goods is characterized by a high number of small firms.

Reduction in transaction costs

A vertical M&A can be motivated by the reduction in the *transaction costs* that a firm sustains acquiring raw materials, components and services on the market, because of the inefficiency of the supply market and of the opportunistic behaviour of suppliers.[1] As is known, transaction costs are the costs a firm has to sustain for stipulating contracts with third parties: costs for defining an agreement, securing its observance and for adjusting and correcting the contract, as well as solving disputes (Williamson, 1975; 1981).

Transaction costs are high especially when managers have an inherent difficulty in managing complex problems and in carrying out totally comprehensive contracts. As the counterparts tend to pursue self-centred interest, sometimes in order to cheat or defraud, that determines an increase in uncertainty of the results of a contract, which are influenced not only by incomplete definition of covenants, but also by the opportunistic behaviour of the other counterpart. It is a matter of actions directed at twisting and hiding information from the other party, taking advantage of asymmetric information (Williamson, 1981).

When the costs of overcoming this limitation are very high, a hierarchical organization can represent the best choice, because it allows the transaction costs to be economized. In this context, a vertical M&A can allow the acquiring firm to obtain a clear advantage, since the possibility for opportunistic behaviour is considerably reduced, with transactions made within the group and with more efficient means for controlling and quickly solving possible controversies among managers of the same group.

The following characteristics of transactions with suppliers or clients will favour the choice of a vertical M&A:

- the specificity of assets of the acquiring firm and the small number of suppliers or clients (typically bilateral monopoly);
- the asymmetry in information;
- the frequency of transactions; and
- the uncertainty on a possible future.

Asset specificity means that an asset can only use a specific raw material or intermediate product, or component. If the specificity of an asset offers the firm the advantage of a higher specialization, it also reduces the possibility of alternative uses of the asset. In such cases, the firm that has made the investment is vulnerable to exploitation from its supplier, because the asset would be worthless in another application. Since this asset is not easily transferable to other activities, the cost sustained for its acquisition can be recovered only by using it for a long time. That creates a strong bond between the firm and its suppliers of raw materials or components, increasing the negative effects of contractual opportunism and so determining high transaction costs. Specificity of assets also modifies the conditions of markets after the transaction from competition to a bilateral relation. Consider a firm that has customized its production facility to use a particular grade of raw material supplied by a producer. The firm considered has no alternatives other than using those raw materials and thus it is bound to the supplier and to its price and delivery policy. It can look for a different supplier, but that implies reconfiguring its production facility for the new grade of material, which would be very expensive.

Asymmetry in information between the buyer and seller of materials, semi-manufactured products, components and services can also favour opportunistic behaviour. In particular, the information asymmetry means a lack of fair information about the quality of the product and the guarantee of the seller's correct behaviour. All this means that a buying firm has to sustain an additional cost for obtaining the necessary information and that can reduce the advantage of buying raw materials, components or services. Thus, a vertical M&A is convenient where a firm has to sustain high transaction costs when using the market, for reducing the asymmetry in information and the opportunistic behaviour of suppliers that exists when there are few operators.[2]

The information market represents a clear example of market failure, because frequently in this market one party knows relevant facts for deciding a transaction, while the other can acquire information only by bearing high costs. These are situations which are characterized by a high risk of opportunistic behaviour by the more informed party. That makes it difficult to find an agreement in a context of limited rationality, contractual opportunism and specificity of resources. As far as know-how is concerned, high transaction costs derive from problems related to the identification, diffusion and organization of information. In fact, in the market of owned know-how there is an objective difficulty in identifying an exchange opportunity which is reciprocally advantageous for the two parties, because of the situation of imperfect information. Furthermore, a market exchange may not work, due to problems regarding the diffusion of the value of the information to the buyer. In some cases there is a problem of information block related to the protection of technological know-how ownership. This happens because the value of know-how is unknown to the buyer while he does not possess the information, but, when he possesses it, he has already obtained it without cost (Arrow, 1974). Finally, a third transaction problem arises because know-how shows strong characteristics of learning by doing, which makes the transfer of human capital necessary.

The high transaction frequency with some suppliers will also favour high transaction costs. This situation can repeatedly hold up a firm, because haggling and negotiation occur more often. In all these cases, a vertical M&A can allow an acquiring firm to eliminate these costs through its organization. Finally, a vertical integration can offer cost advantages with respect to market use, when there is a high uncertainty on possible future eventualities. In fact, the variability of external conditions requires a continuous adaptation both of the design of a product and of production programmes. In these cases long-term contracting does not solve the problem either. In fact, there is the risk that all parties can interpret the contractual ambiguities to their own advantage, so as to require expensive forms for the contract to be respected, including appealing to justice. To avoid disputes, all possible implications deriving from a contract should be specified beforehand, but even if this were possible, it may be quite expensive. Also a sequential and adaptive decisional process, accomplished through a series of short-term contracts, presents high risks if the investments are firm specific, since its interruption would cause high costs and regaining the investment would be impossible. In addition, this situation can offer one of the negotiators an advantageous position, due to the specificity of resources, when the contract has to be renewed, especially when the post contract situation is characterized by a small number of competing firms.

In these situations, a vertical integration strategy through M&A can reduce costs and risks, allowing a process of sequential adaptive decisions to be taken through internal adjustments made by the different organs of the firm and coordinated in order to reach a common objective. Hierarchical structures can allow better results to be obtained, overcoming the problem of limited information and making the rise of opportunistic behaviour easier to combat. To prevent opportunistic behaviour from its suppliers, a firm could write a contract for the duration of the asset. But in this case, uncertainty about all possible future eventualities can make it impossible or prohibitively expensive. This contract would have to cover an enormous number of clauses as well as all possible contingencies that are impossible to evaluate, also for the bounded rationality, that is, the physical limits to which the mind can process information.

In short, some market situations can offer opportunities for reducing transactions costs: these are all durable relationships with suppliers or clients (especially wholesalers or retailers) involving asset specificity, uncertainty and high frequency of transactions. In these cases, a vertical M&A can be regarded as a winning solution to economize on transaction costs, by harmonizing interests and permitting more efficient incentives and control processes to be activated.

Empirical evidence confirms that vertical integration strategies are strongly influenced by high transaction costs (Monteverde and Teece, 1982; Leiblein and Miller, 2003).[3] A classic example of high transaction costs leading to a vertical integration is represented by the relationship between General Motors and Fisher Body for the supply of car bodies (Klein et al.,

1978; Williamson, 1986a). General Motors used to buy all its car bodies from Fisher Body, in accordance with a contract which established the prices on the basis of costs and a margin and required all disputes to be solved by a binding referee. Through this agreement the two parties intended to avoid opportunistic behaviour. As a matter of fact, this relationship worked well until the demand for car bodies largely exceeded the forecast. When this happened, GM evaluated the price agreement as no longer being satisfactory and asked Fisher Body to reduce prices and to build a new plant adjacent to a GM car assembly factory, in order to reduce transport costs and stocks.

Fisher Body refused, fearing that, once the factory was built, it would have had no real choice other than to supply GM, because of the high costs involved in finding and switching to a new customer. Thus the risk of opportunistic behaviour from GM, once Fisher Body had made the investment, led to a market failure. To reach the objective of reducing production costs by having the production plant built next door, GM bought Fisher Body and merged its activity, thereby obtaining a vertical integration (Collis and Montgomery, 2005).

Increase in margins through the integration of wholesale and retail activities

In the case of downstream M&As, the quality of some assets and resources of the acquiring firm can favour the expansion of sales of the target firm and *vice versa*. For example, in an M&A between a manufacturing company and one of its clients, represented by a commercial firm with a retailers network, reputation for quality and reliability and general management skills of the first firm can boost the final sales of the combined firm.

Relevant revenue synergies can arise from a cross-border M&A. For example, acquiring a commercial company operating in a foreign market allows an acquiring firm to establish a direct and durable relation with new customers, using and adapting marketing and selling activities to customers' needs. This is the solution normally adopted for quickly selling instrumental goods or consumption goods in foreign high potential markets. In these cases, by the acquisition of companies already having networks of agents, franchise stores or subordinate vendors at their disposal, a firm can increase the sales of its types or models of product rapidly.

Reduction in costs due to a higher bargaining power with suppliers

A degree of self-sufficiency can also give significant bargaining advantages in respect to other suppliers, with a consequent reduction in costs. Not only does it allow the firm to know the cost structure of an item, a component or service, but it makes the firm a competitor of its suppliers or clients, thereby threatening their businesses (Porter, 1980; Prahalad and Doz, 1986 and 1998).

Increase in product price

Furthermore, an increased control of the value added chain can provide an opportunity for active price management: a more integrated firm can enlarge, for example, the margin it has at its disposal to fight competitive battles.[4] In particular, the control of critical raw materials and components or of distribution channels can allow the vertically integrated firm to gain a larger market power against its competitors and customers.[5]

ADDITIONAL COSTS OF VERTICAL M&As

When deciding to grow through vertical M&A, it is also necessary to consider the additional costs of integrating new activities. High costs for coordinating activities can derive from the necessary modifications of firm structure: the new functions can require an internal restructuring of the organization, with the assignment of new positions of responsibility, the need to develop new knowledge and to motivate employees, etc. A balance sheet of benefits and costs of vertical integration is shown in Table 6.1.

Furthermore, a vertical integration determines a loss in flexibility of the combined firm, with high costs in the case of variations of sales in declining phases of an industry, as it is not possible to transfer the effects of a fall in demand to suppliers.[6]

Table 6.1 A summary of the main effects from vertical M&As

Potential benefits	Potential costs
Cost reduction for higher technical efficiency	Cost of coordinating and integrating new activities
Reduction of transaction costs	Loss of flexibility
Control over value added and margins capture	Loss of focus on a business

TYPES OF VERTICAL M&As AND SYNERGIES

Through a vertical M&A a firm decides to integrate the production of raw materials, components or services for its product, instead of buying them from other firms (upstream M&As). It can also decide to integrate the activities of selling and distribution of its products to retailers or to final customers (downstream M&As). Thus, a vertical M&A implies directly carrying out operations or phases in the production cycle, which before were carried out by external firms. In this way a combined firm will replace the market with an internal organization, extending its activities upstream or downstream in the product cycle.

The potential scope of a vertical integration M&A is shown in Figure 6.1. Therefore, the specific vertical M&A will be characterized by the direction and the scope of vertical integration. According to the output obtained from the target firm, with respect to that required for the final output of the acquiring firm, a vertical integration can be balanced, partial or exceeding (Grant, 1998; Rispoli, 1998).

A *balanced* vertical M&A occurs when a firm acquires and integrates a company that produces the quantities of inputs necessary for satisfying its entire planned production flow or all the services necessary for selling the entire production. A *partial* integration occurs when the quantities of inputs produced by the target firm are smaller than quantities required from the planned production of the acquiring firm. Finally, an *exceeding* integration occurs when the quantities of inputs produced by the target firm are larger than what is required from the acquiring firm, or when the services accomplished after the acquisition exceed the acquiring firm's needs, and it is necessary to sell them on the market.

An *exceeding* vertical integration can be favoured by profit opportunities in upstream or downstream sectors, or forced by minimum efficient dimensions[7] (MES) of upstream or downstream activities which are larger than those characterizing the already developed activities of the acquiring firm. In any case, when a firm enters the market through an M&A with an exceeding production of components or services, it also obtains a production-diversified strategy, with all the features which we will analyse in Chapter 7.

With reference to different types of horizontal M&As, it is a matter of evaluating the reduction in costs and the increase in revenues and margins determined by the M&A. For this purpose, it is necessary to examine and compare the value chain of firms involved in the merger, for identifying which activities are to be integrated, exploited or removed and the expected effects in terms of costs and revenues.

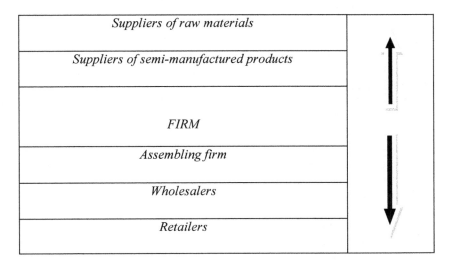

Figure 6.1 The potential scope of a vertical M&A strategy

The expected synergies will vary according to the type of vertical M&A strategy. For our analysis, we distinguish the following forms of vertical M&As:

- upstream M&As;
- downstream M&As.

In Chapter 4 we have presented some schemes for this purpose. They offer useful bases for planning the new value chain of the combined firm and determining the expected effects in terms of cost and revenue synergies.

Upstream M&As

With upstream M&A (backward integration) a firm directly controls the early phases of the product cycle, thereby obtaining unfinished products or components of its product.

In this case the merger can produce a reduction in total costs from making semi-manufactured items, components and products, because of the technological advantages in joining different phases of the operating cycle of a product. This requires the reorganization of the primary activity of the target firm by exploiting relationships with those of the acquiring firm.

The reduction in costs can be favoured also by sharing some support and primary activities and exploiting exceeding assets and resources suitable for being transferred and used in upstream activities. That is true especially for intangible assets such as know-how in planning and finance, information systems, technological platforms, technical and professional qualification of employees, HR management expertise, technological knowledge, and patents. The analysis of the value chains of the companies involved in the merger will offer useful insights in this direction.

Saving in transaction costs for raw materials, components and services, will be obtained in the case of specificity of assets and in the case of inefficient markets of intermediate products.

Finally, an integration of upstream activities, can favour a reduction in prices of components and raw materials because of the increased competition from the combined firm.

In economic terms, this type of vertical M&A causes the increase in the added value for the acquiring firm, but not necessarily the increase of revenues which can remain constant if the total final output does not increase. Therefore, the extent of a vertical integration can be indicated by the ratio of a firm's value added to its sales revenues.

Downstream vertical M&As

With downstream M&As (forward integration) an acquiring firm integrates the terminal phases of the product cycle or those regarding the selling and the distribution of its product. This implies a longer value chain, with additional assets and resources. In this case, the merger will produce an increase in total revenues by sharing distinctive assets and resources in support and primary activities, so as to boost product sales. This is true especially when exploiting some intangible assets, such as know-how in planning and finance, information system and technological platform, HR management expertise, technological knowledge, sales networks and logistic management expertise. The analysis of the value chains and the strategic assets and resources of the companies involved in the merger will offer useful insights in this direction.

RISKS IN VERTICAL M&As

Risks arising from industry structure and dynamics

Risks in vertical M&As are mainly the risks a firm takes when entering a different industry. They depend, first of all, on the structure of the industry and particularly on the dynamics of technical progress and the competitive pressure of incumbent firms. Technical progress can lead to cancelling advantages of joint production and of sharing technical know-how and current patents, whereas the competitive pressure of incumbent firms can quickly reduce initial cost advantages of the merger.

Secondly, risks depend on the adequacy of managerial competencies and firm resources. In effect, to compete successfully and create value in the businesses of raw materials and intermediate products, as well as in those of selling and distributing products, it is necessary to continuously improve strategic and distinctive assets and resources. Besides, this requires increasing managerial capabilities.

Finally, a vertically integrated company presents a more rigid structure with disadvantages in responding quickly to new product development opportunities that require a new combination of technical capabilities.

In short, risks of failure in a vertical merger mainly derive from the strategic dissimilarities between businesses requiring different technological processes and product development capabilities in vertical adjacent activities. In particular, production and marketing activities require different technological and organizational capabilities. Obviously, risks are bigger when an M&A implies an exceeding vertical integration, since in this case the acquiring firm is forced to enter the market of the intermediate products. The analysis of this type of M&A will be similar to that developed for diversified M&As. On this point see Chapter 7.

A MODEL FOR DETERMINING THE VALUE OF VERTICAL M&As

A vertical integration strategy, carried out through the acquisition of firms producing raw materials, components or services used by the acquiring firm, requires the acquiring firm to evaluate the saving in costs and the increase in revenues that the merger will produce.

In particular, the benefits that can be obtained through a vertical M&A can be summarized as follows:

- the lower operating costs of products, which derive from directly making semi-manufactured items, products or services (ΔC_{SY});
- the saving in transaction costs (ΔC_T);
- the higher product price, due to an increased control of distribution channels and a larger market power with respect to retailers and/or customers (ΔR_{SY}).

Obviously, it is also necessary to consider the additional costs, (ΔCo), that the combined firm has to sustain for coordinating new activities.

If ΔC_{SY} is the cost synergy, ΔC_T the saving in transaction costs, ΔR_{SY} the revenue synergy and ΔC_O the additional coordination costs, the total increase in the gross margin, $\Delta EBITDA$, due to the merger, will be:

$$\Delta EBITDA = \Delta C_{SY} + \Delta C_T + \Delta R_{SY} + \Delta C_O \tag{6.1}$$

Therefore, according to the model proposed in Chapter 3, the value of synergies *created* by the merger (V_{SY}), will be as follows:

$$V_{SY} = \frac{(\Delta C_{SY} + \Delta C_T + \Delta R_{SY} + \Delta C_0)(1 - \tau)}{\rho_M} \tag{6.2}$$

where ρ_M is the cost of capital of the combined firm.

In turn, the value created by the effect on the cost of capital of the combined firm, will be:

$$V_{CC} = [\frac{FCFO_A}{\rho_A} + \frac{FCFO_T}{\rho_T}] - [\frac{FCFO_A}{\rho_M} + \frac{FCFO_T}{\rho_M}] \tag{6.3}$$

Therefore, the total value created by the acquisition and merger will be:

$$V_M = V_{CC} + V_{SY} \tag{6.4}$$

Finally, the value created by the merger for the shareholders of the acquiring firm (V_{SA}) will be:

$$V_{SA} = V_{Acq} - P_T = (V_T + V_M) - P_T \tag{6.5}$$

where V_T is the value of the target firm standing alone and P_T is the price of the target firm.

DETERMINING THE VALUE OF A VERTICAL M&A: AN EXAMPLE

In order to determine the value of a vertical M&A, let us consider a target firm T producing a component of the product of the acquiring firm A. The financial characteristics of the two firms are indicated in Table 6.2.

The firm T produces an intermediate product acquired by firm A, so that the revenues of T are purchasing costs for firm A. The value of the acquiring firm is estimated as being equal to €10,000,000, while the value of the target firm standing alone, $V_T(0)$, is estimated as being equal to €500,000.

We assume that the merger does not affect the cost of capital of the combined firm. If there are no synergies in the merger, the combined firm will present a reduction in revenues of €1,200,000 equal to the reduction in costs, due to the integration of the two firms. The value of acquisition will be €500,000 and no value will be created by the merger.

The situation is different if we suppose that the merger produces a net reduction in costs equal to €200,000 due to the synergies. In particular, we consider synergies deriving from a reduction in production costs and from savings in transaction costs, minus the additional costs for coordinating internal activities.

In fact, the total costs of the combined firm without synergies are: 4,000,000 + 1,000,000 − 1,200,000 = €3,800,000. With synergies, the net reduction in costs determined by the integration are estimated as being equal to 200,000; therefore the total cost of the merger is equal to €3,600,000.

The value created by the merger will be:

$$V_M = V_{SY} = \Delta C_{SY}\,(1-\tau)\,/\,\rho_M = 200{,}000\,(1-0.25)/\,0.10 = 1{,}500{,}000 \qquad (6.6)$$

Therefore, the value of the acquisition will be:

$$V_{acq} = 500{,}000 + 1{,}500{,}000 = 2{,}000{,}000$$

In this case, if the price of T is €500,000, the value created for the shareholders of the acquiring firm is 1,500,000. In fact:

$$V_{SA} = V_{Acq} - P_T = 200{,}000{,}000 - 500{,}000 = 1{,}500{,}000$$

The proposed model allows us to explore the effects on the value created by the merger, considering different hypotheses of cost and revenue synergies and additional cost of integration. In this way, through simulation, it is possible to evaluate the effectiveness of a vertical M&A strategy under different hypotheses regarding synergies.

Table 6.2 Vertical M&A: the value of merger

Economic variables (€)	Firm A	Firm T	Firm AT combined	Firm AT – Firm A	Synergy
Revenues	6,000,000	1,200,000	6,000,000	0	
Total assets	8,000,000	2,000,000			
Fixed assets	4,000,000	1,200,000			
Cost x unit	40	50			10
Total costs	4,000,000	1,000,000	3,600,000	400,000	200,000
EBITDA	2,000,000	200,000	2,400,000		
ΔEBITDA				400,000	
Tax rate (%)	25	25	25	25	25
EBITDA $(1 - t)$	1,500,000	150,000	1,800,000	300,000	150,000
DA (Deprec.& Amm)	400,000	120,000	520,000	120,000	
DA t	100,000	30,000	130,000	30,000	
ΔWC (Working Cap.)	50,000	20,000	70,000	20,000	
Capex	550,000	110,000	660,000	110,000	
FCFO	1,000,000	50,000	1,200,000	200,000	150,000
Cost of capital (%)	10	10	10	10	10
Value of firm	10,000,000	500,000	12,000,000	2,000,000	
Value of acquisition				2,000,000	
Value of synergies					1,500,000
Price of target *T*				500,000	
Value created for shareholders of A				1,500,000	

Note: The firm value is calculated by using the following model: $V = FCFO*/\rho$.

NOTES

1. For some fundamental concepts on the theory of transaction costs see Dringoli (2011, Appendix to Chapter 5).

2. According to Williamson (1975 and 1981), failures of intermediate product markets are the most important factors underlying the vertical integration of firms. In fact, if the market works well with low transaction costs, and prices are not distorted by the monopolistic position, market intermediation is to be preferred to internal organization of activities by virtue of specialization advantages.

3. Monteverde and Teece (1982) in an empirical study on the automobile industry show that transaction costs had an important consequence for vertical integration, thereby supporting the transaction cost paradigm.

4. On the vertical integration strategies as an instrument for increasing the market power in the pharmaceutical industry see Pammolli (1996).

5. However, on this subject there is still a theoretical controversy; see in particular Moomaw (1974); Grant (1998).

6. Instead of accomplishing a formal vertical integration through an M&A, a firm can establish various forms of coordination with its suppliers and clients, for assuring stability in procuring semi-manufactured products, components and services (Harrigan, 1986; Rispoli, 1998). These relations take the form of a permanent and organic collaboration with some suppliers for the delivery of semi-manufactured products, components or services, which are of relevant importance for the firm. Close relationships can be made also with clients such as wholesalers and retailers. Consider, for example, the relations between the large production companies in the automobile, clothing and furniture industries and the network of their retailers. All these relations can be regulated by sale with exclusive or franchising contracts or others forms (quasi-vertical integration).

   Finally, a firm can establish systematic and durable exchange relations with suppliers of products or services, which are autonomous but linked together by a substantial and continuous convergence of interests (a network of firms). In this case, a firm frequently assumes the role of "central or leader firm" of the *net* (Vaccà,1986; Lorenzoni, 1990 and 1992).

7. The minimum efficient scale (MES) of production is the smallest output at which average cost is minimized. If a firm A requires a number of units of an item 1 smaller than MES, to meet its own need, it cannot benefit from economies of scale.

Instead, if a firm realizes in-house production of the item through an exceeding vertical integration it can fully exploit minimum cost. However, to increase the production of this item profitably, beyond its own needs, this firm would need to find buyers to sell its excess items.

7. Diversified M&As

INTRODUCTION AND OBJECTIVES

In this chapter we analyse diversified M&As and how to estimate the value created by the merger. In particular, we only consider *related diversified M&As*, that is mergers producing operating synergies by the integration of businesses. We do not consider unrelated M&As, because these are directed at obtaining higher operating cash flows by restructuring firm processes and substituting managers, rather than at obtaining cost and revenue synergies by integrating firms. As diversified M&As imply the entry of the acquiring company into different industries, risks of failure are higher than in other M&A strategies.

The analysis focuses on the conditions under which a diversified M&A can boost competitive advantage and create value for shareholders. Attractiveness of the industry, that the target firm operates in, is the most important external condition for a diversified M&A to create value. Conversely, capabilities of exploiting asset and resource interrelationships for reducing product costs (economies of scope), as well as for increasing revenues, result as being the most important internal factors for successful diversified M&As. In this context, we present a quantitative model for estimating the value of a diversified M&A.

RATIONALES FOR RELATED DIVERSIFIED M&As

A related diversified M&A consists of expanding the activity of a firm by acquiring companies with products that are different but *related* to those which the firm is already producing and selling. The objective of a diversified M&A may be summarized in creating value for shareholders, mainly through the expansion of revenues and the reduction in costs.

A diversified M&A represents a fundamental strategy for the growth of a firm (Penrose, 1959; Gort, 1962; Berry, 1975; Chandler, 1990; Dringoli, 1995). This is confirmed by empirical studies that point out the positive relationships between product diversification and firm size (Gort, 1962; Rumelt, 1982; Utton, 1979; Berry, 1975).

More precisely, an acquiring firm, entering a different industry through an M&A, can obtain a larger competitive cost advantage over the existing firms when it possesses relevant strategic resources, exceeding the needs deriving from the original activity, which can be shared and transferred to new businesses.[1] In particular, these polyvalent or sharing resources can be: plants, commercial network, logistic structures, brands, firm reputation, patents, technological know-how, etc.

Generally, a firm will decide to use the versatility of its excess resources in activities which are different from the present, when there are limits in implementing a horizontal expansion, due to fierce competition from rival firms or to a steady demand for mature products or technologies. In these cases, through a diversified M&A an acquiring firm will be able to accomplish a "lateral transfer" of its excess resources, that is a move towards business areas where these resources can be effectively used and where useful connections and shared inputs may arise.

However, for a diversified merger to be successful, it is also necessary to be capable of removing assets and resources that will become redundant because of the merger.

More precisely, the levers for creating value through a related diversified M&A can be summarized as follows:

- the reduction in total costs by the sharing of excess assets and resources between companies and businesses (*economies of scope*);
- the reduction in total costs by the exploiting of economies of scale, made possible by the larger size in some common activities determined by the acquisition;
- the increase in total revenues by the exploiting of *complementary* assets and resources of companies in cross selling of different products.

Reduction in costs by exploiting economies of scope

By exploiting exceeding assets and resources between the companies, a combined firm can benefit from cost savings, thereby achieving a larger cost advantage over the rival firms. In particular, in the explanation of successful diversification, the economic literature (Panzar and Willig, 1979; Besanko et al., 1996) has emphasized the importance of *economies of scope*. To be precise, the notion of economies of scope refers to the cost savings that a firm can obtain by combining the production of two or more products at a single location or using the same multipurpose equipment. In more general terms, economies of scope are the economies of jointly producing, selling and distributing different products, coming from the use within a single operating unit of processes enabling the production and distribution of different products.

In analytical terms, we can say that these economies arise when the cost of jointly producing and selling products X, Y is lower than the cost of separately producing and selling each product X and Y. That is, where the following condition is true (Besanko et al., 1996):

$$C(Q_X, Q_Y) < C(Q_X, 0) + C(0, Q_Y) \qquad (7.1)$$

In this case, the cost advantage for the firm adding the product Y to its line X, over the firm producing only the product Y, is given by:

$$C(Q_X, Q_Y) - C(Q_X, 0) < C(0, Q_Y) \qquad (7.2)$$

This formula expresses the idea that it is cheaper for a single firm to produce both goods X and Y than for one firm to produce X and another to produce Y.

All that considered, it is clear that the presence of economies of scope *can favour a diversified M&A*, as the joint production of two or three products by the same firm reduces its costs.[2]

However, for these economies to be obtained, a profound and widespread restructuring of the value chain of the combined company has to be carried out. In particular, the assets and resources that might create value, by sharing and transferring in other businesses are:

- tangible assets, such as the technical structure and therefore plant, production facilities, the sales network, the outbound logistic system, the R&D laboratories, etc.;
- intangible assets, such as the brand image and notoriety, firm reputation, patents, etc.;
- capabilities and competences, such as the marketing and administrative expertise, R&D know-how, technological know-how, managerial skills and experience in problem solving, etc.

Such a resource is, for example, the distribution network of the acquiring firm which will be used for selling the products or services of the target firm (or vice-versa) with negligible additional costs or even increasing revenues if the new products or services complete the original assortment, so facilitating the sale of other products and improving the service to the client.

Among the resources with great potential in value creation there is also technological know-how and organizational capabilities. An acquiring firm, which is particularly endowed with these resources, will be able to use them profitably in other businesses where they constitute an important source of competitive advantage. That is they are distinctive resources capable of constituting a key successful factor in the portfolio of businesses (Hamel and Prahalad, 1994).

In particular, process skills are a fundamental key for successful diversification, especially when these skills can be shared across businesses or transferred, thereby producing a competitive advantage. Among them, general managing capabilities have a great relevance in the diversification processes: they are competences that enable more effective management of the business system (Porter, 1985).

Another relevant asset for successful M&As is the R&D. Empirical studies widely confirm the relevance of R&D resources for diversification, showing a positive and statistically significant relationship between the intensity of R&D and product diversification (Gort, 1962; Chandler, 1962 and 1990).

Therefore, it is a matter of evaluating interdependences across businesses and the available resources that can be exploited in a diversified M&A, by identifying the benefits and costs associated with their use (Prahalad and Doz, 1998). For this purpose a comparison of value chains of companies can offer fundamental information. In particular, sharing assets and resources (Figure 7.1) can give a competitive cost advantage to a related diversified merger through:

- a more intense exploitation of a firm's production structure and in general of technical assets and resources;
- a larger scale in buying common raw materials, components and services, etc.;
- the sharing of distribution channels, outbound logistic structure, promotional and advertising investments;.
- the sharing of an R&D department and technical and production know-how;
- the sharing and transferring of managerial resources, knowledge and problem solving experience.

The importance of scope economies, in favouring diversified M&As, is also confirmed by the history of many large enterprises. A clear example is offered by oil companies which diversified their activity by entering the business of alternative energies, mainly leveraging on scope economies generated by the sharing of technological know-how among different energy activities (Teece, 1980).

In short, a firm can have benefits from diversified M&As when there are tangible and intangible resources that can be used in a number of different activities, without sustaining relevant supplementary costs.

| Value chain of | | Value chain of |
Acquiring firm		Target firm
Inbound Logistics		Inbound Logistics
Operations	⟵⟶	*Operations*
Marketing & Sales	⟵⟶	*Marketing & Sales*
Outbound Logistics	⟵⟶	*Outbound Logistics*
Service		Service

Figure 7.1 Interrelationships between activities of value chain concerning two related businesses

Obviously, the economies of scope are not relevant in conglomerate diversification, which is characterized by the aggregation of quite different activities managed according to a purely financial approach aimed at diversifying risk. This type of diversification, that entails a great capability for selecting and controlling businesses, allows only the general managing capabilities and synergies of an exclusively financial nature to be exploited.

Reduction in costs by a larger scale of activity

A larger scale of activity, determined by the merger, can allow economies of scale to be exploited with additional savings in costs. This often happens in some support activities, such as HR management, information system and technological R&D. But also in primary activities economies of scale can be relevant, for example in manufacturing common components of products or in outbound logistics, as well as in marketing and retailers network.

Increase in total revenues

Revenue synergies can arise from the availability of complementary assets and resources, for example advanced technologies or innovative patents, information or knowledge of markets, well-known brands, as well as distribution networks. They can be exploited for the increase in sales of all firms involved in the merger (cross selling of products). Among these, the immaterial assets are very important, since they have the characteristic of being useful for different products. The firm image and reputation, for example, once they have been developed, also become intangible assets which are useful for promoting all of the firm's products. In these cases, an M&A can be the best solution for successfully diversifying, because it allows the position occupied in the industry by the target firm to be exploited, particularly the existing relationships with customers and suppliers. In addition, it also benefits from the quality of its management and the already specialized personnel.

Cost and revenue synergies

In short, in a diversified M&A, the creation of value for shareholders will depend on the synergies that can arise from the acquisition and the merger of firms. In particular, the synergy gains that can be obtained through a diversified acquisition are the following:

- *cost reduction*, that is the lower operating cost of products derived from exploiting the interrelationships between the businesses of the merged firms and the divestiture of redundant assets.
- *revenue synergies*, that is the incremental revenues derived from exploiting complementary assets and resources for different products and businesses.

Regarding cost synergies, we can distinguish between operating, financial and managerial synergies. The operating synergies arise mainly from reducing the redundant resources in activities with strong technological and market relationships. It is a matter of eliminating double structures and assets in all activities of the value chain of products. Financial synergies, expressed by lower financial costs, are mainly due to more convenient contractual conditions generally obtained by a larger firm. That is true both for raising equity and debts. Finally, managerial synergies are represented by lower costs due to the reduction of excess managerial resources as a consequence of the merger.

Regarding revenue synergies, they can derive from the exploiting of relevant and distinctive assets and resources of the companies involved in the merger for boosting sales of the different products.

ADDITIONAL COSTS OF DIVERSIFIED M&As: COSTS FOR INTEGRATING COMPANIES

In all cases, when evaluating a diversified M&A, it is also necessary to consider the additional costs deriving from integrating and managing the production and distribution activities of companies involved in the merger (Porter, 1985; Collis and Montgomery, 2005). They can be particularly high in diversified M&As. In fact, often a diversified M&A fails because the additional costs sustained for organizing and coordinating a firm's activities are larger than the synergies. The integration costs can be distinguished in these components: coordination, compromise and inflexibility costs.

Coordination costs derive from the need to coordinate companies operating in different businesses, in order to create value by transferring and exploiting competences. They arise because managing a shared activity often requires high-cost managers with competence and experience in identifying opportunities and threats in different businesses. High coordination costs come from the number of business units that the firm has in its portfolio: the higher the number of business units, the more complex the coordination among them. In fact, top management has to collect and interpret a large amount of information and that requires extra time to coordinate (i.e. meetings, call conferences, etc.) and specific experience in order to identify the inefficiencies and the potentialities of the different businesses. The complexity of coordinating a number of business units in a portfolio also requires having people dedicated to coordination activities and a specific organizational structure to support the general manager in interpreting a lot of different information, taking decisions and controlling the outcome of division managers.

Compromise costs result from suboptimal decisions, since two different businesses are sharing some activities or resources.

Inflexibility costs are associated with the impossibility for one division to modify its process because of the needs of the other divisions (for example difficulty in reacting to competitors' actions).

In addition to the limits due to resource saturation, a loss of control may also occur as happens in any large organization in which people opt for a decentralized group structure (Chandler, 1962). The greater the organizational costs, the higher the risk that a diversification strategy will incur possible value disruption.

Therefore, the mere existence of synergies does not justify, in itself, entrance into a new business through an M&A. It is necessary that the business, considered singularly, be profitable and that the possible synergies compensate for the greater integration costs.

IDENTIFYING SPECIFIC ASSETS AND RESOURCES TO BE EXPLOITED IN A DIVERSIFIED MERGER

Also with a diversified M&A it is a matter of analytically evaluating the reduction in costs and the increase in revenues determined by the integration of activities. For this purpose, it is necessary to analyse the value chains of firms involved in the merger, so as to evaluate which activities are to be integrated, exploited or removed and the expected effects in terms of costs and revenues.

The schemes shown in Chapter 4 offer a useful basis to this work. It also allows the new value chain of the merger to be planned and the expected costs, revenues and cash flows to be evaluated.

RISKS IN DIVERSIFIED M&As

Risks in diversified M&As are mainly risks deriving from managing firms operating in different industries. First of all, they depend on the positioning of the target firm with respect to other competitive forces and the dynamics of the industry. Secondly, they derive from the resources and capabilities of the acquiring firm.

Risks from the structure and dynamics of industry where the target firm operates

Risks in diversified M&As are mainly risks an acquiring firm takes when entering a different industry. To correctly evaluate them it is necessary, first of all, to understand whether a particular industry offers real opportunities for long-run profitability (Abell and Hammond, 1979; Day, 1990; Saloner et al., 2001). With this aim in mind, we remember that the most relevant competitive forces that influence the competitive landscape and influence the level of profits are the following (Porter, 1980):

- competing firms;
- suppliers;
- clients;
- firms producing substitute products;
- potential entrants.

On the way these forces can represent a threat to profitability, see Chapter 4. The other structural characteristics of industry which are relevant for the long-term performance are the following:

- the balance between aggregate demand and supply;
- the ratio between the aggregate demand and the minimal efficient scale of production;
- the rate of growth of aggregate demand;
- the presence of barriers to exit.

In particular, the relationship between the aggregate demand and the production capacity in the industry is of particular importance. In fact, unused production capacity is one of the critical factors forcing existing firms to compete on product prices. Excess capacity can be the result of a decreasing rate of market growth and an excess of investments on the part of the existing firms. Moreover, the duration of the negative effects arising from an excess production capacity principally depends on exit barriers, that is on the possibility of firms exiting the business and mobilizing their resources to different businesses. When costs or barriers to the mobility of resources are high, it is difficult to exit the sector. So, the condition of having excess capacity, with its negative effects on prices and incomes, may last for a long time.

Conversely, when the aggregate demand exceeds the production capacity of the industry, prices and incomes will be higher, as the result of weaker competition. That will favour the increase in profits, cash flows and firm value.

Therefore, the performance of a diversified merger can significantly increase through the effects of a growing rate of the aggregate demand of products and services. On the contrary a business characterized by a low growth rate will show a greater rivalry among competitors and lower profitability in the long run (Thompson and Strickland, 1998).

In conclusion, the dynamics of aggregate demand will have a determining effect on product prices and sales, determining the success of a diversified M&A, favouring the reaching of planned sales and the increase in product price; conversely, a low growth with a large increase in product supply can produce in-excess product capacity, thereby causing a fall in product price and destructive retaliation from rival firms.

Also the presence of barriers to exit, determined by specialist investments, can be a negative factor for the success of a diversified M&A, because less efficient firms will be able to continue operating in the industry, even bearing a loss for a long time, and consequently preventing the market from returning to balance.

Summarizing, the earnings and cash flows that a firm can gain through a diversified M&A will be strongly affected by the structure and dynamics of the industry into which the target firm operates. In particular, the most relevant variables that an acquiring firm has to evaluate, when deciding to enter a new business are the following:

- the number of competitors, their production capacities and the concentration rate of supply;
- the number of buyers, their purchase capacity and the concentration of demand;
- the number of substitute products;
- the relationship between the aggregate demand for the product and the whole production capacity;
- the growth rate of aggregate demand.

Risks arising from the inadequacy of firm resources and capabilities

It is well known that for creating value in a business a firm has to adequately position itself with respect to the competitive forces, so as to achieve a competitive advantage. In particular, to create a sustainable value, a firm must be structured in such a way to emphasize its differential elements compared with its competitors.

Therefore, it is particularly important, for the acquiring firm, to evaluate the current competitive positioning of the target firm and its capability to improve through the merger, in order to gain a larger competitive advantage (Day, 1990). On this subject, we recall that the competitive advantage may be of two different forms: a) cost advantage; b) differentiation advantage (Porter, 1980).

The cost advantage arises when a firm succeeds in organizing the activities for manufacturing and selling the product more efficiently, so that the product costs less, even if it is basically equal to competitors' products. The cost advantage may result from different factors: input costs, operating efficiency, scale economies, employment capabilities and competencies, outsourcing of some production activities, etc. The cost advantage enables the firm to create value by selling a product, which is more or less equal to those of its competitors, at lower prices thereby obtaining higher sales volumes.

The differentiation advantage depends on the greater benefits provided by the product, compared with those offered by competitors. The differentiation advantage may derive from different factors: the innovation of products or services, distribution and logistic activities and brand policies, so as to make the firm's supply more valuable than that of its competitors. The differentiation advantage allows value to be created making leverage on the product, in terms of quality or image, so that customers are willing to pay a premium price, or to buy higher quantities (Porter 1980 and 1985; Day, 1990; Grant 1998).[3]

Having said that, for creating value through a diversified M&A, an acquiring firm will have to create larger advantages in terms of costs or differentiation or a combination of them, in comparison with the situation before the merger. In the first case, the merger will create value through a lower cost of product and higher volumes of production and sales. In the second case, leveraging on a higher product differentiation, the combined firm will be able to establish a higher price for the product, with higher unit margins.

But all that will depend on the adequacy of technical and managerial resources of firms involved in the merger.

The analysis of value chains of firms will allow assets and resources, suitable for producing potential synergies by the merger, to be identified and the effects in terms of additional operating cash flows to be estimated.

Risks arising from the complexity of the integration process

As diversified M&As imply the entry of the acquiring company into different industries, risks of failure are higher than in other M&A strategies. In effect, a complex interaction among multiple variables is necessary for a diversified M&A to be able to create value for shareholders. Many of these variables are internal to the firm, but many are external and their estimation and control is highly uncertain. Therefore, the potential synergies could in the end be overvalued.

Furthermore, it is necessary to highlight that potential synergy benefits are not sufficient for ensuring the success of a diversified M&A; they must be larger than the additional costs of integration of activities regarding different businesses. Therefore, the success of a diversification strategy also depends on the capability of implementing the integration processes and particularly on how effectively linkages between different business units are designed and managed.[4] In the end, the success of the merger requires managerial capabilities of managing different businesses and quickly facing environment changes and aggressive strategies of rivals. The analysis presented above suggests that these qualifications are difficult to obtain and develop, especially in low related diversification.

With this belief, in Chapter 9 we will examine the changes to be carried out in the organizational structures of firms, in order to solve the complex organizational problems that a diversified M&A produces, and for making a full deployment of potential synergies possible.

THE ADVANTAGES OF A DIVERSIFIED M&A IN RESPECT TO INTERNAL DEVELOPMENT

A product diversification strategy can be also implemented through internal development. This strategy consists of building a new business unit through direct investments aimed at manufacturing a different product and organizing a new sales and distribution structure.

With respect to internal development, a diversification implemented through the acquisition of existing companies offers some important advantages. The main advantages of this option are provided by the greater speed and ease of entering into a different industry and its neutrality related to the industry supply capacity, that remains the same. On the contrary, internal diversification implies a production capacity increase at the industry level. The consequent supply increase can determine a significant sale price reduction, if the increase in aggregate supply is larger than the increase in product demand. In these circumstances, the reaction of incumbent competitors can also cause a price war, with negative effects on the outcome of all firms operating in the market.

Besides allowing an acquiring firm to easily overcome the barriers to entry in an industry, an M&A strategy will also offer the acquiring firm the benefits deriving from the possibility to increase capabilities and competences through resources available at the acquired companies. However, external growth through M&A exposes the firm to other risks, as we have observed above.

UNRELATED (CONGLOMERATE) M&A: THE VALUE OF CONTROL

Diversified M&As can be unrelated, or conglomerate. We remember that an unrelated M&A is characterized by the acquisition of firms with products or services that have characteristics different from the technological, commercial, organizational and managerial specialization of the acquiring firm. In an unrelated M&A the increase in value of the acquiring firm mainly arises from the higher operating cash flows obtained by restructuring firm processes and substituting managers, rather than from cost or revenue synergies by integration. For these reasons, this type of acquisition and merger are not the object of the present study. Situations favouring these M&As are the following:

- a target firm with a managerial group pursuing objectives which are not coherent with the creation of value for shareholders;
- a target firm with a top management endowed with inadequate competences to run the actual business and the availability of superior managerial competences in the acquiring firm, capable of improving the performance level of target firms.

Indeed, managerial capabilities are the determinant resource for the success of conglomerate acquisitions, mainly in industries where the complexity of the competitive environment and the dynamics of evolution processes require high managerial competences and know-how. In this case, the transfer of managerial resources between companies, both purchased and purchaser, can contribute to increasing the economic value of entities involved in the operations of extraordinary management. Other assets and resources, suitable to be shared and transferred for increasing the economic value of the merger, can be present in support activities, such as know-how in planning accounting, legal, and government affairs, HR management expertise, firm reputation, etc.

Conglomerate M&As are often justified by speculative reasons, market imperfections and asymmetric information. In some cases the possibility of creating economic value depends on the capability of exploiting advantageous prices in the negotiations. In this case a takeover (change of shareholders) is launched by raider investors, when market prices do not mirror the real business value or the value that can be obtained by different managers.

Finally, a conglomerate acquisition can also be realized for reducing variance of cash flows and creating firm value through the reduction of the firm's cost of capital, as an effect of the decrease in comprehensive risk following the diversification in business portfolio. However, as the capital asset price model shows, diversification lowers unsystematic risk not systematic risk. Therefore, shareholders can also reduce their risk through a diversified portfolio of securities.

A MODEL FOR DETERMINING THE VALUE OF A DIVERSIFIED M&A

As we have seen in Chapter 3, for an M&A to create value, first of all, the value of synergies must be positive.

Precisely, *revenue synergies* (ΔR_{SY}) depend on the increase in sales and eventually the increase in the price of products (Δp) as a consequence of the merger (for example of the higher image and reputation of the acquiring firm).

Cost synergies (ΔC_{SY}) depend on exploiting the interrelationships between activities and the divestiture of redundant assets and the resource redeployments. They can also result from scale economies made possible by the merger.

Additional costs (ΔC) depend on the complexity in integrating different activities and coordinating different businesses.

As far as revenue synergies are concerned, where the merger generates synergies both for the business unit T (target firm) and the business unit A (acquiring firm), we will have: [5]

$$\Delta R_{SY,T} = [p_T(0) + \Delta p_T] \Delta Q_T + \Delta p_T Q_T(0) \tag{7.3}$$

$$\Delta R_{SY,A} = [p_A(0) + \Delta p_A] \Delta Q_A + \Delta p_A Q_A(0) \tag{7.4}$$

$$\Delta C_{SY,T} = [Q_T(0) + \Delta Q_T] \Delta Cu_T \tag{7.5}$$

$$\Delta C_{SY,A} = [Q_A(0) + \Delta Q_A] \Delta Cu_A \tag{7.6}$$

Therefore, the total *revenue synergies* for the merger will be:

$$\Delta R_{SY} = \Delta R_{SY,A} + \Delta R_{SY,T} \tag{7.7}$$

The total *cost synergies* will be:

$$\Delta C_{SY} = \Delta C_{SY,A} + \Delta C_{SY,T} \tag{7.8}$$

Therefore, the incremental *EBITDA* produced by the merger will be:

$$\Delta EBITDA = \Delta C_{SY,A} + \Delta R_{SY} + \Delta C_0$$

As a consequence, the net value of synergies created by the merger can be determined as follows:

$$V_{SY} = \frac{(\Delta C_{SY} + \Delta R_{SY} + \Delta C_O)(1 - \tau^*)}{\rho_M} \qquad (7.9)$$

The value created by a change in operating risk and thus in the cost of capital will be:

$$V_{CC} = \frac{(FCFO_A + FCFO_T)}{\rho_M} - [\frac{FCFO_A}{\rho_A} + \frac{FCFO_T}{\rho_T}] \qquad (7.10)$$

As a consequence, the total value created by the merger will be:

$$V_M = V_{SY} + V_{CC} \qquad (7.11)$$

Finally, the value created for the shareholders of the acquiring firm A will depend on the price paid for the target firm (P_T). Precisely, it will be equal to the value of acquisition minus the price paid for the firm T.

$$V_{SA} = V_T + (V_{SY} + V_{CC}) - P_T \qquad (7.12)$$

where $V_T + (V_{SY} + V_{CC})$ is the value of the acquisition and P_T the price paid for the acquisition.

DETERMINING THE VALUE CREATED THROUGH A DIVERSIFIED M&A: AN EXAMPLE

For further clarification, let us consider two firms A (acquiring) and T (target) independently operating in different industries and having the financial characteristics indicated in Table 7.1.

To simplify the analysis let us assume that the merger of the two firms will produce:

- cost synergies (ΔC_{SY}) equal to a 10% reduction in the total costs of products sold;
- revenue synergies (ΔR_{SY}) equal to a 5% increase in total revenues;
- additional costs (ΔC_O) for integrating and coordinating activities of the merger equal to 2% of the total costs of products sold.

Let us also assume that the combined firm has a lower cost of capital (12%) than the target firm standing alone (15%), because of the reduction in operating risk.

Table 7.1 A simulation of value created by a diversified M&A

Variables (€)	Firm A	Firm T	Firm AT combined	Firm AT − Firm A	Synergies
Product price	60	40			
Sales (tons)	100,000	80,000			
Revenues	6,000,000	3,200,000	9,660,000	3,660,000	460,000
Total assets	8,000,000	2,000,000			
Fixed assets	4,000,000	1,200,000			
Cost per unit	40	30	32.7		
Total costs	4,000,000	2,400,000	5,888,000	1,888,000	512,000
EBITDA	2,000,000	800,000	3,772,000	1,772,000	972,000
Tax rate	25%	25%	25%	25%	25%
EBITDA $(1-t)$	1,500,000	600,000	2,829,000	1,329,000	729,000
DA (Dep.&Am)	400,000	120,000	520,000		
DA t	100,000	30,000	130,000		
ΔWC (Work. Cap.)	10,000	5,000	15,000		
Capex	90,000	25,000	115,000		
FCFO	1,500,000	600,000	2,829,000		
Cost of capital	12%	15%	12%	12%	12%
Firm value (1)	12,500,000	4,000,000	23,575,000		
Value of synergies					6,075,000
Value by the cost of capital change					1,000,000
Value of acquisition				11,075,000	
Value created by M&A					7,075,000
Value of cost synergies (net value)					3,200,000
Value of revenue synergy					2,875,000

Notes:

(1) The values of firms A, T and AT have been calculated considering *FCFO* constant for an unlimited period of time.
(2) Value of synergies: cost synergies = 512,000 $(1-0.25)/0.12 = 3,200,000$; revenue synergies = 460,000 $(1-0.25)/0.12 = 2,875,000$; value from cost of capital change = $-(600,000/0.15) + (600,000/0.12) = 1,000,000$.

Applying the model shown above, on the basis of our assumptions the value of the combined firm results in being equal to €23,575,000 and the total synergies from the merger result equal to €6,075,000, of which €2,875,000 are revenue synergies and €3,200,000 are net cost synergies. The increase in value due to the reduction in cost of capital (cost of capital synergies) results as being equal to €1,000,000. In fact, *the value of the merger* is:

$$V_M = V_{SY} + V_{CC} = 7,075,000$$

where:

$$V_{SY} = 3,200,000 + 2,875,000 = 6,075,000$$

$$V_{CC} = 1,000,000$$

If the price of the firm T is equal to the value of the firm stand alone (€4,000,000), the value created by the merger will be entirely gained by the shareholders of firm A and it will be equal to €7,075,000.

In fact we have:

$$V_{SA} = V_{acq} - P_T = 4,000,000 + 7,075,000 - 4,000,000 = 7,075,000 \quad (7.14)$$

If the price of T is larger than €4,000,000, a part of the value of merger will be transferred to the shareholders of firm T.

Under our assumptions, the shareholders of firm A will find the merger convenient only if the price of firm T is lower than €11,075,000. In fact, this is the value of the target firm standing alone (€4,000,000) plus the total value produced by the merger (€7,075,000) (Table 7.1).

NOTES

1. According to Porter (1985), the interrelationships between the relevant activities of the value chain of business units are the basis of diversification. In particular, sharing activities can lead to a sustainable competitive advantage for a diversified firm, by lowering costs and enhancing differentiation. However, sharing does not necessarily lower costs unless it favourably affects the other cost drivers of an activity. According to Porter, sharing has the potential of reducing costs if the cost of an activity is driven by economies of scale, learning or the pattern of capacity utilization. Focusing on the firm's activities rather than on firm resources, Porter distinguishes between tangible, intangible and competitors' interrelationships and proposes to analyse the

interrelationships between the value chains of different business units.

2. Economies of scope occur when a single firm producing a specific combination of different products is more efficient than specialized firms separately producing one single good. To illustrate the economic logic of exploiting the economies of scope, let us suppose the following cost functions of a hypothetical manufacturer of a product X and of a manufacturer of a product Y:

$$C(Q_X, 0) = 200 + 0.30\ Q_X$$
$$C(Q_Y, 0) = 50 + 0.10\ Q_Y$$

To produce the good X the first manufacturer must sustain a fixed cost of $200 million and a unit variable cost of $0.30 for each product. Producing a quantity equal to 500 million units this firm will have a total cost of $350 million. The second manufacturer must sustain a fixed cost of $50 million and a unit variable cost of $0.10 for each product Y. Producing a quantity of 200 million units it will have a total cost of $70 million.

Now, let us suppose that the first firm X decides to acquire the firm Y and to exploit its know-how and its plant capacity jointly producing the goods X and Y, with an increase in fixed cost equal to $20 million and a unit variable cost of good Y equal to 0.09 (-0.01).

The function of the total cost of the combined firm will be:

$$C(X, Y) = 220 + 0.30\ Q_X + 0.09\ Q_Y$$

If the combined firm produces a quantity of 500 million units of product X and 200 million units of product Y jointly, it will sustain a total cost of $388 million. On the contrary, the two firms standing alone would sustain a total cost of $420 million (350 + 70). Thus, the cost synergies are equal to $32 million. The additional cost for adding product Y to its line is only $38 million ($388 million − $350 million). This will give a competitive cost advantage of $32 million over firm Y.

3. Porter (1980) considers cost leadership and differentiation strategies mutually excludible: 'firms trying to pursue both, risk ending up "stuck in the middle". For these firms the almost certain result is low profitability. Either they lose clients which ensure high volumes, or they assist in the volatilization of the greatest part of profits in the attempt to compete with firms with lower costs. At the same time, they will also lose those clients that ensure higher margins − the cream of the market − leaving them to firms that have focused on higher margin segments or that have succeeded in a substantial differentiation. The firm that stops in the middle of the ford has probably a less defined business culture, and operates in a conflicting organizational and motivational structure' (p. 42).

4. On this position see Larsson and Finkelstein (1999); Haspeslagh and Jemison (1987); Gary (2005).

5.   In fact, for the business unit T the revenue synergies will be:

$$\Delta R_T = [p_T(0) + \Delta p_T] \, [Q_T(0) + \Delta Q_T] - p_T(0) \, Q_T(0) =$$
$$= [p_T(0) + \Delta p_T] \, \Delta Q_T + \Delta p_T \, Q_T(0)$$

And the cost synergies will be:

$$\Delta C_T = [Q_T(0) + \Delta Q_T] \, \Delta Cu_T(0).$$

It will be similarly for the business unit A.

8. Financing M&As and effects on merger value

INTRODUCTION AND OBJECTIVES

In M&A operations the form of payment of the target firm is crucial for the success of the merger. This chapter examines the main alternatives of payment: by cash and by new stocks issued by the acquiring firm. The payment by new shares requires the exchange ratio between the shares of the acquiring firm and those of the target firm to be determined. The analysis indicates how to calculate the maximum exchange ratio the shareholders of the acquiring firm can pay without destroying value, and the minimum exchange ratio that makes the merger neutral for the shareholders of the target firm.

The choice between alternative forms of payment is also analysed with particular reference to debt financing, taking into consideration the relative fiscal advantage, due to the interest exemption from income tax, and the effects on financial risk. The choice between payment by cash and by the issue of new shares is also evaluated considering the tax effects on the shareholders of the acquiring firm and of the target firm. Finally, a numerical example is presented for comparing the effects of financing acquisition through debt or new shares.

FINANCIAL PLANNING OF AN ACQUISITION

Under a financial profile the acquisition of a company is an investment decision and therefore it has to be evaluated as an investment. In this context, a first amount of capital is required at the closing of the deal for the payment of the price to the vendor and a second amount of capital is required to carry out the integration of companies and the implementation of merger activities. More precisely, the total capital required is the sum of the following components (Reed-Lajoux and Weston, 1999):

- the direct financial requirements for the acquisition, inclusive of the acquisition price and the contingent net financial assets, in addition to legal and transaction costs;
- the indirect financial requirements due to the integration costs for the improvement of the efficiency of the merger.

However, this total capital can be reduced through the disinvestment of non-strategic assets.

CHOOSING BETWEEN DIFFERENT FORMS OF PAYMENT

In M&A operations the form of payment can be crucial for the success of the merger (Hitt et al., 2001). The main alternatives of payment are the following:

- by new stocks issued by the acquiring firm;
- by cash using debt;
- by cash using firm liquidity.

The three alternatives can present some variants. For example, in the case of payment by cash, instead of a single cash payment, a series of payments can be established which are distributed over time and subject to the achievement of precise performance objectives. In the second case, the issue of convertible bonds can be agreed on the basis of a fixed exchange ratio. A list of different forms of payment is presented in Table 8.1.

Obviously, combining the different alternatives it is possible to obtain a number of customized solutions. In this respect, the flexibility offered by the different forms of payment can be quite useful for balancing the different needs of the parties, those, for example, concerning the liquidity of the investment, the price level, the fiscal position, etc. In particular, the payment of part of the price, bound to the future incomes of the merger, can allow the vendor to prove the real value of the company and the acquirer to justify the price paid.

PAYMENT THROUGH NEW SHARES ISSUED BY THE ACQUIRING FIRM: HOW TO DETERMINE THE EXCHANGE RATIO

After having estimated the value of acquisition (*Vacq*) and defined a possible price of the target firm (P_T), it is a matter of evaluating how to finance the acquisition.

Payment through new shares requires, first of all, determining the exchange ratio, that is the number of new shares of the acquiring firm A to be issued for the payment of the shares of the target firm T. Precisely, it is a case of determining the number of new shares the acquiring firm has to give to the shareholders of the target firm in exchange for each share of this firm.

Table 8.1 Different forms of payment for an acquisition

Payment offered by the buyer:	The shareholders of the acquired firm receive:
Liquidity (cash)	Cash in exchange for shares of the target firm.
Deferred cash payment (earn out)	Cash in exchange for shares in different tranches over time, in relation to the checked performance of the acquired firm.
Shares exchange	Shares of the acquired firm in exchange for the target firm's shares according to the agreed exchange ratio.
Liquidity through new shares (vendor placing)	Shares of the acquired firm in exchange for the target firm's shares according to the agreed exchange ratio, that are subsequently sold to an institutional investor for cash.
Bonds exchange	Bonds issued by the acquirer in exchange for each share of the target firm according to an agreed exchange ratio.
Privileged shares exchange, convertible bonds or warrants	Convertible bonds, warrants or privileged shares issued by the acquirer for each share of the target firm, according to an agreed exchange ratio.

Source: P.S. Sudarsanam (1995).

The current exchange ratio $ER(C)$ will be given by the ratio between the current value of a share of the target firm w_T and the current value of a share of the acquiring firm w_A. In other words, the current exchange ratio is determined on the basis of the current values of the companies A and T interested in the M&A (V_A, V_T) and consequently of the values of equity (E_A, E_T) and thus the value of each share (w_A, w_T).

Precisely it will be:

$$E_A = V_A - D_A \qquad (8.1)$$

$$E_T = V_T - D_T \qquad (8.2)$$

where D_A and D_T are the value of debts of firms A and T.

And thus:

$$w_A = E_A / N_A \qquad (8.3)$$

$$w_T = E_T / N_T \qquad (8.4)$$

where N_A and N_T are the number of shares of the two companies.

Thus, the *current exchange ratio* will be:

$$ER(C) = w_T / w_A \qquad (8.5)$$

On the basis of the current exchange ratio, we can determine the number of the new shares (ΔN_A) to be assigned to the shareholders of the target firm, as the payment of the agreed price, by multiplying the exchange rate $ER(C)$ by the number of shares of the target firm, N_T:

$$\Delta N_A = N_T \ ER(C) \qquad (8.6)$$

Obviously, the current values of the interested companies are only a basis for the determination of the *real exchange ratio* between the shares of the firms, and consequently of the number of new shares to assign to the shareholder of the target firm as payment of the price. In fact, the *real exchange ratio ER(C)* will be determined considering, besides the current values of the firms standing alone, other factors such as the expected synergies and the general interest of the two parties.

The maximum exchange ratio for the shareholders of the acquiring firm

As we have seen, the current exchange ratio is determined on the basis of the current stand-alone values of the the interested companies. If these values are accepted in the deal, the shareholders of the companies involved in the merger will enjoy the value of synergies produced by the merger in proportion to the stand-alone values of their firms.

However, to conclude the acquisition, it may be necessary to agree upon a higher level of the exchange ratio, with respect to the current values, to meet the request of the target firm's shareholders. So, in this case, what is the maximum exchange ratio that the shareholders of the acquiring firm can pay for the target firm, without a loss in value?

This maximum exchange ratio is the one that makes the share value of the company A, after the merger, (w_{AT}) equal to the share value of company A, before the merger (w_A). In fact, in this case, the shareholders of A will maintain the same value for each share owned.

In analytical terms, the following conditions must be satisfied:

$$w_{AT} = w_A \tag{8.7}$$

As the theoretical value of a share after the merger (w_{AT}) is given by[1]:

$$w_{AT} = (w_A N_A + w_T N_T + V_{SY}) / (N_A + ER N_T) \tag{8.8}$$

where V_{SY} is the value of expected synergies, the maximum *ER* for the shareholders of A is the value that satisfies the following condition:

$$(w_A N_A + w_T N_T + V_{SY}) / (N_A + ER(\text{Max}) N_T) = w_A \tag{8.9}$$

This occurs when[2]:

$$ER(\text{Max}) = (w_T / w_A) + (V_{SY} / w_A N_T) = (w_T + V_{SY} / N_T) / w_A \tag{8.10}$$

In other words, the maximum exchange rate occurs when all the value of synergies, produced by the merger, is attributed to the shareholders of the target firm. That means that the price paid for the shares of the target firm PE_T will be equal to the value of shares of the firm *T* standing alone (E_T), plus the value of total synergies produced by the merger.[3] This is when:

$$PE_T = E_T + V_{SY} \tag{8.11}$$

Therefore, the maximum price to be paid for firm T will be:

$$P_T = PE_T + D_T = V_T + V_{SY} \tag{8.12}$$

The minimum exchange ratio for the shareholders of the target firm

The minimum value of the exchange ratio is the one that makes the merger neutral for the shareholders of the target firm. This is the value which satisfies the following relationship:

$$w_T = ER(m) \, w_{AT} \tag{8.13}$$

that is:

$$ER(m) = w_T / w_{AT} \tag{8.14}$$

Therefore, it will be:

$$w_T = ER(m) \frac{(E_A + E_T + V_{SYN})}{N_A + ER \, N_T} \tag{8.15}$$

and thus:

$$ER(m) = \frac{w_T N_A}{E_A + E_T + V_{SYN} - E_T} = \frac{w_T}{w_A + V_{SYN} / N_A} \tag{8.16}$$

As a consequence, the price of firm T can be smaller than the value standing alone, because the shareholders of firm T will benefit from the synergies created by the merger, as new shareholders of the combined firm.

We note that when:

$$ER(C) = w_T / w_A \tag{8.17}$$

the synergies produced by the merger are not incorporated in the price of the target firm (as w_T and w_A are determined only by the stand-alone value of the companies). However, the shareholders of the target firm will participate in the synergies produced by the merger, in proportion to the value of their shares, because they become new shareholders of the merger company, also taking the relative risk upon themselves.

An intermediate value of the exchange ratio

An intermediate value of $ER(R)$, as a consequence of the bargaining power of the two parties, will recognize a price of the target firm which is higher than its stand-alone value. Therefore, the shareholders of the target firm will enjoy part of future synergies to be produced by the merger, as soon as the deal is made, reducing the merger's risks. In addition, this intermediate value will also allow the shareholders of the combined company (the old shareholder of the acquiring firm and the new shareholders) to benefit from the residual part of synergies actually produced by the merger.

The cost of the merger for the shareholders of firm A (CM_{SA}) will be given by the premium paid to the shares of shareholders of the target firm over its stand-alone value, E_T. That is precisely:

$$CM_{SA} = E_T(R) - E_T \qquad (8.18)$$

where:

$$E_T(R) = ER(R) N_T (E_A + E_T + V_{SY})/ (ER(R) N_T + N_A) \qquad (8.19)$$

being: $ER(R)$ the agreed exchange ratio between the two parties; $ER(R) N_T$ the number of new shares issued for the change; $(E_A + E_T + V_{SY})$ the post-merger value of the shares of the combined firm and $(ER(R) N_T + N_A)$ the number of shares after the merger.

Therefore:

$$ER(R) N_T / (ER(R) N_T + N_A) \qquad (8.20)$$

is the portion of total shares given to the shareholders of the target firm.

Obviously, if the shareholders of the acquiring firm are optimistic about the expected synergies of the merger, they will pay a higher price for the shares of the target firm, with respect to the value corresponding to the stand-alone value of the company, but they will avoid paying too much, with respect to the expected synergies.

On the contrary, the shareholders of the target firm will prefer to be paid in cash, if their expectations are not positive about the merger performance. In this case, they will limit their risk.[4]

Note that the price of shares after merger (p_{AT}) will depend on the total value of the company resulting from the merger (combined firm) and therefore from the synergies produced, the total value of debt (D_{AT}) and on the number of shares on the market. In fact, we will have:

$$p_{AT} = (V_{AT} - D_{AT}) / (ER(R) N_T + N_A) \qquad (8.21)$$

where $(V_{AT} - D_{AT}) = E_A + E_T + V_{SYN}$ is the value of equity.

Thus, it is evident that, given the synergies, the higher the $ER(R)$, the lower the price of shares after the merger. In other words, the larger the number of shares issued, the lower the price of shares after the merger.

FINANCING THE ACQUISITION THROUGH DEBT

Technical forms of debt

When the acquisition is financed by debt, the most used banking instrument is the *senior debt*, that is a privileged debt accompanied by a real and/or a personal guarantee. The technical forms are represented by the medium–long-term debt, such as mortgage loan, stand-by credit, over green credit or short-term banking credit. The choice among these is based on the need for flexibility and on the nature of the investment. For example, to finance an investment in working capital, a short revolving credit is preferable, because of its flexibility. On the other hand, in the case of a leveraged acquisition, a senior debt, that is renewable at maturity, may be preferable as the company can adapt the payments to the cash flows produced by the investment.

In the case of a relevant debt, a syndicate debt may be the best solution, because it allows the high debt to be shared among a number of lenders. A particular form of these loans are the so called *jumbo* loans, characterized by an exceptional level of debt, which are required by large international groups. Among the senior debts, *bridge* loans have a particular importance: they are short-term funds directed at covering immediate needs. Soon after, they will be replaced by cheaper and more suitable financing.

Sometimes, the funds required for an M&A are collected by the issue of bonds on the financial market; they are mainly directed at institutional investors and can be secured loans (with real guarantee), zero coupon bonds (with the payment of coupons at maturity) or pay in kind bonds (with the payment of coupons with the issue of new bonds). In this context, particular attention should be paid to high yield bonds, which are bonds characterized by no-guarantee and high rate of interest. The use of high yield bonds presents some advantages for the debtor, among which there is the presence of only financial covenants, the speed with which the operation is set up and the flexibility of the repayment modes.

With regard to debt financing, it is also necessary to consider the effect of the total increase of debt ($D_T + \Delta D$) and thus of financial leverage on the weighted average cost of capital ($WACC$) of the combined firm.

Effects of increasing debt on the average cost of capital

The payment of the target firm through the issue of bonds or a bank debt on one hand offers the acquiring firm's shareholders the advantage of a lower cost of debt and then the fiscal advantage due to the interest exemption from income tax. On the other hand, the increase of debt can worsen the risk profile of the combined firm, with an increase in the cost of debt and in the cost of equity and thus in the weighted cost of capital.

In fact, as we noticed in Chapter 3, the value of a merger depends both on the increase of net free cash flows obtained by the acquisition (Δ *FCFO*) and the weighted cost of capital (ρ). Therefore, it is also necessary to evaluate the effects of the different forms of financing on the weighted average cost of capital (*WACC*).

We remember that the cost of capital (*WACC*) is expressed by the following:

$$WACC = \rho_M(D) = k_d\,(1 - t_c)\,D/V + k_e\,E/V \tag{8.22}$$

where $k_d\,(1 - t_c)$ is the unit cost of debt after tax and k_e is the unit cost of equity.

In particular, the debt will increase the risk for creditors and thus the cost of debt of the combined firm. We remember that the cost of debt, *kd*, will increase as the financial leverage rises (see Chapter 3). Therefore, it is a matter of evaluating the new rating of the combined firm, as the effect of the planned financial leverage, and then the credit spread to be added to the risk-free yield of Treasury bonds (i_f). Precisely, it will be:

$$kd = i_f + cs \tag{8.23}$$

where:

$$cs = f\,(D + \Delta D) \tag{8.24}$$

Also the cost of equity, *ke*, will be influenced by the increase in financial leverage. Precisely, according to the CAPM (Capital Asset Pricing Model) theory (Sharpe, 1964; Lintner, 1965; Fama, 1968; Levy and Sarnat, 1986; Brealey and Myers, 1996), the cost of equity can be expressed as follows:

$$k_{e,i} = i_f + (r_m - i_f)\,\beta_i \tag{8.25}$$

where i_f is the return on free risk investment, for example US Treasury bills, r_m the return on the investment in the market portfolio of common stocks; ($r_m - i_f$) is the market risk premium required for investing in the market portfolio and β_i is an index expressing the relative risk of firm i with respect to the risk of the investment on the market portfolio of common stocks, considered equal to 1. So, the second addend of the expression indicates the premium required to invest in the firm i over the return on the risk-free investment i_f.

As we pointed out in Chapter 3, the Beta of a firm (β_i) is influenced by the type of business in which a firm i operates, its operating leverage and its financial leverage. In particular, we can consider that, other things remaining unchanged, an increase in financial leverage will proportionally increase the equity Beta of the firm. In fact, intuitively the fixed payments on debt increase the variance in net income, because a higher leverage increases income during good times, but decreases income during bad times.

If all of the firm's risk is borne by the stock holders (i.e. the beta of debt is zero) and debt has a tax benefit for the firm, it results that:

$$B_L = \beta_U [1 + (1 - \tau) \, D/E] \tag{8.26}$$

where: B_L is the levered beta of the firm; β_U the unlevered beta of the firm (i.e. the beta of the firm without any debt); τ the corporate tax rate and D/E the debt to equity ratio.

The unlevered beta of a firm is determined by the types of business in which it operates and by its operating leverage. In practice, statistical data on returns of shares allow us to calculate r_m, ke and B_L, that is the *leveraged beta* value of every company (for those listed on the official market and then approximately for the comparable others). From the current $\beta_L\,(C)$ of a firm it is possible to calculate the new $\beta_L\,(P)$ corresponding to the planned level of financial leverage $(D + \Delta D)/E$, as the consequence of financing the acquisition by additional debt. To do this, it is a matter of deriving the value of beta unlevered β_U from the same firm, as follows:

$$\beta_U = \frac{\beta_L(C)}{1 + (1 - \tau)D/E} \tag{8.27}$$

And then we can calculate the new beta corresponding to the planned level of financial leverage $(D+\Delta D)/E$. It will be:

$$\beta_L(P) = \beta_U [1 + (1 - \tau) \, (D + \Delta D)/E] \tag{8.28}$$

Now, we can obtain the new value of cost of equity, $k_e\,(P)$, according to the following expression:

$$k_e\,(P) = i_f + (r_m - i_f)\,\beta_L(P) \tag{8.29}$$

In other words, knowing the current value of the Beta of the firm, in correspondence to a given value of leverage (current value), we will determine the value of the Beta of the same firm without any debt, and then the new value of Beta corresponding to the planned level of debt. Soon after, we will determine the cost of equity $k_e(P)$ in correspondence of the new level of debt.

Finally, we will recalculate the *WACC*, being:

$$WACC = \rho_M(D) = K_e(P) \ E/V + K_d(1-\tau) \ (D + \Delta D)/V \qquad (8.30)$$

Therefore, if $\rho_M(D)$ is the average cost of capital of the merger financed by debt (ΔD) and ρ_A and ρ_T are the average costs of capital of firm A and T, stand alone, the value created (or destroyed) by a reduction (or an increase) in the cost of capital, as a consequence of the additional debt necessary for financing the acquisition, the following expression will be given:

$$V_{\Delta D} = \frac{FCFO_A + FCFO_T}{\rho_M(D)} - [\frac{FCFO_A}{\rho_A} + \frac{FCFO_T}{\rho_T}] \qquad (8.31)$$

If $\rho_M(D)$ is smaller than ρ_A and ρ_T, there is an advantage in financing the merger by debt, because the reduction in cost of capital creates additional value. On the contrary, if $\rho_M(D)$ is larger than ρ_A and ρ_B, financing the acquisition by debt will destroy value, thereby reducing the value created by synergies.

FINANCING THROUGH DEBT OR THROUGH NEW SHARES?

Effects on the merger value

The choice between debt and new shares requires a comparison between the value created (or destroyed) financing the M&A by additional debt with the value created (or destroyed) by issuing new shares.

On one hand financing the acquisition by debt, $(\Delta D = P_T - D_T)$, the additional debt causes the cost of equity, (ke), to rise; on the other hand it raises the weight of debt, the cheaper component of financing (kd). So the problem is how much will the required return on equity (ke) increase for hedging the higher risk, due to the larger financial leverage. In this case, the total value created, or destroyed, by the merger financed by additional debt will be given by the following expression:

$$V_{AD} = \frac{FCFO_A + FCFO_T}{\rho_M(D)} - [\frac{FCFO_A}{\rho_A} + \frac{FCFO_T}{\rho_T}] + \frac{\Delta FCFO}{\rho_M(D)} \qquad (8.32)$$

where: $\rho_M(D)$ is the average cost of the combined firm financed by additional debt and ρ_A and ρ_T are the cost of capital of the two companies standing alone.

On the contrary, by financing the acquisition with new shares, ($\Delta E = P_T - D_T$), on one hand the weight of the more expensive component of firm capital increases, on the other the financial leverage reduces and with it the unit cost of equity. The combined effect can be an increase or a decrease in the average cost of capital of the merger. Precisely, if $\rho_M(E)$ is the average cost of the combined firm financed by new shares and ρ_A and ρ_T are the cost of capital of the two companies standing alone, the total value created (or destroyed) by the merger, financed through new shares will be:

$$V_{AE} = \frac{FCFO_A + FCFO_T}{\rho_M(E)} - [\frac{FCFO_A}{\rho_A} + \frac{FCFO_T}{\rho_T}] + \frac{\Delta FCFO}{\rho_M(E)} \qquad (8.33)$$

Therefore, the difference in value between financing by debt and by new shares will be:

$$V_{AD} - V_{AE} = \frac{FCFO_A + FCFO_T}{\rho_M(D)} - \frac{FCFO_A + FCFO_T}{\rho_M(E)} + \frac{\Delta FCFO}{\rho_M(D)} - \frac{\Delta FCFO}{\rho_M(E)} \qquad (8.34)$$

In conclusion, the final effect on the weighted average cost of capital will depend on the way the cost of equity is influenced by the different levels of financial leverage.

On this subject, it is well known that, according to the Modigliani-Miller theory, in the absence of fiscal benefits on debt, the weighted cost of capital is not influenced by the different form of financing, but only by the operating risk. This means that the cost of equity will rise in proportion to the increase of debt, because the increase in risk premium on equity requires compensating the larger risk. Consequently the weighted cost of capital would remain unchanged. All that would be obtained by arbitrages between prices of shares with different values but the same operating risk. On the contrary, according to this theory, if fiscal benefits of debt are taken into consideration, the weighted cost of capital will continue to decrease, making debt more advantageous than equity.

Other scholars deny this conclusion and argue that it is true only as far as a certain level of leverage is reached, but over this level the cost of bankruptcy causes the cost of equity to rise considerably, also dragging up the weighted cost of capital.

Without entering into this complicated theoretical controversy, we will follow the pattern adopted in real life, considering the average cost of capital greatly rising with the increase of financial leverage up to a threshold believed to be acceptable by the financial institutions.

COMPARING THE VALUE CREATED THROUGH FINANCING BY NEW SHARES AND BY DEBT: AN EXAMPLE

Let us consider that firm A is evaluating how to finance the acquisition of firm T operating in the same industry (horizontal M&A). The basic data regarding the two firms are shown in Table 8.2. In particular, the estimated *FCFO* for firms A and T standing alone, prior to merger, are respectively equal to €5,330 and €4,225 million.

The average cost of capital is calculated according to the formula:

$$WACC = kd(1 - \tau)\ D/V + Ke\ E/V \tag{8.35}$$

In particular, the cost of debt is calculated on the basis of the rate of interest for risk free bonds and the credit spread for the firms. The risk free interest is assumed equal to 2.7% and the cost of debt of firm A and firm T is given by the following:

$$kd(A) = 2.70\% + 1.32\% = 4.0\% \tag{8.36}$$

$$kd(T) = 2.70\% + 3.30\% = 6.0\% \tag{8.37}$$

being the credit spread respectively equal to 132 basis points and 330 basis points (Table 8.3) due to the ratings of *A* and *T*.

The cost of equity *ke* has been calculated on the basis of the CAPM:

$$ke = i_f + (r_m - i_f)\,\beta i \tag{8.38}$$

Beta (A) and *Beta (T)* being respectively equal to 1.1 and 1.25. The values of firms A and T standing alone are €86.2 and €67.87 million.

Table 8.2 Basic data of the acquiring company A and the target firm T

(000 euro)	A	T
Revenues	60,000	50,000
Cost of sold products (% of revenues)	45%	45%
Operating costs (% of revenues) net from the depreciation costs	38%	39%
Depreciation costs	2,000	1,500
Tax rate	35%	35%
Working capital investment (percentage of revenues)	0%	0%
Fixed capital investment	2,000	1,500
Free operating cash flow (*FCFO*)	5,330	4,225
Beta current levered	1.10	1.25
Rate of interest risk-free	2.7%	2.7%
Equity risk-premium	5.5%	5.5%
Cost of equity	8.75	9.58
Cost of debt	4.02	6.00
Net cost of debt	2.61	3.909
WACC	6.19	6.22
Expected rate of growth of operating incomes	0%	0%
Firm value	86,149	67,872
Debt value	36,000	40,000
Equity value	50,149	27,872

Table 8.3 Leverage ratio, rating and estimated credit spread

D/E	Rating	Spread values
25% or less	Aaa/AAA	42
	Aa1/AA+	54
25% to 43%	Aa2/AA	65
	Aa3/AA-	69
	A1/A+	72
43% to 67%	A2/A	77
	A3/A-	89
	Baa1/BBB+	115
67% to 90%	Baa2/BBB	132
	Baa3/BBB-	165
	Ba1/BB+	248
90% to 233%	Ba2/BB	330
	Ba3/BB-	413
	B1/B+	495
233% and above	B2/B	578
	B3/B-	660
	Caa/CCC+	743
	US Treasury yield	2.73

Note: Spread values represent basis points (bps) over 10 yr. US Treasury securities of the same maturity, or the closer matching maturity.

Source: Our calculation from *Reuters Corporate Spreads for Industries* (28.03.2014).

The price of acquisition of firm T has been assumed equal to €70 million. The expected synergies from the M&A are represented by a reduction in operating costs equal to €2.7 million, as shown in Table 8.5. As a consequence, the additional free cash flow $\Delta FCFO$, that firm A estimates to obtain from the acquisition of firm T, is equal to €1.755 million.

Financing the acquisition through new shares

In a first hypothesis we consider the acquisition to be financed by the issue of new shares. In particular, we assume that the price for the target firm, equal to €70.0 million, is paid by the *issue of new shares* of firm A. As the current debt of the target firm is equal to €40 million, the value of new shares will be equal to €30 million.

On the basis of these data and assumptions the value of synergies, V_{SY}, as well as the value of the combined firm AT, are calculated applying the model proposed above (Table 8.4). The value of the combined firm AT results as being equal to €175.7 million of which the value of debt is equal to €76 million and the value of equity is €99.7. The value created by the merger results as being equal to €21.7 million, while the value of *synergies results equal to €27.2 million.* This is because the combined firm presents a higher *WACC*, due to a larger financial leverage as a consequence of the integration of firm *T*, which has a debt equal to €40 million. This increase in the cost of capital of the combined firm destroys value by €5.5 million (Table 8.4).

In fact, we must remember that the value created by the merger is the sum of two components: the value created by synergies and the value created (or destroyed) by a cost of capital of the combined firm, ρ_M, smaller (or larger) than the cost of capital of the two firms standing alone, ρ_A and ρ_T, according to the following expression:

$$V_M = V_{SY} + V_{CC} = \frac{\Delta FCFO}{\rho_M} + \left(\frac{FCFO_A + FCFO_T}{\rho_M(D)} - [\frac{FCFO_A}{\rho_A} + \frac{FCFO_T}{\rho_T}] \right) \quad (8.39)$$

As the price paid for the target firm, P_B, is equal to €70.0 million, the net value created for shareholders of firm A results as being equal to €19.5 million, while the premium paid to the shareholders of T (by new shares of the combined firm) is €2.24 million (30 million − 27.76 million).

Financing through additional debt

In a second hypothesis, we consider the acquisition to be entirely financed by debt, while all other data remain unchanged. As we consider paying the target firm at a price P_T = €70 million, being the debt of *T* equal to €40 million, the price to be paid to shareholders of firm *T* is equal to €30 million. Therefore, the acquiring firm will raise a new debt equal to €30 million. This will further increase the financial leverage of the combined firm and consequently the cost of debt and the cost of equity.

In particular, the net cost of debt of the combined firm will increase at

3.90% because of the reduction of firm rating and the increase in credit spread as indicated in Table 8.3. Also the cost of equity will increase, from 8.75% to 10.1%, because of the increase in Beta leverage of the combined firm (from 1.1 to 1.34), due to the increase in financial leverage (Table 8.5).

On this point we must remember that the cost of equity of the combined firm is calculated on the basis of its beta levered, considering the new level of debt. To do this, first we calculate the beta unlevered of the combined firm, β_U, on the basis of the current beta of firm A, β_L (C), according to the formula (8.27). Then, we calculate the beta levered of the combined firm, after the merger, applying to the beta unlevered the higher level of leverage determined by the acquisition of firm T, according to the formula (8.28).

Finally, we calculate the *WACC* of the combined firm resulting from the increased level of the financial leverage.

As the expected synergies from the M&A are represented by a reduction in operating costs equal to €2.7 million and the additional free cash flow ($\Delta FCFO$) is equal to €1.755 million, we have all the data necessary for calculating the value created by the merger.

Applying the model proposed above, the value of the combined firm results as being equal to €145.1 million and the value created by the merger equal to €–8.9 million (Table 8.5).

Of this value, the value of synergies results as being equal to €22.5 million while the value destroyed by the increase in the average cost of capital is equal to €–31.4 million. This is the effect of the increase in the average cost of capital (*WACC*) of the combined firm, from 6.19% to 7.79%, due to the additional debt. We note that the merger reduces the equity value of shareholders of the acquiring firm by –€11million. On the contrary, the premium paid to the shareholders of the target firm is equal to €2.12 million.

The example highlights the relevant effects on the value created by the merger, deriving from the way the acquisition is financed. In particular, financing the acquisition by new shares, the merger creates a value equal to €21.7 million, whereas financing by debt destroys the value by €8.9 million (Table 8.6). As the price paid for the firm T is equal to €70 million, the equity value of shareholders A increases by €19.5 million, when financing acquisition by new shares, but it is reduced by 11.1 million, when financing acquisition by debt.

Table 8.4 Valuation of an M&A financed by new shares

(000 euro)		A	T	A+T	merger	AT	Synergies
Revenues	1.00	60,000	50,000	110,000		110,000	
Cost of product sold	0.45	27,000	22,500	49,500		49,500	
MOL	0.55	33,000	27,500	60,500		60,500	
Operating costs	0.38	22,800	19,500	42,300	0.360		2,700
						39,600	
EBITDA		10,200	8,000	18,200		20,900	2,700
Tax rate		0.350	0.350	0.350		0.350	0.350
EBITDA (1-t)		6,630	5,200	11,830		13,585	1,755
D&A		2,000	1,500	3,500		3,500	
A t		700	525	1,225		1,225	0
CFO		7,330	5,725	1,3055		1,4810	1,755
Investiment in working capital		0	0	0		0	
Investiment in fixed capital		2,000	1,500	3,500		3,500	
FCFO		5,330	4,225	9,555		11,310	1,755
Market value of equity		50,200	27,760	77,960		77,960	
Value of debt		36.000	40.000	76.000		76.000	
Value of firm		86,200	67,760	153,960			
Financial leverage D/E		0.72	1.44	0.97		0.97	
Credit spread %		1.32	3.30			3.00	
Beta current (data)		1.1	1.25	1.166		1.165	
Beta unlevered		0.75	0.65	0.71		0.71	
Rate of interest risk-free		2.70%	2.70%	2.70%		2.70%	
Equity risk-premium		5.50%	5.50%	5.50%		5.50%	
Cost of equity (according to CAPM)		8.75%	9.58%	9.04%		9.11%	
Cost of debt		4.02%	6.00%	5.06%		5.70%	
Cost of debt (net of tax benefit)		2.61%	3.90%	3.29%		3.71%	
WACC		6.19%	6.22%	6.20%		6.44%	6.44%
Rate of growth = g		0%	0,00%	0,00%		0,00%	0,00%
Estimated firm value		86,149	67,872	154,021		175,694	27,263
Estimated value of equity		50,149	27,872	78,021		99,694	
Price paid for firm T					70,000		
Price paid for shares firm T					30,000		
Increased debt to buy shares T					0		
Increased equity to buy shares T					30,000		
Value created by M&A		21,674					
Value created for shareholders A		19,546					
Value of cost synergies		27,263					
Value from cost of capital		-5,589					
Premium to shareholders of T		2.128					

Note: Weights used to calculate *WACC* are the values of firms A and T stand alone.

Table 8.5 Valuation of an M&A financed by debt

(000 euro)		A	T	A+T	Merger	AT	Synergies
Revenues	1	60,000	50,000	110,000		110,000	
Cost of product sold	0.45	27,000	22,500	49,500		49,500	
MOL	0.55	33,000	27,500	60,500		60,500	
Operating costs	0.38	22,800	19,500	42,300	0.360	39,600	2,700
EBITDA		10,200	8,000	18,200		20,900	2,700
Tax rate	0.35	0.35	0.35	0.35		0.35	0.35
EBITDA (1-t)		6,630	5,200	11,830		13,585	1,755
D&A (Deprec. and Ammort.)		2,000	1,500	3,500		3,500	
A t		700	525	1,225		1,225	
CFO		7,330	5,725	13,055		14,810	1,755
Investiment in working capital		0	0	0		0	0
Investiment in fixed capital		2,000	1,500	3,500		3,500	0
FCFO		5,330	4,225	9,555		11,310	1,755
Market value of equity		50,200	27,760	77,960		77,960	
Value of debt		36,000	40,000	76,000	30,000	106,000	
Value of firm		86,200	67,760	153,960			
Financial leverage D/E		0.72	1.44	0.97		1.36	
Credit spread %		1.32	3.30			3.30	
Beta current (data)		1.1	1.25	1.17		1.34	
Beta unlevered		0.75	0.65	0.71		0.71	
Rate of interest risk-free		2.70%	2.70%	2.70%		2.70%	
Equity risk-premium		5.50%	5.50%	5.50%		5.50%	
Cost of equity (according to CAPM)		8.75%	9.58%	9.04%		10.10%	
Cost of debt		4.02%	6.00%	5.06%		6.00%	
Cost of debt (net of tax benefit)		2.61%	3.90%	3.29%		3.90%	
WACC		6.19%	6.22%	6.20%		7.79%	7.79%
Rate of growth = g		0%	0.00%	0.00%		0.00%	0.00%
Estimated firm value		86,149	67,872	154,021		145,110	22,517
Estimated value of equity		50,149	27,872	78,021		39,110	
Price paid for firm T					70,000		
Price paid for shares firm T					30,000		
Increased debt to buy shares T					30,000		
Increased equity to buy shares T							
Value created by M&A		-8,910				-8,910	
Value created for shareholders A		-11,038					
Value of cost synergies		22,517					
Value from cost of capital		-31,427					
Premium to shareholders of T		2,128					

Note: Weights used to calculate WACC are the values of firms *A* and *T* stand alone.

Table 8.6 Comparing the value created financing an M&A through new shares and through debt

Effects produced by a merger (€ million)	Financing through Shares (1)	Financing through Debt (2)	Difference (2) – (1)
ΔFCFO	1.75	1.75	0
Net cost of debt (%)	3.71	3.90	0.19
Cost of equity (%)	9.11	10.10	0.99
WACC (%)	6.44	7.79	1.35
Value of synergies	27.2	22.5	-4.7
Value by cost of capital	-5.5	-31.4	-25.9
Value created by merger	21.7	-8.9	-29.9
Value of acquisition	89.5	58.9	-30.6
Price paid for firm *T*	70.0	70.0	0
Value created for shareholders of firm *A*	19.5	-11.1	-30.2
Premium to shareholders of firm *T*	2.1	2.1	0

PAYING BY CASH OR PAYING BY SHARES?

The choice between paying by cash or paying by shares is quite complex, because of the different effects on the shareholders of the acquiring company and the vendor, on the basis of different situations. The main aspects that have to be considered can be summarized as follows.

Cash payment

Surely, cash payment is the most transparent form of payment, because the value is clearly determined. In this case, the net cost of the acquisition (CA) for the acquiring company will be:

$$CA = P_T - V_T \qquad (8.40)$$

where: V_T is the value of the target stand-alone company and P_T is the established price for this firm.

The net investment to be financed is given by:

$$I = P_T - D_T \tag{8.41}$$

where D_T is the existing debt of the target firm.

If the acquisition is paid by cash, the buyer can choose to use its liquidity or to finance it by additional debt.

Self-financing is surely the most rapid and reserved form for an acquisition; it allows the acquiring firm to take the right opportunity on the market immediately. If it is possible, a firm will use its current liquidity or the revenues from the disinvestment of some non-strategic assets. In this case the cost of capital will be a function of the operating risk and the financial structure of the combined firm.

Differently, the acquiring firm can use its debt capability (leveraged acquisitions) to finance a cash payment. In this case, the effect of an increased leverage on the average cost of capital has to be considered in evaluating the effect on the merger value, as we have seen in preceding paragraphs.

Payment by cash allows a definitive distribution of value between the two groups of shareholders. For the shareholders of the target firm, payment by cash allows a definitive price to be received and therefore they may in part participate immediately in the potential synergy, if the price is higher than the value of the stand-alone company. But, if the merger generates synergies larger than those expected when the price had been defined, shareholders of the target firm will not participate in the distribution of the major value created by the merger. Vice versa, if the merger does not create additional profits, the shareholders of the target firm will not participate in the unexpected losses, leaving the shareholders of the acquiring firm to bear all the losses.

In other words, payment by shares exposes the vendor to the risk of the merger. It benefits from a good performance of the merger, but it also bears the losses of value if the merger does not work as planned.

For the old shareholders of the acquiring firm there is also the risk that the new shareholders will decide to sell the new shares after the merger, therby reducing their market value.

Share payment

If the shares of the acquiring company are correctly priced by the market or overvalued, paying by shares can be more attractive than by cash for the acquiring firm. In fact, in this way this form of payment avoids a high exit of cash or a huge increase in debt. This alternative can be advantageous also for the shareholders of the target company, because they can became investors of the combined firm and benefit from a firm without a high debt.

But financing a merger by shares can be disadvantageous for the shareholders of the acquiring firm. That happens, for example, when the shares of the acquiring firm are undervalued. In this case, paying by shares is not profitable, because it determines the distribution of a higher number of shares with a high revaluation potential to target shareholders. This will produce a strong *dilution of earning per share* (EPS) and of unit value of shares after merger, damaging the shareholders of the acquiring firm. In particular, the *dilution of earnings per share* for the shareholders of the acquiring firm occurs when, evaluating the companies by the *multiple method* (see Chapter 3), the earnings of the target firm are valued more than the earnings of the acquiring company, that is when the multiple *P/E* of the target firm is larger than that of the acquiring firm. In this case, a more favourable exchange ratio to the vendor will result; the consequence is that a larger number of new shares will be issued than those that would be proportional to earnings. In this way, the target firm's shareholders are favoured at the expense of the shareholders of the acquiring firm. The consequence is a reduction in the earnings per share (dilution of EPS) for the shareholders of the acquiring firm, with the advantage for the target shareholders.

Obviously, the managers of the acquiring company can benefit from asymmetric information, that is information which is not available to the external investors. Therefore, if they are optimistic about the potential synergies, they will prefer to pay by cash; on the contrary, if they are pessimistic they will prefer to pay by shares. But the shareholders of the target firm and the investors can understand the situation and behave consequently. As a matter of fact, the price of an acquiring firm generally falls when mergers financed by shares are announced, while the price of the target firm generally increases. Franks et al. (1991) found an average market adjusted fall of 3.2% on the announcement of acquisitions financed by shares, between 1975 and 1984. On the contrary, there was a small gain, about 0.8%, for a sample of deals financed by cash.

Effects of tax on shareholders

Finally, the choice of payment has to consider the tax effects of the different alternatives for the shareholders. In fact, an acquisition paid by cash also causes tax effects on shareholders. In particular, the shareholders of the target firm are obliged to pay income tax on the increase of the shares' value made by the sale. On the contrary, in the case of payment by shares, they are not

obliged to immediately pay tax, because they have only changed their shares
with new shares of equal value. Taxes will be paid when they sell their new
shares.

NOTES

1. To be precise, the expression (8.10) is true when the value created by the
    merger is equal to the value of synergies, that is when the change in the
    average cost of capital, as a consequence of the merger, is not relevant.
2. In fact, developing the expression (8.11) we have:
    $$w_A N_A + w_T N_T + V_{SY} = w_A N_A + ER(\text{Max})\, w_A N_T$$
    Therefore:
    $$ER(\text{Max}) = w_A N_A / w_A N_T + w_T N_T / (w_A N_T) + V_{SY} / w_A N_T - w_A N_A / w_A N_T$$
    $$= w_T / w_A + (V_{SY} / N_T) / w_A$$
3. In the case the company A already owns a share on the target company, the
    number of A's new shares to give to the shareholders of the target firm will be
    equal to the number of new shares to give per share of the target firm (ER)
    multiplied by the number of shares of the target firm, minus the number of
    these shares owned by the acquiring firm A. That is: $\Delta N_A = ER\,(N_T - N_{T,A})$.
    Therefore, the ER does not change, but only changes the number of shares to
    be given to shareholders of the target company.
4. If the number of the new shares of the acquiring firm, to give to shareholders
    of the target firm, is not a whole number, a balance in cash will be necessary.
    Generally, the law decrees the maximum balance in cash, in relation to the
    value of each share.

9. Organizational structures and procedures for implementing merger

INTRODUCTION AND OBJECTIVES

For synergies to be effectively produced, appropriate changes have to be carried out in organizational structures of firms involved in M&As. The focus of this chapter is on the choice of the organizational structure and procedures that allow the combined firm to obtain the desidered outcomes, according to different types of M&As.

The fundamental choice to be made regards the level of *integration* and *autonomy* of companies involved in the merger. The level of integration indicates the degree to which functional activities are integrated across the merger firm, as part of the implementation of the acquisition. The level of autonomy measures the extent to which the acquirer delegates or defers to the target firm managers decisions to be made within target functional activities.

So, it is a fundamental challenge for top level managers to select the appropriate organizational structure and then to adopt managerial and control procedures for an effective implementation of the merger.

GOVERNANCE MECHANISMS FOR IMPLEMENTING SYNERGIES: INTEGRATION VERSUS AUTONOMY

As we have already seen, the decision to acquire a firm is based on the expectation of increasing firm value by unifying and exploiting activities and resources of various companies. But, to produce synergies effective integration is necessary between activities and processes of the companies involved. This integration requires a complex interactive and dynamic process in which organizations and persons have to collaborate to obtain the expected benefits. Therefore the integration must be organized with extreme care and attention to be successful (Datta, 1991; Pablo, 1994; Walsh and Ellwood, 1991; Marks and Mirvis, 2010).

In effect, there are two main alternative forms, which vary according to the level of integration, that is to the extent to which the existing organizations, resources and procedures of companies are related, aligned or centralized within the companies involved in the merger:

A. a total formal integration through a merger of activities and structures, either a merger by incorporation or a merger by union, so that just one company will result from the companies involved;

B. an integration of organizations only, maintaining separate legal identities of the companies involved.

The choice has to be made mainly by considering two main requirements that a merger has to meet (Haspeslagh and Jemison, 1991; Weber et al., 2010):

- the strategic interdependence between companies;
- the level of company autonomy.

The first alternative (A) is preferred when there is the need for a high level of strategic interdependence among companies and a low level of autonomy. In this case, a total integration allows all potential synergies to be exploited, through a consolidation of activities, organizations and cultures. A total integration is favoured by a high level of similarity between the companies, in particular with reference to their organizations, markets and products. A high level of relatedness favours a complete merger because there are more opportunities for exploiting economies of scale. In this case, some resources will be substituted by those of higher value.

The second alternative (B) is preferred when it is necessary to maintain a high level of autonomy for the companies involved; in other words it is necessary to maintain different cultures, capabilities and know-how. In this case, an integration of organizations only is the best solution, because maintaining separate companies allows specific cultures, market relationships, brands and know-how to be exploited, whereas being a part of a group means benefitting from some common activities and resources. These can be shared and transferred, when necessary, according to a unitary vision of businesses and a joint effort to create value for the group. This solution is favoured by a low level of relatedness between companies, in particular with reference to markets and products.[1]

For the reasons we have explained, mergers by incorporation or by union are more frequent in the case of horizontal and vertical acquisitions. On the contrary, simple integrations of organizations with a holding structure and separate autonomous companies are more frequent in diversified acquisitions. In these cases, also an intermediate form of integration can be used, such as the divisional organizational structure, where a formal merger of companies is accompanied by the setting up of business units with a relative autonomy in the management of different related business. This solution allows economies of scope and economies of scale to be exploited by activities that can be unified and shared with the other business units.

The characteristics of these organizational structures can be summarized as follows.[2]

ADAPTING THE FUNCTIONAL ORGANIZATIONAL STRUCTURE FOR IMPLEMENTING HORIZONTAL AND VERTICAL M&As

As authoritative literature has pointed out, in order for a firm to create value, it is necessary for the organizational structure to be coherent with the strategies and the tasks a firm must perform, interacting with its environment (Abell, 1993: Hitt et al., 1997; Collis and Montgomery, 2005). Therefore, in the case of horizontal M&As, top management has to design an organizational structure to effectively manage a larger amount of activities and to rule and control the greater complexity of relationships determined by a firm which is larger in size.

An effective and simple solution can be obtained by adapting the functional organizational structure. As known, this organizational structure is characterized by a firm system divided into units which specialize in the different activities carried out: production, human resources, logistics, marketing, R&D, etc. These functional units are assigned to line managers to which the entrepreneur or the general manager delegates decisional power regarding the operating management. Because the differences in orientation among organizational functions can impede communications and coordination, the central task of a general manager is that of integrating the decisions of individual business functions for the benefit of the entire firm (Galbraith, 1977).

A horizontal M&A can be implemented effectively by consolidating the functional departments, such as production, marketing or sales of the companies participating in the merger. Obviously, consolidation can also regard other functional departments, for example logistics, R&D and administration. This will allow the combined firm to reduce operating costs, by optimizing the use of plant, machinery and personnel. In particular, the concentration of resources that share homogeneous specializations in the same organizational unit means using these resources in the most efficient manner and avoiding their dispersion in many different structures.

Benefit can also be drawn from economies of scale at a single function level and from specialization, by concentrating specialists in the same unit thereby creating a "critical mass" which is necessary for having up-to-date knowledge and competences in every functional activity.

An example of a functional organizational structure adapted by a firm for implementing an international M&A is represented in Figure 9.1. The Figure shows a chart (or a graphic description) of the organizational model of a firm, providing essential information about the sub-units into which the firm is divided, the number of hierarchical levels, the coordination relationships among them and the top management, etc. In this case, the acquisition of a firm operating in the UK by an Italian firm was followed by consolidation of the production departments in a single factory in Italy and by setting up a commercial subsidiary in the UK, for a more efficient sales policy.

Generally, after a merger it is also necessary to have a larger and more complex central structure, with new functions, such as finance, engineering, etc. and a larger staff office for the CEO, to increase coordination and control activities expecially in sales and marketing. To improve the level of horizontal coordination among functional managers, which is a classical limit of functional organizational structures, the use of joint committees, task forces or teams can be provided for conflict resolution, by increasing horizontal relationships and favouring a continuous flow of information.

More significant changes in the organizational structure are necessary when the target company operates in different geographic markets and in countries having different characteristics with respect to the existing firm markets, to the point of requiring differentiated promotional and selling activities.

In these cases a traditional functional structure, such as that represented in Figure 9.1 can present important drawbacks for successfully dealing with additional local issues and for coordinating and monitoring day-to-day operations. In this case, more complex organizational structures may be necessary for implementing an international M&A. They must be designed to effectively integrate the work of the manufacturing and marketing personnel operating in each country, thereby facilitating the tailoring of products and services to local markets.

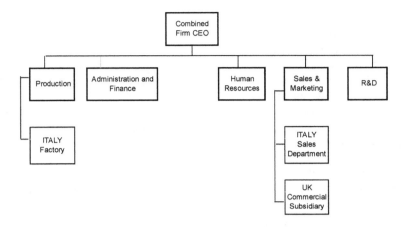

Notes: (1)   In a functional structure most functions are decentralized, but Administration and Finance may have centralized staff that work closely with the general manager;

        (2)   Production and Sales & Marketing are often the main functions.

Figure 9.1 Adapting a functional structure to implement horizontal M&As

In these cases, a worldwide geographic area structure can be used successfully by the consolidated company to implement a multi-domestic M&A strategy. For this purpose, subsidiaries can be set up to manage production and sales in a country or in a group of countries, so as to satisfy different local needs in production and service. In this case, it is necessary to reinforce the company's headquarters by consolidating common activities (R&D, Administration, HR, etc.), for coordinating financial resources among different country area managers, defining the general investment policy and controlling activities and results.

This is an organizational structure that can progressively evolve into a holding structure, as differences in products become bigger and bigger.

DIVISIONAL STRUCTURES TO IMPLEMENT DIVERSIFIED MERGERS

When a firm grows through diversified mergers, efficiently managing a number of products and markets is quite difficult with a functional structure, because of the complexity of knowledge required by different products and markets and the need for coordination and integration of different firm functions.

The most effective and efficient solution for ruling a company, which has carried out a diversified M&A, is adopting a multidivisional organizational structure (M-form).[3] This is characterized by a firm system divided into sub-units which are relatively autonomous (divisions), each of them specialized in operating a determined business (a line of product).

With this solution, a formal merger between companies is accomplished, with all benefits from the consolidation of companies. But the assets and resources of the acquired company remain separate in a specific organizational unit or division inside the combined firm, in order to produce, sell and distribute the assigned product or line. The decisional power for day-to-day operations regarding each business will be delegated by the chief executive manager (CEO) to a specialized organ, the divisional manager, having both the power to rule the division (business unit) and the responsibility for its performance (Figure 9.2). The corporate CEO will maintain the decisional power concerning strategic resources, over all human and financial resources, assigning them to different divisions, according to their specific needs in order to reach the ultimate company objective. The corporate officer will also define the corporate strategy and carry out coordination and control activities on the various divisions. For this job, staff organs have to be provided and made up of personnel specialized in the various firm functions.

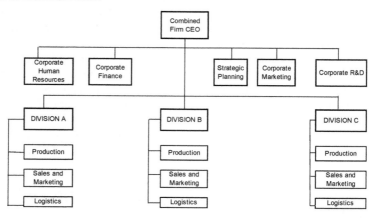

Figure 9.2 A typical multidivisional structure for diversified M&As

This organizational structure, designed around businesses rather than functions, will allow the acquiring firm to remove the disadvantages of a functional structure in managing diversified businesses. In fact, under such conditions a functional structure is not capable of elaborating the amount of information the combined firm receives from the different markets, and of making forecasts and suitable evaluations, or of deciding the tasks each product line has to carry out. Conversely, with a divisional structure it will be capable of quickly elaborating information and making decisions, since each business is followed by a manager who has the authority to run the division and to use the assigned resources and who is responsible for the outcome. A divisional structure also allows competences and resources to be assigned more efficiently, according to the specific needs of each business. It offers high managerial and organizational flexibility, enabling an easier coordination of activities within each division and an easier focus of the activities on cost and time objectives.

In addition, the corporate office, being relieved of the operating problems of different products and markets, can concentrate its activity on strategic decisions involving the company as a whole, as well as on the coordination and control activities of different divisions.

At the same time, all common and similar activities will be concentrated in corporate organizational units, thereby favouring a reduction in costs. This will also allow the combined firm to avoid the duplication of assets and resources and to exploit economies of scale.

For example, basic R&D will be concentrated in a corporate organizational unit, while the amount of experimentation on new knowledge processes and practices will be assigned to product divisions.

In a multidivisional structure the mechanism, by which coordination among divisions has to be achieved, is of upmost importance. The basic solution is the hierarchy, in which a superior guides the direct subordinates and imposes the objectives to be reached. However it will be integrated by joint committees of divisional managers and corporate office managers. Besides centralization, a number of structural links have to be used to foster cooperation among divisions. Direct contact between division managers must be frequent in order to encourage and support cooperation and the sharing of strategic assets. Temporary teams or task forces may also be formed around projects to achieve the desired levels of coordination.

Nonetheless, introducing coordination in autonomous businesses can be very difficult, because it requires the divisional managers to limit their power and to accept the choice of optimizing corporate not divisional performance, thereby changing attitude and behaviour. Transferring resources and skills across businesses can also be a powerful way to create value, for example moving highly skilled managers.

In effect, a multi-business structure will be able to create value only if it will favour a more intense exploitation of corporate resources across the divisions. It is necessary not only for reducing costs, but also for providing greater benefits to the customers, improving the level of differentiation in products.

In conclusion, a divisional structure offers a good response both to the need of integration between companies and businesses and that of autonomy. It generally makes it easier to integrate the target company and to allow the combined firm to cope with the organizational complexity of a large diversified company operating in different businesses. In this way, the combined company benefits from the cost synergies and, at the same time from revenue synergies, as this organizational structure increases the flexibility of the business system and its capability to quickly adapt to the changes in the external environment. In fact, the divisions have a substantial authority for their own decisions, so these may be made by those who possess the relevant knowledge, while minimizing the amount of information transfer to the hierarchy. Moreover, each division or business unit can also be specialized in succeeding in its own competitive environment; in particular it can develop and tailor its resources and shape the details of its own organization to fit its unique tasks. Finally, the motivation of managers who are given control of an entire division will be high, particularly when they are rewarded directly for the performance of that unit.

The limits of this organizational model are given by the larger need for resources in divisions and the corporate office, due to the central organizational structure required for the corporate activity of leadership and coordination. Therefore, a divisional structure may lead to inefficient functional activities, for example multiple sales forces calling on the same customer. In this way, the advantages of functional specialization are reduced and the risks in managing the different divisions increase.

HOLDING ORGANIZATIONAL STRUCTURES TO IMPLEMENT DIVERSIFIED MERGERS

When more initiative, power and autonomy are necessary, the integration of companies has to be limited to organizational aspects. The best solution is maintaining autonomous firms, open to market, but directed and controlled by a holding company (holding organizational structure). In this case, the companies controlled by the holding remain autonomous from a legal point of view, so as to create a stronger incentive to innovation and more competitive behaviour, with a less centralized bureaucratic structure (Figure

9.3). In this way, each company remains a source of ideas, resources and knowledge: it can operate successfully in its business and be better exploited by the entire group structure.

The integration process is partly carried out and especially concerns support activities, such as basic R&D, Corporate marketing, Finance and Human Resources. Consolidation of assets and resources in these activities can offer relevant cost synergies, by removing duplication and inefficiencies, as well as by exploiting economies of scale.

This organizational structure is more flexible than a divisional structure, but at the same time it permits a control link with the acquired firms to be maintained. The central direction also gives these firms strategic and operating responsibility, delegating to them the management of the selected business area and the pursuing of innovative development lines.

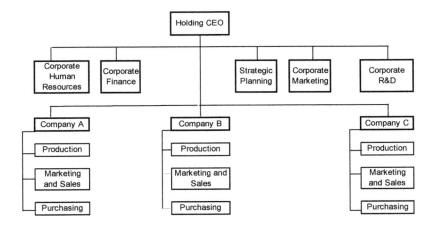

Notes:

(1)   Structural integration among companies, but independence among them;
(2)   Strategic planning and human resource assignation are prominent functions of CEO corporate office;
(3)   Culture emphasizes cooperation between companies.

Figure 9.3 A holding structure for diversified M&As

This organizational structure will be used especially when it is necessary to improve the development of the entrepreneurial capacity of the companies' managers through a more direct rapport with the market, so stimulating capabilities of learning and innovating, in order to exploit all the opportunities offered by the business.

The greater operating flexibility of this structure is also increased by the fact that the business units are juridically distinctive companies. Generally, this organization is set up through the acquisitions of companies which maintain their own autonomy as distinctive companies. In addition, as a part of a group, the single company will benefit from common and transferable resources, such as company image and reputation, financial capability, technological know-how, etc., with cost and revenue synergies.

A holding organizational structure is the most appropriate solution also to implement a low-related diversified M&A. In this case different businesses have to be managed by separate and autonomous firms controlled from a legal point of view by a holding company and competing one against the other for corporate capital. To gain benefits from efficient resource allocations, companies must have separate identifiable profit performance; the headquarters office does not intervene in single firms' affairs except to audit operations and to discipline managers whose firms perform poorly. The corporate office sets the rate of return targets and monitors the results of controlled companies. In this case, corporate headquarters has a small staff, finance and auditing are the most prominent functions of corporate headquarters. Companies are independent and separate for financial evaluation purposes; they retain strategic control, but compete for corporate financial resources. The entire organization emphasizes competition rather than cooperation between member companies of the group.

INCENTIVES AND CONTROLS FOR AVOIDING MANAGERS' OPPORTUNISTIC BEHAVIOUR

A firm's growth through M&As often requires a radical change in its *governance system*, because a progressive delegation of decisional power is necessary for managing a larger-sized firm and a more complex set of activities. But, when decision rights are delegated, self-interested managers may act in a way that maximizes their interests or the interest of functional areas or divisions at the expense of the company's and shareholders' interests.

The extreme situation is where the property and governance of a firm are totally separate and the property is largely divided. In this case, the property delegates decision rights to managers, only maintaining the right of defining general objectives and controlling the outcomes. So, managers concentrate not only on the operating decisions but also on the strategic decisions regarding the development of the firm (the so-called managerial company).

Since managers may favour growth only for satisfying personal objectives, therefore destroying equity value, it will be necessary to carefully discipline the internal relationship between property and management. For this reason, a system of rules of behaviour and incentives must be defined in order to reduce or mitigate the intrinsic divergence of interests between property and management, so that the objective of creating value for shareholders can be constantly pursued.[4]

In order to reach this objective, that is avoiding the opportunistic behaviour of managers, it will be necessary to introduce certain mechanisms, such as the setting up of a board of directors composed of expert members, in addition to proprietors, and powerful control organs, such as an internal control committee, audit company, etc. On a different level, the definition of incentives for managers bound to firm performance can represent an important instrument for manager objectives to meet those of the proprietors.

Finally, we must remember that the efficiency of the financial market can play a fundamental role in reducing manager behaviour that conflicts with shareholders' interests, thereby reducing the equity value. This situation can cause a hostile takeover from new investors interested in restructuring the company and creating value, removing the current managers (Marris, 1964; Marris and Wood, 1972). Therefore, also listing the combined firm on the stock market can be a useful instrument for managers operating to create equity value.

PLANNING AND CONTROL SYSTEMS TO INCREASE PERFORMANCE IN LARGE AND DIVERSIFIED COMPANIES

After the acquisition, specific planning and control systems are necessary for the combined firm to be able to prevent the abuse of delegated decision-making authority, or by functional managers or by managers of autonomous divisions. Specific planning and control systems are also necessary for providing coherence to the corporation activity, by deploying resources across otherwise structurally differentiated units.

In particular, it is necessary for all the organs of companies involved in the merger to work as a consistent system, so that their impact is interactive and mutually reinforcing, rather than creating conflict. With this aim in mind, it is necessary that the planning and control systems be re-designed in such a way that objectives are clearly defined and assigned to different organs of different companies, divisions or functions.

Even if these systems may add bureaucracy to functional activities and the entrepreneurial activities of divisions, and may therefore cause additional costs, such systems are a powerful discipline for managers of different companies and a necessary instrument for enabling the interests of the whole company to be able to prevail over the interests of functional units or product divisions (Collis and Montgomery, 2005).

The most pervasive form of corporate control is the use of systems and processes that continually lead, monitor and regulate the behaviour and performance of functional units or divisions. Typically these are strategic planning, budgeting, and measurement and reward schemes.

Therefore, after the merger deal, it is a matter of setting the targets that the sub-unit managers have to reach and then of monitoring the progress towards those targets. Managers will be motivated and rewarded for reaching the targets. The system will also include mechanisms for intervening when performance deviates from acceptable boundaries, assisting or even replacing the unit manager, rather than adjusting the goal.

The value of the system lies in setting an appropriate incentive structure for managers and a control mechanism for intervening when performance is not satisfactory. In this respect, control systems have to be differentiated on the basis of the characteristics of companies, the organizational units and the emphasis on *outcome* or *behaviour control.*

In a system based on *outcome control* managers will be evaluated on the outcome of activities assigned. This requires structuring the organization into autonomous and self-contained organizational units and aligning responsibility and managerial authority as closely as possible. Conversely, managers will be improperly stimulated and motivated, if they are held accountable for events and actions beyond their control. This is of particular importance for divisional managers. For this reason, it is necessary to select an appropriate performance measure for evaluating divisional executives, for example the return on investment (ROI) or value-base measures.

A system based on *outcome control* is preferable when there are simple interdependencies among divisions and when there are few exogenous influences on the business outcome.

On the contrary, this system is less feasible when there are complex interdependencies among divisions. In these cases a *behaviour control* system is more effective. It consists of monitoring multiple operating and financial measures of performance, such as delivery lead times, reject rates, sales statistics, and cash flows as well as qualitative goals. Obviously, it does not allow the results of divisions to be evaluated, but it permits solving the "agency" problem, by directly evaluating the behaviour of divisional managers. In this control mode, the role of corporate officers becomes more similar to a coach rather than a monitor. They offer constructive advice and criticize behaviour in a way that improves the decisions of divisional managers.

In practice, it can be useful, for a combined firm, to adopt elements of both systems, placing a relative emphasis on one or the other according to the characteristics of the activities and markets.

LEADERSHIP AND COMMUNICATION

Imposing a strong leadership

Leadership is a decisive capability to take decisions, to impose control and assume risk. In an M&A, a strong leadership capability is essential for integrating different employees, facilitating acculturation and reducing uncertainties. Papadakis (2007) and Gomes et al. (2013) point out that a determining critical success factor in M&A's integration is to impose leadership quickly. It is fundamental a top executive capable of imposing his leadership immediately after the M&A and obtaining an organizational and cultural alignment and good management between both organization (Vermeulen and Barkema 2001). In fact, a high number of acquisition failures do not derive from lack of strategic choice, but from a leadership team which is incapable of addressing the major challenges (Prichett et al., 2007).

A strong leadership is also necessary because, as Haspeslagh and Jemison (1991) explain, "the immediate post-acquisition is pregnant with expectations, questions, and reservations, among the personnel and the managers of both the acquired and acquiring organizations".

In short, leadership is crucial when an M&A closes, because it is necessary to adjust speedily complex situation, change management and facilitate the employees' new tasks and activities.

Generating a clear communication of M&A

Communication is one of the main issues of a successful deal (Schweiger and Very, 2003; Carr et al., 2005, Papadakis, 2007). In particular, it is necessary to generate sufficient and clear communication with all employees and stakeholders of the new economic subject, managing in such a way that all components of the whole hierarchical scale feel equally important (Jemison et al., 1996).

In fact, employees are often kept in the dark about the sale of the corporation; they often hear about the acquisition on a less than timely basis, through the press or through the "corporate mutterings". This can lead to a misinterpretation or distorted picture of the acquisition's sense and to counterproductive activities by employees, who may be anxious about probable job losses, especially in cross-border merger and acquisition. It is necessary to remember that in the acquired firm there are people who produce profits, represent the company, establish rapport with the customers, and, ultimately, are the ones that will make the combined company successful. Therefore, the most talented employees, having an important value to their firms, have to be retained, and cultural conflicts, integration and communication problems have to be solved.

Wherever possible, firms interested in M&A should inform all employees at the same time, to avoid shock and subsequent feelings of resentment or depression. To reduce this effect, any layoffs or downsizing should be conducted, as soon as possible, to alleviate anxiety and reduce rumours, allowing employees to return to business as usual. During this period, it is essential that top managers continue to listen to and communicate with employees and transmit detailed and complete information.

However, in this context, a lack of information is better than inexact or even incorrect information. Therefore, it is necessary to find the right proportion of communication and mutual respect for the other culture and business customs (Bower, 2001). Good communication can create a positive atmosphere among all employees after and during the deal, overcoming the differences in cultures and exchanging knowledge. In fact, as Haspeslagh and Jemison (1991) suggest, the knowledge should be principally transferred through interactions between the acquired and target firms, and demand teaching and learning from both sides.

In conclusion, as many studies underline, communication has to reinforce the positive utility of the merger and to promote a sense of belonging. In particular, managers of both firms should quickly put into operation efficient and comprehensive communication programmes, involving all organizational members in order to favour the integration process. The messages between top and middle management should be particularly clear and regular, as it is important that the lower levels of management and employees are not kept in the dark about M&A issues and their implementation. The managers of the two parties should communicate frequently and implement integrated communication plans, because both can have a decisive impact on M&A integration (Appelbaum et al., 2009).

INVOLVING KEY PEOPLE AND CONSIDERING CULTURAL DIFFERENCES

Involving the HR department and the key people

The involvement of Human Resources Department is essential for the synergies to be accomplished, because they know and distinguish very well all the key people. These persons are the main talent and the persons who can preserve the relationship with many key customers and also maintain skills and knowledge (Haspeslagh and Jeminson, 1991; Very, 1999). It is important that the key people remain in the "new" combined firm and don't leave it, as often happens. In fact, frequently the turnover of management and employees in M&As is a relevant problem, especially, when it is on a voluntary basis, without a choice from the firms. The motivations why some key people leave the firm after M&A can be many and not totally clear, but often it is because they had not been involved in the M&A process.[5] In short, Human Resources Department should be constantly involved in the integration process of an M&A, because they know all members of the organization well, so they can easily understand their problems and try to resolve them. They should help employees to cope with uncertainty.

Taking into careful consideration multicultural differences between firms

Integration has to be carried out carefully considering cultural differences between the firms involved in the merger and evaluating what is necessary to favour a cultural fit between the acquiring and the target firms (Chatterjee et al., 1992; Weber and Camerer, 2003). In fact, incompatible management styles of the two merged firms can damage and delay integration. So it is important that the acquiring firm has tolerance for multiculturalism, especially in cross-border M&As. Teerikangas and Very (2006) recommend developing detailed integration plans to overcome cultural differences. This is crucial in all types of M&A. Therefore, managers should always consider this factor because it has a considerable impact on M&A performance.

In particular, as the integration of two different cultures is a very problematic issue, managers have to identify a new vision for the company and create a united mission, integrating the teams made up of components from both firms. For this purpose, the acquiring firm must not impose its culture, but should try to merge the two cultures, trying to take the best capacities and knowledge from both firms. On the contrary, the acquiring firm often tends to enforce its own rules.

Although many of the acquiring firms state the importance of retaining and acquiring key talent, 47% of senior management in the acquired firm leave within the first year and firms experience on average a 50% drop in productivity in the first six–eight months of the integration process. Intervention must be made with considerable diplomatic skill; great attention has to be paid to communication, speed of integration and managers' skills to involve human resource departments. In fact, while employee skills can be transferred easily from one firm to another, employee motivation is far more difficult to transfer.

Among authors who pointed out the lack of integration of the different cultures as the main factor of the failures are: Datta (1991); Haspeslagh and Jeminson (1991); Chatterjee et al. (1992); Cartwright and Cooper (1992); Gertsen et al. (1998); Vlasic and Bradley (2001); Schweiger and Very (2003); Weber and Camerer (2003); Conn et al. (2005); Papadakis (2007); Appelbaum et al. (2009).

According to some scholars and advisors, cultural issues can be the single most decisive factor that can make the deal a success or failure (Miller, 2000; KPMG, 1999; Marks and Mirvis, 2001 and 2012). They point out that language and culture appear to be the biggest barriers for successful completion of the deal, and underline that the problem of cultural integration is ignored in the majority of the M&A process, while this is a principal reason why about 50 to 80% of all takeovers result in failure.

Therefore, it is important to underline the critical importance of cultural integration for the success of M&As.[6] Every firm undertaking an M&A needs to acquire a clear vision of both organizations and needs to resolve problems of cultural conflicts well ahead of time. As suggested by Weber and Camerer (2003): "Post-merger integration and performance are related to the cultural similarity and ability to capitalize on synergies of pre-merger firms". These possible difficulties always have to be considered by executive management in the M&A integration phase to accomplish estimated synergies.

Using an appropriate speed of integration

The integration process in a merger means human and task integration. Human integration refers to the process of creating a united vision between the employees of both firms. Task integration indicates the value added by combining activities of the two firms that, when united, obtain synergies sharing resources, knowledge and capabilities.

Human and task integration represent the integration process that is fundamental for avoiding an M&A failure. Haspeslagh and Jemison (1991) describe the integration process as "an interactive and gradual process in which individuals of both organizations learn to work together and cooperate in the transformation of strategic capabilities".

However, the integration process has to be implemented with an appropriate speed. In fact, synergies can be compromised by the *slowness in integration*. That occurs because a low integration process can limit the reduction in costs and increases the uncertainty among the employees of the combined firms. Speed of integration is considered especially important in marketing and sales for customer trust. The dominant beneficial effect of a quick integration is to reduce indecision among customers, related to price, quality and services.

On this subject many authors agree. Bragado (1992) observes that the appropriate speed of integration depends on cultural fit of the two combined firms. Haspeslagh and Jeminson (1991) indicate that the effect of integration speed on M&A depends, in particular, on the level of relatedness. In a recent research, based on the survey of 232 horizontal M&As, Homburg and Bucerius (2006) show that *speed of integration* influences M&A success mainly when the *external relatedness* between two organizations is high.

AN EMBLEMATIC CASE OF FAILURE IN MERGER IMPLEMENTING: DAIMLER-BENZ AND CHRYSLER

Daimler-Benz and Chrysler joined together in November 1998. The two companies were two leaders in their respecticve markets. Daimler-Benz was the largest industrial group in Germany operating in four businesses (automotive, aerospace, services and directly managed businesses), with 1997 revenues of $68.9 billion. It was a luxury vehicles producer deriving 63% of sales from Europe and it had less than 1% of the US market. It had an excellent reputation for quality and engineering. Chrysler was a highly profitable automotive firm with 2.1 million units produced annually (light truck, van and large sedan). Chrysler mainly depended on North America with a 93% share of all sales and a market share of 23% in the US. It was characterized by low cost production and a successful marketing organization.

There were several economic reasons for the merger. Both companies had product ranges, with world class brands, that complemented each other perfectly. Daimler wished to increase its market share in North America, through a rapid expansion of its product range, and to reduce its manufacturing costs. Chrysler desired to extend its international position and benefit from Daimler technology. In short, their goal was to become a global player with interests outside their traditional bases. In effect, the combined firm had, on paper, the potential for obtaining high levels of sales, participating in all segments of the car market, innovation capability, adaptability and technology and quality excellence.

Relevant synergies in costs and revenues were expected, because of economies of scale and economies of scope in operating activities and in R&D of new products and processes. Table 9.1 shows annual benefits expected from merged operations and in particular from shared technologies, distribution, purchasing and know-how.

The merger was considered the biggest merger in the industry, creating a global giant with 470,000 employees and sales of $120 billion. The objective of the two companies was to consolidate their position in the worldwide automotive industry and to become, within five years, one of the three largest automotive companies in the world.

It was announced as a "merger of equals", but in effect it was never reality. Daimler treated Chrysler as a mere subsidiary not as a partner.

Despite the widespread expectations of a successful combination of two well performing firms, that did not happen. On 5 May 1988, one day before the merger announcement, the market value of Daimler-Benz was $58.1 billion, whereas the market value of Chrysler was $26.8 billion.

Based on these market capitalizations, Chrysler's share of the combined firm would be equal to 31.6% (Blasko et al., 2000). The actual exchange ratio, based on several valuation techniques (DCF, multiple, comparables, etc.), put Chrysler's share of the new company at 41.4%. Thus, shareholders of Chrysler received a 31% premium over the closing prices of their shares on 5 May 1998. Daimler paid Chrysler $37 billion with a stock-swap deal. The merger shares value was approximately equal to $ 95 billion. Two days after the worldwide announcement (7 May 1998), the combined value increased to $95.2 billion.

After a positive starting period, with about 12% increase of sales revenues, at the end of 1999 Chrysler began to lose money. Disharmony grew in the firm; many senior key managers left the company and many more of Chrysler's managers were dismissed or exchanged with Daimler veterans.

At the end of July 1999 much of initial merger returns had been dissipated; in December 1999 the market capitalization of the entire Group DaimlerChrysler reduced to $65 billion. Also in the following years the "marriage" was not a happy one. In late 2000, six plants were closed and 26,000 employees were laid off. In the meantime, competitors improved their market positions. At the end of 2000 the market capitalization of DaimlerChrysler was only $44 billion, roughly equal to the value of Daimler-Benz alone, before the merger! Three years after the deal, the failure of the merger was already clear, as can be seen from some reports (for all see: Blasko et al., 2000; Finkelstein, 2002).

Table 9.1 Expected synergies in Daimler Chrysler merger

Expected synergies	1999 ($bill.)	from 2000 ($bill.)
Purchasing	0.4	1.3
Integration/financial services	0.2	0.4
Research and technology/platform technologies	0.1	0.4
Sales/distribution infrastructure	0.3	0.3
Higher sales	0.3	0.6
Total	1.3	3.0

Source: DaimlerChrysler merger prospectus, 1998.

In the following years poor performance of Chrysler subsidiary continued; the value of shares of the combined firm remained around $40 billion. In 2006 Chrysler registered further heavy losses and a drop in total market share. Plans to lay off over 13,000 employees in the future year were prepared. Finally, in April 2007 Daimler Chrysler sold 81.1% of the US Chrysler subsidiary to a private equity investment firm (Cerberus Capital Management) at a price of $7.4 billion. Daimler also had to pay $810 million for debt repayment of Daimler-Chrysler.

As numbers clearly tell, the merger produced a dramatic destruction in value.

Although it is extremely difficult to identify what roles different factors have played in a merger failure or success, in the case of Daimler-Chrysler analysts agree that cultural differences of the two firms were one of the main reasons for the failure. Daimler was a German company which could be described as "conservative, efficient and safe", while Chrysler was known as "daring, diverse and creating" (Appelbaum et al., 2009 p.44). In particular the main factors that are believed to have caused the merger failure can be summarized as follows:

- differences in culture and values between the two organizations;
- lack of coordination between the different levels of managers;
- severe lack of trust between the employees.

All three resulted in culture clash (Finkelstein, 2002), communication failures and poorly integrated management structure, which in turn caused a sharp reduction in productivity. Operational activities and organizational structures were not successfully integrated because of the entirely different ways in which the German and American managers operated. While Daimler-Benz culture stressed a more formal and structured management style, Chrysler culture favoured a more relaxed, freewheeling style (Weber and Camerer, 2003). Daimler's rigid and bureaucratic German direction style did not match with Chryslers more modern and informal approach to management.

The failure of the Daimler-Chrysler merger perfectly illustrates the difficulties in implementing mergers, especially when they are cross-border. As we have said before, these mergers involve higher risks due to the differences between the firms coming from different nations: differences in language, organizational culture, management style, regulations and technical know-how. The failure of the DaimlerChrysler merger was really the effect of cultural conflicts and mismanagement between the two firms. Potential relevant synergies between the two firms existed, but they were not carried out, because of an unclear and inadequate integration process, mainly due to cultural difference, lack of communication and leadership, and incorrect managerial decisions.

NOTES

1.   On the appropriate level of integration and autonomy for successful mergers, see also: Vancil, 1979; Datta and Grant, 1990; Datta, 1991; Pablo, 1994; Haspeslagh and Jemison, 1991; Zaheer et al., 2013.

2.   While referring to specialist texts in organization for a more complete and exhaustive analysis of these topics (Galbraith 1977; Mintzberg, 1983; Gerloff, 1985; Daft, 2001), we recall that the fundamental elements of organization design are the following: a) formal organizational structure; b) planning and control systems; c) human resource management.

3.   Chandler's study of strategies and structures of large American firms documented the M-form development as an innovative response to coordination and control problems that large firms such as DuPont and General Motors had during the 1920s, using functional structures to implement diversification strategies. Chandler's studies showed that these firms found significant difficulties in coordinating the conflicting priorities of the firm's new and different products and markets, while using a functional structure. On this topic, see Chandler (1962) and Sloan (1963).

4. On the importance of incentive contracts as a response to the moral hazard problem see Milgrom and Roberts (1992).
5. It has been shown, for example, in a survey conducted in 2001 on 134 human resource executives, that only 59% of human resources staff members in the acquired firms were asked to participate before the merger and only 58% were asked after the merger (Larsson and Finkelstein, 1999).

10. Conclusions: how to make M&As create value

INTRODUCTION AND OBJECTIVES

According to a considerable amount of empirical research, management's personal interests, inaccurate evaluation of synergies and ineffective implementation result in generating an M&A failure rate of more than 50%. In the light of the poor performance of M&As, as empirical research showed, we have drawn up some managerial directives to make M&As successful.

First of all, it is necessary that M&As be undertaken on correct and clear theoretical fundamentals. Certainly, M&A remains a very complex and difficult decision with high risk of failure, but it has not to be taken on generic expected strategic advantages and on supposed benefits of growth. It requires being driven by the objective of creating value for shareholders and it must be based on a deep analysis of the economic effects and cash flows produced over the long period. While it is not possible to cancel the risk of the investment, we think it is possible to reduce the risk of failure by carefully considering all the effects an M&A can produce on the shareholder value.

On the basis of the analysis developed and the models presented in the previous chapters, in this chapter, we summarize the main conditions necessary for M&As to create value. As different types of acquisitions are associated with different sources of value creation, in determining M&A strategies it is necessary to examine the potential for specific sources of value creation. The estimate of the potential for value creation will help to define the maximum premium that the bidder will pay for the target firm.

Finally, according to the type of M&A, it is necessary to design the appropriate organizational structure and adopt effective managerial and control procedures for successfully implementing the merger.

THE VALUE CREATED THROUGH AN M&A: THE BASIC MODEL

The analysis developed previously and the models presented highlight that the value created by an acquisition and merger mainly depends on the following variables, according to specific relationships:

- cost and revenue synergies;
- additional costs of merger (governance costs);
- cost of capital.

With regard to *synergies*, they are the determining factors for the success of M&A deals. First of all, synergies have to be properly explored, calculated and evaluated. Estimates have to be precise and complete, and integration problems have to be correctly evaluated, considering the possible costs and the timing of gains. In particular, a realistic estimate of synergy value has to be made taking into account the difficulties associated with combining the two organizations. In fact, integration is an "interactive and gradual process in which individuals from two organizations learn to work together and cooperate in the transfer of strategic capabilities" (Haspeslagh and Jeminson, 1991).

As for the *additional costs of managing integration*, this is a thorny issue: they are often underestimated in M&A deals. In fact, after M&A, the target firm and acquiring firm have to be coordinated in operations and structures so as to obtain a number of positive outcomes. Therefore, it becomes very important to understand the costs of coordinating companies and businesses after the M&A deal.

As for the *cost of capital*, this is a fundamental variable, as we explained in Chapter 8. The different forms of financing should be considered, because of their influence on the cost of capital.

In synthesis, the value created by the merger V_M can be analytically determined according to the following basic model:

$$V_M = \frac{(FCFO_A + FCFO_T)}{\rho_M} - [\frac{FCFO_A}{\rho_A} + \frac{FCFO_T}{\rho_T}] + \frac{\Delta FCFO}{\rho_M} \qquad (10.1)$$

where: $\Delta FCFO$ is the incremental operating free cash flow determined by the merger (net synergies); $FCFO_A$ and $FCFO_T$ are the the free cash flows of firms A and T stand alone and ρ_A, ρ_T, ρ_M are respectively the cost of capital of firms A, T and the combined firm M.

TYPES OF M&As, SOURCES OF VALUE AND PROBABILITY OF SUCCESS

According to the type of M&A, the synergies of costs, the revenue synergies and the additional coordination costs originate from different sources and economic conditions and assume different weights as we explained in the previous chapters.

Horizontal M&As

As shown in Chapter 5, the ability to create value through horizontal M&A strategies principally depends on the *economies of scale* in the industry. Economies of scale are present whenever large-scale production, distribution or administrative processes have a cost advantage over small-scale processes. In these cases, a firm exploiting economies of scale can drive out its smaller rivals and increase its supply, market share and margins.

Therefore, the presence of economies of scale in an industry affects the size of firms, favouring internal development strategies and M&A operations. This explains why in some industries, such as aluminium production, cement, steel and chemical-based products, a few large firms account for an extremely large share of industry sales and there are virtually no viable small firms. The recent M&As in the European cement industry are emblematic. We have seen the merger between the French Lafarge and the Swiss Holcin (2014) and the one between the German Heidelberg Cement and the Italian Italcementi (2015).

However, the possibility of achieving a long-term advantage in a market through horizontal expansion strategies generally reaches a limit due to the diseconomies of scale, that is the increasing average cost as output increases beyond a certain scale of activity.[1]

Diseconomies of scale can arise for a number of reasons, the most relevant of which are the following (Besanko et al., 1996):

- rising labour costs;
- spreading of specialized resources;
- bureaucracy costs and agency costs.

First, larger firms generally pay higher wages compared to smaller firms, because they are more unionized than smaller firms. That progressively reduces the advantage of expanding the scale of activity. Second, the expansion, spreading specialized resources to several activities, reduces the effectiveness of these resources, making costs rise as production runs up against capacity constraints. In other words, if a specialized resource input is a source of advantage for a firm, the expansion of activity and operations without duplicating the input may overburden the specialized input with a consequent reduction in performance. Finally, larger firms generally have increasing bureaucracy and agency costs. As the firm grows, difficulties in monitoring and communicating with workers increase too. So, a firm has to adopt work rules to ensure that workers do not slack off. While these rules may lead workers to perform specific tasks as desired, they may also stifle creativity and lead workers to feeling detached from the organization. Drawbacks are typically associated with the bureaucracy of large-scale organizations that impede efficient information processing.

However, probably the greatest costs of larger firms are what are called *agency costs*.[2] These are costs that arise where individuals act in their own interest rather than acting to maximize corporate performance. The increasing size of a firm generally favours a divergence of interests between shareholders and managers and between the general manager and functional executives.

The resulting behaviour may involve simply slacking on the job, but it will more likely involve actions to reach targets that trigger managers' bonuses even at the expense of corporate profits. Such behaviour incurs both additional production costs resulting, for example, from inappropriate decisions, as well as the governance costs of the monitoring and control systems, such as budgets, capital expenditure approvals and HR reviews set up to prevent such behaviour. To these costs we must add the expenses involved in the design and operation of any incentive scheme required to align the interests of division managers with those of the shareholders. This is necessary in order to minimize self-interested behaviour that cannot be prevented by direct monitoring.

An important source of value creation in horizontal M&As is associated with the higher *market power*, deriving from a larger size of the combined firm. In particular, the larger size and the reduction in the number of market participants will offer greater opportunities for collusion to control the price and the quantities of product sold, thereby generating extra-normal profits. The classical model of oligopoly suggests that prices in an industry rise following an increase in concentration and a reduction in the number of participants.

However, limits to horizontal expansion are imposed by the antitrust authorities, in order to impede the emergence of a firm with a dominant position in the industry, capable of cancelling any competition in the market, and therefore seriously damaging its customers.

Internal causes of unsuccessful horizontal M&As are mainly the shortage of resources for managing a larger-sized firm and the increasing complexity of organizational structure, especially in the case of international expansion. External causes of unsuccessful M&As are mainly the fall in aggregate demand and the unexpected dynamics of technology.

Vertical M&As

As shown in Chapter 6, in vertical M&As synergies mainly derive from *economies of scope* and from reducing *transaction costs*. In general terms, a vertical M&A can create value if the *corporate hierarchy* is more efficient in making activities than conducting them through a market exchange. In other words, a vertical M&A strategy will create value when a company "hierarchy" is more efficient than the market, that is, when the organizational arrangement minimizes the sum of production and governance costs. Therefore, the success of a vertical M&A will be principally determined by the economies of scope and the organization costs associated with the activities concerning the production and distribution phases of the existing products.

Diversified M&As

In diversified M&As the most important source of value creation is represented by *economies of scope*. These exist when the cost in joint production of two goods by one firm is less than the sum of production costs of these goods by two single-product firms. The condition for the existence of economies of scope is the presence of exceeding and shareable inputs and resources (production capacity, know how and other intangible assets) that are available without costs, for use in the production or sale of other products. Efficiencies for economies of scope are typically expected in the case of related M&As, where both partners bring complementary assets, resources and skills to the combination, so that the value is created as a result of the integration.

If synergies mainly depend on the economies of scope, it follows that the more the business of the target firm is distant from that of the acquiring firm, the smaller are the synergies and the larger the integration costs. Therefore, only companies operating in closely related businesses are potential candidates for successful M&As.

However, managers should also approach these mergers with great care and not put too much faith in their success. In fact, also when mergers are considered "related", because firms share some customers, synergies are difficult to achieve, expecially when processes are complex and firms are difficult to integrate because of the organizational constraints and cultural differences (Chatterjee, 1986 and 2007).

In diversified M&As, hierarchy costs increase in a more significant way, as the firm expands its scale by entering into new businesses. In particular, these costs derive from the bureaucracy necessary for providing efficient information processing to solve the difficulties that the corporate executive has in leading a corporation operating in a number of businesses and in controlling businesses that may have different dominant logics.

Frequently, in diversified firms the greatest costs of a corporate hierarchy are *agency costs*.[2] In fact, as a firm increases the number of businesses, the expenses of minimizing self-interested behaviour by the direct monitoring of division managers progressively increase, as well as the expenses for aligning their interests with those of the corporate office, through appropriate incentives (variable compensation and stock options).

In conclusion, limits to M&As creating value occur when the *economies of scope* become minimal or non-existent and the expenses of hierarchy become high. When this happens, a diversified M&A is no longer consistent with the creation of value for the shareholder. Rather than incur the agency costs of operating a new division or department inside the corporate hierarchy, it will be more convenient to employ outside specialized firms. Empirical studies support this conclusion. They present increasing evidence that firms often lose some of their efficiency and earn declining rents when they grow, diversifying away from their core business.[3] In particular the scope of diversified firms is limited by the transferability of firm-specific resources and skills. As a consequence, they reduce their diversification by refocusing on their core business to improve profitability, after over-diversified M&As (Ollinger, 1994; Markides, 1995).

Sometimes, the existence of extra profits in oligopolistic markets acts as an incentive for companies to enter markets that are technologically related, even if this is inefficient in terms of costs. High rents can lead to an *over-diversification*, in the sense that companies end up being more diversified than they would be based on pure cost efficiency.[4] In particular, when the capital market is imperfect, the investment opportunity could arise not for the most efficient producer, but for the producer that possesses the funds to finance it. A company endowed with enough funds could diversify in such an industry even though a multi-product production is more expensive than specialization. This motivation arises especially in large companies endowed with relevant capital, and mostly in those industries in which start-up costs are very high.

Also the interests of managers may spur towards over-diversification; in fact, they can act in order to favour the dimensional development of the firm through diversification, even reducing the equity value for shareholders. A manager can be induced to diversify for increasing the power and prestige more strictly linked to the size of a firm rather than to its profits (Marris, 1964; Marris and Wood, 1972).

Risks in M&As

Risks of failure are different according to the type of M&A. In general, *horizontal M&As* are less risky. In fact, if the two firms are in the same business, it is easier to understand the dynamics of the activity and the development of the industry. The main reasons for being more successful are already acquired knowledge, economies of scale and transferred expertise (Porter, 1987). In particular, an M&A can favour a reduction in costs by the combination of the firms, because synergies in cost reductions are easier to realize, optimizing general costs. Moreover, M&A directed to consolidate the capacity in the same market or industry can achieve revenue increase from an increased market power.

Differently, *related diversified M&As* are more problematic. In effect, they present higher cost of coordination and experience integration difficulties and consequently more uncertain cost synergies. In addition, it is more difficult to identify the source of revenue increase and to come to a definite conclusion in advance about the potential for revenue increase (particularly for related M&A). Finally, managers can overestimate their ability to achieve synergies or at least the fact that synergies take time to be achieved (Miller, 2004). Surely, diversifying can be an easy way to grow rapidly, but is not an easy way to create value, as we have already demonstrated.

All this is confirmed by wide empirical evidence (Rumelt, 1974; Peters and Waterman, 1982; Grant, 1998). These authors also found that firms that diversified into businesses closely related to their core business were significantly more profitable than those that pursued unrelated diversification. At the same time the problems associated with wide-ranging unrelated diversification were highlighted by the poor performance of conglomerates.[5]

The price to be paid for the target firm: a critical variable for the acquiring shareholders

For the shareholders of the acquiring firm, an M&A creates value only when the value of acquisition is larger than the price paid for the target firm T. That is when the following condition is satisfied:

$$V_{SA} = (V_T + V_M) > P_T \qquad (10.2)$$

where: V_{SA} is the value created for shareholders of the bidder, V_T the stand-alone value of the target firm, V_M the value created by the merger and P_T is the price paid for the target firm T.

A considerable amount of empirical research has indicated that "paying too much" is a main cause of failure. In particular, Sirower (1997) shows that the greatest winners in M&A are the target firm's shareholders, because the premiums paid tend to be around 30% above the market value of the target firm, so the shareholders of the acquiring firm rarely gain from the transaction.

Sometimes, the price paid results excessive after the deal, because it does not only include the value of the target firm, but also an estimated value of synergies that results as being over-valued (Moeller et al., 2005; Papadakis, 2007). That in part derives from a failure in the integration process.

However, synergies are not easy to obtain. Very often change of management structures and control mechanism are not obtained and so the acquirer results as having paid too much. This has already been shown by Inkpen et al. (2000), Bower (2001), Hayward (2002), and Schweiger et al. (1993). Even if the main reason for the exceeding high price paid is an incorrect synergy evaluation, sometimes it is the personal interest of managers (agency conflicts) which can lead to overpayment of the deal.

FINANCING M&As: SHARES OR DEBT?

As we noticed in Chapter 3, the value of a merger depends both on the increase in net free cash flows obtained by the acquisition ($\Delta\,FCFO$) and the weighted cost of capital ρ_M. In its turn, this also depends on the financial leverage. Therefore, it is necessary to evaluate the effects of the different forms of financing on the average cost of capital. In particular, we have highlighted that financing by debt increases the financial leverage and with it the risk for creditors and shareholders. That determines a consequent increase in the cost of equity and in the average cost of capital.

The model we proposed in Chapter 8 allows us to evaluate, case by case, which alternative is preferable for the shareholders of the acquiring firm, according to the effect on the cost of capital and, finally, on the value created by the merger. The analysis highlights the importance of the choice regarding the financing of acquisition.

ORGANIZATIONAL STRUCTURES AND PROCEDURES FOR INTEGRATING COMPANIES

In Chapter 9 we studied the appropriate organizational structures and procedures for managing the integration process and for favouring efficient coordination between different activities and functions. We showed that according to the type of M&As, a different level of integration between the companies is necessary for implementing the synergies and exploiting the existing resources and competencies.

Control systems and managerial procedures are necessary for coordinating decisions and preventing the abuse of functional managers and of managers of divisions and companies, as well as for providing coherence to the combined firm's activity. Such systems are a powerful discipline for managers and a necessary instrument for integrating different companies and enabling the interest of the whole company over the interests of companies involved in the merger and their functional or divisional managers.

The analysis pointed out that the integration process is fundamental to avoid an M&A failure. Surely it is difficult to obtain these synergies in an M&A so much so that Damodaran (2005) refers to them as "often promised and seldom delivered". On this topic, Chatterjee (2007) explains: "Synergistic mergers may, at least in theory, create competitive advantage when their complexity makes imitation difficult by would-be competitors. But this same complexity can also lead to integration problems".

Management should not only base their predictions on the excellent results of their calculations; in fact, it is far more difficult to realize synergies and achieve targets, than it seemed on paper. The possible difficulties always have to be considered by executive management in the M&A integration phase, to actually realize estimated synergies. Besides, there are mistakes that are to be avoided in running the integration process. The most relevant *recommendations,* for overcoming difficulties and managing a successful integration process, are taking into consideration the cultural differences between firms and using an appropriate speed of integration (Marks and Mirvis, 2012).

ADOPTING A CORRECT INCENTIVE COMPENSATION SYSTEM

A correct incentive compensation system and appropriate human resources related to rewarding management are also necessary for a positive M&A performance. In many M&As it is necessary to change some of the key people and retain some qualified employees. Long-term incentives, such as a stock option plan, can determine the necessary motivation of members of the firms and thus guarantee a successful M&A deal. Clearly, post-deal integration success depends on the activities made by management to integrate the different tasks, as well as on paying attention to the right integration process of human resources. Both task and human integration, as indicated by many research projects, are positively associated with the firm performance. Chatterjee et al. (1992) point out that "management of a buying firm should pay, at the least, as much attention to issues of cultural fit during the premerger search process as they do to issues of strategic fit".

PREVENT THE OPPORTUNISTIC BEHAVIOUR OF MANAGERS

Failure in M&A often depends on the personal hubris and ambition of the management, not considering synergies, inability to communicate internally, overpaying and not respecting the other culture in the integration process (Seth at al., 2000; Jensen and Meckling, 1976; Roll, 1986; Hietala et al., 2003).

Sometimes M&As are made only because of the management's desire to pursue their own interest and prestige. Managers place their self-interests above those of the shareholders, and often make decisions that will benefit them alone at the expense of the rest of the organization (Marris, 1964; Jensen, 1986; Jensen and Murphy, 1990).[6] Managers can easily convince shareholders of the opportunity of a promising M&A, using a well-calculated spreadsheet and a good business plan and complementing it with the right words and convincing motivations for the operation. They can also highlight the synergies that could be created, in addition to the reduction of costs and benefits deriving from economies of scale. Smart management easily finds spot-on words to make a deal appear "palatable".

Moreover, if management follows self-interests it will pay a higher price to complete the M&A, so as to earn a good incentive as a premium for having achieved an appropriate size target in a short time period.

As things stand, a system of behavioural rules and incentives has to be introduced, in order to reduce the divergence of interest between shareholders and managers. On a different plane, opportunistic behaviour of managers can be limited by setting up a board of directors composed of experts and independent members.

THE ROLE OF CAPITAL MARKETS IN LIMITING GROWTH THROUGH M&As

The efficiency of capital markets can also play an important role in disciplining corporate executives' behaviour. In particular, takeovers can be an imminent threat for companies quoted on the stock markets and carrying out poorly performing growth strategies. This threat can limit a growth strategy through M&As when this does not create value. Conversely, aggressive takeovers will happen, followed by the removal of top executives and the sell-offs of business units and substantial fractions of the target over-sized and over-diversified firm.[7]

Today hostile takeovers[8] are becoming an accepted tool in the business arsenal. As a consequence, we can consider virtually no company to be free from the threat of takeover. In this way, we believe that one more lever, in an elaborate system of checks and balances, is currently in place for reducing the immunity of even the largest firms and conditioning managers to pursue growth strategies that are more consistent with the creation of value for shareholders.

NOTES

1. Some economists disagree about the severity of diseconomies of scale. When diseconomies of scale are minimal or non-existent, that is when average costs are L-shaped instead of U-shaped, a firm that has reached the minimum efficient scale (MES) may continue to grow without experiencing increases in average costs. If it did a company could extend its scope indefinitely, but that does not correspond to reality.

2. On the agency approach see: Jensen (1986); Jensen and Meckling (1976) and Milgrom and Roberts (1992).

3. On the low performance of many diversified M&As, with respect to single-business firms see: Rumelt (1982); Berger and Ofek (1995); Lins and Servaes (1999); Rajan et al. (2000).

4. The low performance of many diversified M&As, with respect to single-business firms, can be explained by the phenomenon of *over-diversification*. On this subject see Markides (1995); Miller (2004). Among the numerous empirical studies on the performance consequences of diversification strategies, see: Christensen and Montgomery (1981); Montgomery (1985); Grant et al. (1988); Hill et al. (1992).

    Agency theory clearly explains why managers would over-diversify (Jensen, 1986; Jensen and Murphy, 1990; Tosi et al., 2000).

5. Other studies have less consistent results. See, for example: Christensen and Montgomery (1981); Luffman and Reed (1984); Michel and Shaked (1984).

6. Among the empirical studies we cite, in particular, Seth et al. (2002). They investigated a sample of US cross-border acquisitions and found indication that 26% were accomplished by managers for their own utility, rather than

shareholders' interest. In addition, they established evidence of hubris in cases where managers overvalued the target firms by mistake.

7. By the end of the 1980s investment banks and LBO funds took over a number of conglomerates without any size restrictions and then obtained value by breaking them up and selling part of the existing divisions on the market (Ollinger, 1994; Shleifer and Vishny, 1994; Collis and Montgomery, 2005; Markides, 1995).

8. On takeovers and defence tactics see Jensen (1988) and Weston et al. (1990).

PART II

Three emblematic cases of successful M&A strategies

INTRODUCTION AND OBJECTIVES

In Part II three cases of successful M&A strategies are presented: L'Oreal, Campari and Luxottica. These enterprises, even if operating in different industries, are all characterized by a decade of continuous growth, mainly through M&As, accompanied by a systematic creation of value for shareholders. The M&A strategies of these enterprises are described in their characteristics and in their economic and financial effects, as well as in their consequences on organizational structure.

Each company is characterized by specific M&A strategies and reveals its own original pattern of growth, making leverage on different resources and exploiting different environment and industry conditions.

L'Oreal has adopted closely related diversified and horizontal strategies carried out both by internal development and by acquisition of specialized firms and trademarks worldwide.

Campari has followed a growth pattern based on diversified and horizontal expansion strategies in different market segments and countries, mainly through M&As.

Luxottica has implemented a growth model based on horizontal expansion in different markets and a vertical integration in the retail distribution business, mainly through M&As.

Despite the differences, some constant characteristics are shown in the enterprises examined: a continuous growth through M&As and a constant creation of value based on exploiting strategic and complementary assets and distinctive resources of firms involved in the mergers.

The direct analysis of strategies carried out by these enterprises confirms that M&A is a fundamental instrument for increasing competitive advantage and creating value for shareholders.

11. The M&A strategies of L'Oreal

COMPANY PROFILE

L'Oreal is a France-based global cosmetics company, engaged in the production and marketing of a range of perfume, make-up, hair and skin care products. With 100 years of existence L'Oreal is today the top world company in cosmetics. The company operates all over the world with a wide range of products and brands covering almost all segments and all distribution channels.

The company's products are sold under a unique portfolio of prestigious brands, such as L'Oreal Paris, Garnier, Maybelline, Vichy, Kerastase, Redken, Matrix and Mizani, Lancome, Biotherm, Helena Rubinstein, Kiehl's, Shu Uemura and Giorgio Armani.

In 2014, L'Oreal reached €22,530 million consolidated sales and €3,891 million operating profits. In the cosmetic market, L'Oreal has a leading position with a market share of approximately 15%. The following data complete the firm profile of L'Oreal: 78,611 employees and 40 establishments all over the world.

In the cosmetics industry, consumer demand depends on the season, on the social and cultural environment and on the effects of previous marketing communication for fashion items or substitute products. Customers demand products with innovative styles, accomplished with exclusive physical attributes and top level quality by scientists and designers. Responding in a timely way to these changing demands is thus vital for success in this industry; cosmetic firms need to improve products constantly in order to stay ahead in a highly competitive market.

The strategy of L'Oreal has been that of concentrating all its resources on the cosmetics industry. This focus has allowed the firm to exploit and improve its resources progressively covering the major businesses and the different market segments worldwide, with a wide range of products and brands.

L'Oreal's competitors present different strategic profiles. There are companies focused exclusively on perfumes and cosmetics businesses, such as Estée Lauder, Avon, Shiseido or Beierdorf, while other world leaders are diversified conglomerates, such as Johnson & Johnson, Colgate Palmolive, Unilever, Procter & Gamble which also operate in food, personal care goods and household goods (Kumar et al., 2006).

THE GROWTH STRATEGY: RELATED DIVERSIFICATION AND HORIZONTAL EXPANSION

The industry in which L'Oreal operates is the *cosmetics* industry. In February 2014, L'Oreal sold to Nestlé its minor stake of the company Galderma Laboratories (dermatological company), a joint venture with Nestlé in the dermatology industry. L'Oreal also operates in cosmetics retail through The Body Shop, a chain of cosmetic stores specializing exclusively in hair and skin care products based on natural ingredients, with a total of 3,119 stores (of which 1,120 are total company owned and 1,999 franchisees) in 62 countries worldwide. By the end of the financial year 2014, L'Oreal consolidated sales reached €22,530 million, of which €21,658 million are in cosmetics and €872 million are in cosmetic retail distribution.

In the cosmetics industry L'Oreal over time has developed a closely related diversification strategy, progressively entering into and growing within the five major cosmetics businesses: skin care, hair products, make-up, fragrances, toiletries. Sales of the cosmetic products by business segment are shown in Table 11.1.

For each class of products, L'Oreal has distinguished four different market segments, to cater for the differences among professional clients (for example hair salons), and private consumers, thus offering different product lines through different market channels:

- professional products,
- consumer products,
- luxury products,
- active cosmetics.

The professional products are hair care products directed at professional hairdressers, who use or sell these products in their hair salons. Therefore the sector's key focus is to serve the greatest number of hair salons around the world, firstly by offering differentiated brands for different individuals and secondly by increasing targeted innovations to improve the quality of services in hair colourants, permanent waves, styling and hair care. The consumer products are products directed at mass-market retailing channels. The luxury products are premium products directed at customers requiring high quality and service. Luxury products are sold through select retail outlets. The active cosmetics products are derma-cosmetic skin care products, sold through specialist retailers, and pharmacies; pharmacists and dermatologists. Sales and profits of different product lines by market segment are shown in Table 11.2.

Table 11.1 Consolidated sales of the cosmetic products by business segment

Business segments	Sales (€mill.) 2014	%
Skin care	6,489	30.0
Make-up	4,751	21.9
Hair care	4,449	20.5
Hair colourant	2,860	13.2
Perfumes	2,123	9.8
Other (hygiene products, etc.)	0,986	4.6
Total	21,658	100.0

Source: L'Oreal, *Annual Report* 2014.

Table 11.2 Breakdown of cosmetics sales and operating profits by product line in 2014 (€million)

	Sales	%	Operating profit (€million)	Operating profit /sales (%)
Professional products:	3,032	14.0	609	20.1
Hair colourants	1,039			
Styling and textures	328			
Shampoos and hair care	1,665			
Consumer products:	10,767	49.7	2,186	20.3
Hair colourants	1,821			
Hair care and styling	2,722			
Make-up	3,205			
Skin care	2,489			
Other	530			
Luxury products:	6,198	28.6	1,269	20.5
Skin care	2,754			
Perfumes	2,040			
Make-up	1,404			
Active cosmetics:	1,661	7.7	376	22.6
Skin care	1,286			
Hair care	105			
Make-up	109			
Other	161			
Cosmetics total	21,658	100.0	4,440	20.5
Non-allocated cosmetic			−615	−2.8
Total	21,658	100.0	3,825	17.7

Source: Our elaboration on L'Oreal, *Annual Report 2014*.

The company has also pursued a horizontal expansion strategy both in new geographical markets and in new market segments through a policy of multiple brands. In particular, L'Oreal has carried out a geographical expansion, by strengthening its presence or by becoming established in emergent countries, in particular Brazil, Russia, India, Mexico and China.

In the last years the company has developed its sales especially in Eastern Europe, Asia and Latin America. The increase in sales in B.R.I.C (Brazil, Russia, India and China) countries and in Eastern Europe has been favoured both by the increase in consumption and by the growth strategy implemented by L'Oreal through acquisitions of firms operating locally.

Horizontal expansion in new geographical markets

The growth of L'Oreal in emergent markets (New Markets) is clearly highlighted by the increase in sales obtained in the period 2001–2014 (Table 11.3).

Table 11.3 Cosmetics sales growth by geographical area, 2001–2014

Sales by geographical area	2001 (€mill.)	2009 (€mill.)	2014 (€mill.)	2001–2014 growth rate (%)
Western Europe	6,581	7,036	7,698	17.0
North America	4,257	3,802	5,389	26.6
Rest of the world:	2,556	5,419	8,571	335.3
Asia Pacific		2,148	4,564	
Latin America		1,138	1,853	
Eastern Europe		1,213	1,585	
Africa, Middle East		920	569	
Total sales	13,394	16,257	21,658	61.7

Source: Our elaboration on L'Oreal data from *Annual Reports 2001–2014*.

In particular, the percentage of cosmetic sales generated by the Group in the New Markets (Latin America, Africa and Middle East, Eastern Europe, Asia Pacific) was 15.5% in 1995, 27.1% in 2006, 33.3% in 2009 and 39.6% in 2014. The sales in the New Markets increased by nearly 335% between 2001 and 2014.

Horizontal expansion in different market segments through multiple product lines

The company has also pursued an expansion strategy in the different market segments of the cosmetics industry through a policy of multiple types of products and brands: consumer products, luxury products, professional products and active cosmetics.

At present, in the professional products business the company operates with five brands: L'Oreal Professional, Kerastase, Redken, Matrix and Mizani.

In the consumer product business, L'Oreal has successfully used the core brand "L'Oreal Paris" which progressively became the foremost beauty brand worldwide. The company also focuses on differentiating and enhancing the value of the sector's product ranges through innovation, while developing blockbuster products to drive market growth. Other leading brands introduced over the years in this segment include Garnier, Maybelline and SoftSheen Carson.

In the luxury products business leading brands include Helena Rubinstein, Shu Uemura, Lancome, Biotherm, and Kiehl's, as well as perfume brands such as Giorgio Armani, Ralph Lauren, Cacharel and Viktor & Rolf. Finally, in the active cosmetics sectors L'Oreal brands include Vichy, La Roche-Posay, Inneov and Skinceuticals.

Over the years the company has continually expanded to new market segments to meet consumers' needs in all their diversity. In this context, since the male and seniors market segments are exponentially growing, the company has developed and commercialized new product lines adapted to the specific patterns of these populations.

In developed countries (Western Europe, the USA and Japan), as the market share of ageing populations (over 50) is increasing, more and more care products that prevent ageing are being proposed.

During the period examined, all businesses of L'Oreal have obtained significant growth, with a total increase from 2001 to 2014 of 61.7%, as proof of its successful strategies. In particular the active cosmetics products show the most significant increase (254.4%), for the success of new products in the pharmaceutical channel, but also the luxury products show a strong growth with a rate of increase in sales of more than 74% (Table 11.4).

*Table 11.4   Cosmetics sales growth by product lines in the period
           2001–2009*

Cosmetics sales	2001 (€million)	2009 (€million)	2014 (€million)	2001–2014 % growth rate
Consumer products	7,282	8,555	10,767	47.8
Luxury products	3,550	4,080	6,198	74.6
Professional products	1,811	2,388	3,032	67.4
Active cosmetics	653	1,234	1,661	254.4
Total sales (1)	13,394	16,257	21,658	61.7

Note: (1) excluding the dermatology business.

Source: Our elaboration on L'Oreal data from *Annual Reports 2001–2007*.

THE M&A STRATEGIES

L'Oreal's growth strategy has been carried out both through internal development and through acquisition of companies already operating in the cosmetics industry. In particular, external growth by M&As is part of L'Oreal's long-term strategy, with a long-term annual growth goal of 10%. This option has also been facilitated by the group's liquidity and low debts. Purchases of more companies allowed the group to reach the critical size needed for exploiting economies of scale both in R&D activities and in marketing and distribution.

The acquisition of companies also allowed L'Oreal to quickly expand its geographical horizon and develop its market segments. The actual portfolio of 17 prestigeous brands is the result of a series of acquisitions that began many years ago (Table 11.5).

All M&As, related to firms already operating in the cosmetics industry, were nearly always implemented by maintaining the operative autonomy of the acquired firm. These are the general characteristics of the acquired firms:

- operating in different geographical markets from those in which L'Oreal is already operating;
- operating in geographical markets in which L'Oreal intended to reach a leadership position;

- offering types of products that completed the portfolio of L'Oreal products or brands;
- having technologies and competences complementary to those of L'Oreal, both on products and on markets segments.

The acquisitions carried out by L'Oreal allowed the firm to reinforce its presence in the world and to maintain its leadership position in the sector (Table 11.5). Through acquisitions and mergers L'Oreal has also obtained important objectives, such as:

- reaching a critical size needed for exploiting economies of scale both in R&D and in marketing and distribution, thereby improving its competitive capacity, through the control of larger market shares;
- satisfying local needs through a more direct contact with the market and by adapting products to the local context (multi-domestic policy);
- creating a portfolio of distinctive but complementary products and brands;
- quickly acquiring new resources, competences and technologies;
- overcoming the entry barriers in some markets, where normative obstacles and tariff barriers were present.

Here, we indicate the most important M&A deals in the last decades and the objectives the acquisitions were directed to reach.

In 1964, L'Oreal acquired Lancome; through this acquisition L'Oreal entered the field of maquillage and perfume and obtained access to the selective channels of perfumeries. In the same year L'Oreal carried out the takeover of Garnier, an important consumer brand. In 1970, L'Oreal acquired Biotherm, a company specialized in biological cosmetics products, to cover this specific segment of demand. In 1980, L'Oreal acquired Vichy, a luxury brand with a range of products sold in pharmacies. In 1988, L'Oreal acquired Helena Rubinstein and Laboratoires Farmaceutical La Roche-Posay, specializing in skin care. In 1993, L'Oreal acquired the American Redken Laboratories, producing products for professional hairdressers. In 1994, L'Oreal acquired the Spanish Procasa, producing products for professional hairdressers.

Table 11.5 L'Oreal horizontal acquisitions in different market segments

Year of acquisition	Consumer products	Luxury products	Professional products	Active cosmetics
1964	Garnier	Lancome		
1970		Biotherm		
1980		Vichy		
1988		H. Rubinstein		Laboratoires Le Roche Posay
1993			American Redken Laboratories	
1994			Procasa	
1995	Jeda			
1996	Maybelline, Unisa			
2000	MissYlang			
2001	Colorama			BioMedic
2002			ARTec	
2003	Mininurse			
2004	Yue-Sai	Shu Uemura Cosmetics		
2005	Delial			Skinceuticals
2006				Body Shop, Sanoflore
2007		PureOlogy Research		
2008		YSL brand licences		
2010	Essie Cosmetics		Declear and Carita	
2011	Clarisonic			
2012	Urban Decay			
2014	Magic, Niely, Nyx, Carol's Daughter			

Source: Our elaboration of L'Oreal *Annual Reports*.

In 1996 L'Oreal acquired Maybelline, an American company specializing in *maquillage* products. In 1996, L'Oreal acquired the Chilean Unisa. The year before the Group took over the German company Jeda. With these acquisitions L'Oreal became the world leader in the field of large diffusion maquillage. In the same year L'Oreal created a joint venture with the Suzhou Medical College, one of the oldest Chinese universities in medicine.

In 2000, L'Oreal acquired Miss Ylang, a leader in large diffusion maquillage in Argentina. In 2001, L'Oreal acquired BioMedic and Colorama. The first acquisition was directed at enriching the active cosmetics division, while the second acquisition was directed at growth in the Brazilian market. BioMedic is a firm which specializes in products for skin care after plastic and dermatologic surgery; it is present in more than 1,500 medical studios in America and it is distributed in 25 countries. Colorama is a Brazilian leader company in the mass-market of make-up and hair care products. The acquisition of Colorama from the competitor Revlon was directed at reinforcing the position on the Brazilian market where L'Oreal was already present with the brand *Maybelline*. This acquisition allowed production capacity to increase thanks to the Brazilian plant and to the fast expansion of L'Oreal brands on the Brazilian market. In 2002, L'Oreal acquired *ARTec*, a firm producing professional products for hair care and colouring. The superior image of ARTec products in American hairdressers allowed the L'Oreal Professional division to develop new products and reinforce its presence in the most prestigious beauty salons of America. The fast increase in professional products sales and the increase in sales of hair care and hair colour segments in America after the acquisition clearly confirm the success of this strategy.

In 2003, L'Oreal acquired the Chinese *Mininurse*. This company specializes in skin care products for young women; Mininurse has an excellent image, based on a correct quality–price ratio and it is among the first three companies operating in skin care with a share of 5% of the Chinese market and a distribution in more than 280,000 shops all over the country. In 2004, L'Oreal acquired the Chinese *Yue-Sai*. This is a cosmetics firm specializing in skin care and make-up products directed uniquely at Chinese women. The Chinese brand benefits from a great reputation and an excellent competitive position. Yue-Sai products are sold in more than 800 hyper-markets, located in the largest 240 Chinese towns. The acquisition of the Chinese companies gave great opportunities to L'Oreal; besides the economic benefits, these acquisitions allowed L'Oreal to overcome the high entry barriers and to quickly obtain leadership on the market with its core brands: *L'Oreal Paris* in hair colour, *Maybelline* in make-up, *Vichy* in products sold in pharmacies and *Lancome* in selected perfume shops. The acquisition also permitted the extension of knowledge on the particular characteristics of the Chinese customers and finally the expansion of production capacity and increase in productivity. The two acquisitions also produced a rapid increase in sales of *Mininurse* and *Yue-Sai*, as a consequence of the relevant synergies produced by the merger. In 2004, L'Oreal acquired *Shu Uemura Cosmetics*. This acquisition concerned one of the most famous cosmetic brands in Japan and in other Asian countries. This acquisition enabled L'Oreal to reinforce its position in the luxury segment, accelerating the expansion of the brand in Japan.

In 2005, L'Oreal acquired *Delial* and *Skinceuticals*. *Delial* is a brand which specializes in products for solar protection and it is a leader in this sector in southern Europe and particularly in Spain, where it is among the first three brands. This acquisition allowed L'Oreal to reinforce its position in the solar products market and to gain know-how and technological resources developed in *Delial* laboratories. *Skinceuticals* is a US firm specializing in professional skin care, with a growth rate among the highest in the US market. This firm uses a highly specialized distribution network, including plastic surgeons, dermatologists and other professionals. This brand was acquired for enriching the active cosmetics division and increasing the brand portfolio of American brands (including *Ralph Lauren, Redken, Maybelline, SoftSheen-Carson, Matrix* and *Kiehl's*). The sales of *Skinceuticals*, after the acquisition by L'Oreal, increased by 45.7%, as proof of the important synergies produced by the merger. In 2006, L'Oreal acquired *The Body Shop* and *Sanoflore*. The two acquisitions showed the interest of L'Oreal in responding to the demand from consumers for natural products. As far as *The Body Shop* is concerned, this is an international distribution chain of body products composed of natural ingredients, with more than 2,100 sales points all over the world. This chain has an important reputation at international level, thanks to its defence of values in the field of human rights and animal protection; it serves a target of clients who are particularly interested in the chemical composition of cosmetic products. The operation gives evidence of L'Oreal's commitment regarding ethical themes as well as the will to improve its reputation in terms of social responsibility. The acquisition of *The Body Shop* has determined the entry into a new type of business, in addition to the cosmetics and dermatology businesses. The acquisition has produced a strong increase in the sales of *The Body Shop*, as the effect of important synergies with the group. The same can be said for Sanoflore, because this brand also specializes in products made of completely natural ingredients. After the acquisition, Sanoflore became part of the active cosmetics division.

In 2007, L'Oreal acquired *PureOlogy Research*. This is a luxury American brand of hair care products. This company was bought because of its high reputation among American hairdressers. With this acquisition L'Oreal aimed at exploiting the enormous potentialities of the brand, reinforcing its position in hairdressing salons. The acquisition was also justified by the strong complementarities between *PureOlogy* and the brand portfolio of the professional division. In 2008, L'Oreal acquired the operating licences of the group brands *YSL Beauty*. Over the last two years the company has also acquired several distributors of professional products in the United States (Beauty Alliance in 2007, Idaho Barber and Beauty Supply in 2009). In 2010, L'Oreal acquired *Essie Cosmetics* a producer in the USA. In 2011, L'Oreal acquired *Clarisonic*. In 2012, L'Oreal acquired *Urban Decay*, which is an important luxury brand in USA.

In 2013, L'Oreal acquired through the Body Shop 51% of Emporio Body Store in Brazil. In 2014, L'Oreal acquired *Magic Holdings*, a cosmetic firm specializing in skin care in China. In the same year L'Oreal acquired *Niely* a firm operating in hair colour segment in Brazil and Latin America; in 2014 there were the acquisitions of *NYX* a firm operating in make-up in America and of *Carol's Daughter*, a firm operating in the cosmetics industry with beauty expertise in order to serve multicultural customers.

THE ORGANIZATIONAL MODEL FOR IMPLEMENTING M&As

Through a long series of M&A deals L'Oreal succeeded in obtaining synergies and increasing shareholder value, both unifying and exploiting activities and resources of the various companies acquired, and maintaining an appropriate level of autonomy in different businesses, in order to take advantage of all opportunies offered by different markets and products. To this purpose, L'Oreal has implemented a decentrated organization model based on major geographical poles, capable of knowing the specific market needs and autonomously deciding which products to develop, in order to match the different needs of consumers in different countries, on the basis of physical, cultural and economic differences.

L'Oreal has developed an organizational structure characterized by four business divisions, professional, consumer, luxury and active cosmetics, to cater for the existing differences between professional clients (for example hair salons) and private consumers and between mass and affluent consumers and between consumers of cosmetics and dermatological products. In each division different brands are managed, each of them characterized for matching a specific culture and concept of beauty.

The consumer division operates in the mass market with cosmetic products directed at the mass market using wholesale and retail distribution; the most important brands are: L'Oreal Paris, Garnier, Maybelline and SoftSheen Carson. The products of this division are distributed in over 7,600 hypermarkets, 40,000 supermarkets and 74,000 drugstores.

The luxury division operates through selective channels in the highest cosmetics market segment with luxury brand and specialized products. These channels are cosmetic boutiques, other specialist outlets and department stores. Consider that this division is present in 2,500 selected perfumeries with exclusive rights and in department stores with brands like: Lancome, Biotherm, Helena Rubinstein, Giorgio Armani, Guy Laroche, Shu Uemura, Kiehl's, Diesel, Ralph Lauren, Cacharel and Paloma Picasso, Yue-Sai, VictorRolf.

The professional division operates with products directed at hair-dressing salons; the most important brands are: Kerastase, L'Oreal Professionnel, Redken, Matrix, Mizani, Pureology. Consider that more than 3 million hairdressers use and sell the brands of this division in their salons.

The active cosmetics division operates in the derma-cosmetic market with special products sold through pharmacies. All products of this division derive from the research carried out in scientific laboratories of L'Oreal and the collaboration with international dermatologists. This division operates in the derma-cosmetic market through 75,000 pharmacies and in spa companies with brands like: Vichy, La Roche-Posay, Innéov, SkinCeuticals and Sanoflore.

The Body Shop has been operating together with these divisions since 2006; this is a cosmetics firm which, in its 30 years of life, has specialized in selling products not tested on animals with a well-known brand name in 59 countries and a sales network of over 2,426 shops, offering products of excellent quality at the right price.

More in particular, L'Oreal organizational structure is multicentric, with a strong corporate centre based in France. It acts as a holding company with approximately 150 subsidiaries: the holding has a primary role of strategic coordination and marketing coordination of the Group on a global basis. At the corporate level a number of staff departments, such as Finance, HR and Legal Affairs help the corporate CEO to run and govern the group and to ensure all activities are coordinated effectively.

Then, there are two levels of divisions within the Group: a series of divisions according to geographical areas or zones (Asia, the USA, Latin America, etc.) and a series of divisions according to business units.

In particular, there are eight homogeneous strategic regions: Western Europe, the Americas, Asia Pacific, Eastern Europe, Africa and Middle East.

Each major region of the world has its own centre of expertise which groups together the Research and Marketing activities.

Each geographical zone has operational responsibility for the subsidiaries in the countries of its region. The subsidiaries develop the Group's business activities in the country or the region in which they are located. On this aspect, they manufacture or commercialize the products that they decide to sell in their markets. Production is organized by geographical areas; the Group has 43 factories located in different countries: 19 factories are located in Europe, eight in North America, three in Latin America, four in Africa and the 'Pacific Orient' and 4 in Asia. All factories are specialized in certain products: 22 factories are specialized in consumer products, five in luxury products, three in professional products and two factories in active cosmetics (Cogmap.com/loreal, 2010). In 2014 four new factories were added, two of which are in China, with the acquisition of Magic Company, one in France with the acquisition of Decleor and Carita and one in India.

In turn, businesses are organized in division units, each of them responsible for distinctive market segments and brands and with a specific functional structure for pursuing specific objectives. All brand units are supported by specialist staff operating at the division level: Consumer, Professional, Luxury, Active cosmetic. Each business division implements its strategy by adapting its business model to the realities and opportunities in each of major regions. Figure 11.1 represents L'Oreal's organizational structure at the first managerial level of authority.

This complex decentralized organization enabled the group to seize and exploit opportunities more effectively at any location and to significantly reduce the market access times for the launching of new products in each zone.

M&As, GROWTH AND CREATION OF VALUE IN THE PERIOD 1999–2014

Data shown in Table 11.6 clearly highlight the growth of L'Oreal from 1999 to 2014. Sales increased from €10,751 million to approximately €22,530 million, with a growth rate of 32%; invested capital grew from €12,137 million in 1999 to €32,063 million in 2014 (164%). In the period 1999–2014 the company sales grew by more than 5% a year compared with an average growth rate of 3.5% in the cosmetics industry.

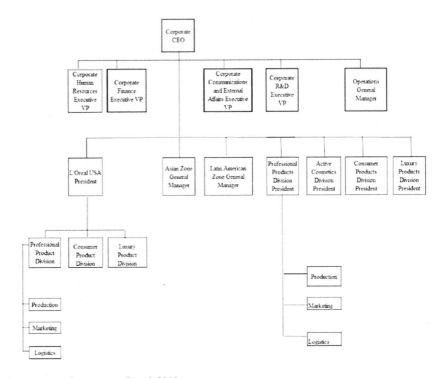

Source: www Cogmap.com/loreal, 2010.

Figure 11.1 L'Oreal organizational structure

The growth strategies created a remarkable value. In this period the operating profit increased by 367% and shareholders' equity value increased from €5,470 million to €20,920 million, providing clear evidence of the effectiveness of M&A strategies in creating equity value. Over the last 20 years an initial capital of €100 invested in L'Oreal shares in 1989 had at 31 December 2009 a value of €1,493 with an average rate of return of 69.6% per year.

Table 11.6 L'Oreal main financial data from 1999 to 2004 (€million)

Year	Sales	Net Profit	Cash Flows	Invested Capital	Equity	Net Profit (€) x share
1999	10,751	827	n.a	12,137	5,470	1.22
2000	12,671	1,028	n.a	15,449	6,179	1.52
2001	13,740	1,229	1,418	16,818	7,210	1.82
2002	14,288	1,456	1,579	17,189	7,434	2.15
2003	14,029	1,653	1,763	17,315	8,136	2.45
2004	14,534	1,656	1,923	20,160	10,564	2.46
2005	14,533	1,972	2,130	23,886	14,657	2.60
2006	15,790	2,061	2,410	24,783	14,624	2.98
2007	17,063	2,656	2,720	23,132	13,622	3.36
2008	17,542	1,948	2,746	22,907	11,563	3.49
2009	17,473	1,792	2,758	23,291	13,598	3.42
2010	19,496	2,240	3,171	24,045	14,866	4.01
2011	20,343	2,438	3,226	26,857	17,637	4.32
2012	21,638	2,868	3,507	29,234	20,185	4.73
2013	22,124	2,958	3,758	30,878	22,637	4.99
2014	22,530	4,908	3,808	32,063	20,920	5.34

Note: Data according to French accounting standard.

Source: Our elaboration on L'Oreal *Annual Reports* from 1999 to 2014.

STRATEGIC ASSETS AND RESOURCES FOR SUCCESSFUL M&As

We think the main strategic assets and resources on which L'Oreal has based its success in M&A strategy are the following:

- the R&D laboratories and research facilities, with top level competences of its scientists;
- company and product brands and reputation for quality and reliability;
- firm reputation, general mangement skill and HR management expertise.

In fact, cosmetics is a volatile and turbulent fashion industry, where customers always demand products with innovative characteristics and styles. That requires a continuous flow of new items produced with exclusive physical attributes and top-level quality. In addition, the competitors that operate in the mass segment are target fashion followers and they tend to imitate the high performing products of top brands, making the competitive advantage of top brands recede over time and the product life cycle shorter. Therefore, in order to avoid the decline of sales, it is necessary to continuously adapt products to the new demands of customers.

L'Oreal's R&D structure is the true key of its competitive success. R&D at L'Oreal is carried out in 18 research centres and 16 evaluation centres on all continents. L'Oreal has research centres in France, in the USA, in Asia and in Latin America to ensure that products match consumers' expectations perfectly and provide inspiration for new products. Furthermore, it has over 100 collaboration agreements with academic and research institutions. In these centres, over 3,000 scientists operate in R&D with 30 scientific specializations. The research and innovation laboratories, the number of research employees and the number of patents demonstrate the strong commitment of the company and the effectiveness of cosmetics and dermatological research (Table 11.7).

The effects of R&D activity are impressive: consider that half of L'Oreal's annual revenues is determined by new products launched on the market, 20% of products are renewed every year, so that all the product portfolios are renewed after five years on average, and that on average 500 new requests for patent registration are presented each year. R&D resources and competences are reinforced every year by relevant investments, allowing the firm to maintain and improve its leading position in the global market through continuous innovations in products. Such is the importance of new product development for L'Oreal that it tries to grab the maximum market share through the introduction of innovative products that are not only differentiated but also cater to satisfying the different segments of the international market.

The growth in sales and revenues carried out through M&As also allowed the firm to reinforce the original and distinctive competence of L'Oreal in cosmetics R&D every year, by the significant financial means granted to the R&D department. Consider that in 2014 the R&D budget obtained €761 million, equal to 3.4% of the company's total sales, and L'Oreal registered 501 patents (Table 11.7).

In this way L'Oreal's laboratories allowed the firm to create innovations capable of covering all price segments, by launching product lines accessible to the greatest number possible, attracting new clients to markets with strong growing potential such as the hairdressing business, body care, or products for men. That made it possible for L'Oreal to exploit new geographic markets and new market segments through the acquisition of different cosmetic firms.

Table 11.7 Patents, R&D expenditures and employees at L'Oreal

	2001	2003	2005	2007	2009	2014
Registered patents	493	515	529	576	674	501
R&D exp. (mill. €)	432	480	496	560	609	761
R&D employees	2,743	2,921	2,903	3,095	3,313	3,782

Source: Our elaboration on L'Oreal data from *Annual Reports 2001–2009*.

The second strategic firm asset for M&As success is given by L'Oreal's brand and reputation. Over the years L'Oreal has strengthened its image as an innovative and high quality firm through heavy investment in advertising and promotion (approximately 30% of sales) also by the means of world-famous personalities (Diane Kruger, Patrik Dempsey, Anne Hathaway, Penelope Cruz, Beyoncé, etc.).

Finally, general mangement skill and HR management expertise have been fundamental assets and resources at the basis of the success of the M&A strategy. Over a long period of time the success of M&A deals has been continuous and that proves the ability to integrate assets and personnel of the acquired firms, exploiting the characteristics of different brands and markets, as well as different cultures.

In conclusion, in the period examined (1999–2014) the growth of L'Oreal in both sales and profits has been constant. The growth has been characterized by horizontal expansion and related diversification, mainly through acquisitions of firms and trademarks all over the world (Figure 11.2).

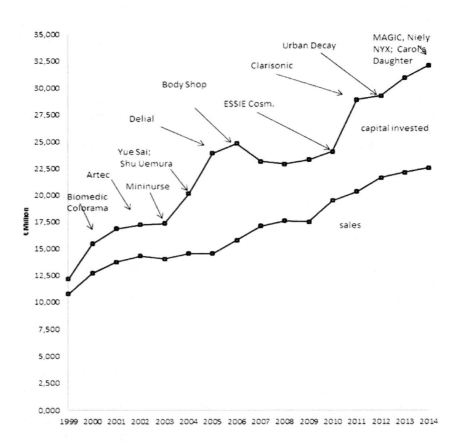

Source: Our elaboration on L'Oreal *Annual Reports* from 2004 to 2009.

Figure 11.2 L'Oreal sales, invested capital and main M&As

On one hand, the closely related diversified strategy allowed L'Oreal to operate in the main cosmetics businesses, hair care, make-up, fragrances and toilet products, exploiting relevant *economies of scope*, made possible from the intense relationships (complementarity) between these businesses, concerning customers, distribution channels, marketing and R&D activities.

On the other hand, the horizontal expansion strategy enabled L'Oreal to enter into new geographical markets, characterized by high growth rates, and to develop new segments in traditional markets, through an increasing number of types and models of products and brands, suitable for matching different customer needs and preferences.

This strategy also allowed L'Oreal to exploit remarkable *economies of scale*, especially in R&D, marketing and distribution activities. Synergies in operating costs and in capital expenditures have been relevant in these activites. Those concerning R&D activities have been particularly important. Even in the last decade the L'Oreal business model, based on product innovation, quality and globalization, has kept on showing its outstanding ability to sustain external growth through M&As and create value for its shareholders.

12. The M&A strategies of Campari

COMPANY PROFILE

Campari is a medium-sized company operating in the beverage industry and particularly in the spirits, wine and soft drinks businesses. It was founded by Gaspare Campari who invented the famous red aperitif Campari with many other liqueurs. Then he passed the activity to his son Davide Campari who opened the new factory in Sesto San Giovanni near Milan in 1904; it remained productive until 2005. Davide Campari changed the firm policy, limiting the production only to drinks with a strong identity and image: the aperitif Campari and the liqueur Cordial Campari. In addition, he gave an international impulse to the company making Campari products appreciated all over the world. In 1960 Campari products were already wide-spread and well known in more than 80 countries; in subsequent years distribution covered 190 countries with leadership in the Italian and Brazilian market and an important position in the USA, Germany and Switzerland. However, it was at the beginning of the 1990s that Campari made its major transformation, becoming one of the main players in the world market of the beverage industry. Today the group is directed by managers while the majority of shares are owned by the Garavoglia family. As from 6 July 2001 Campari has been quoted on the Milan stock exchange.

In 2014 Campari registered net sales equal to €1,560 million, *EBITDA* and net profits equal to €294.4 million and €128.9 million respectively. Campari has its headquarters in Sesto S. Giovanni, near Milan (Italy), and carries out its production in many factories located in Italy (Novi Ligure, Alghero, Sulmona, Canale, Crodo), Brazil (Jabotao and Sorocaba), the UK, Greece, Argentina and the USA (San Francisco). Campari also owns vineyards in Sardinia and Tuscany.

At present the company operates in four businesses: spirits, wines, soft drinks and other. Campari sales in 2013, divided by business areas, are shown in Table 12.1.

Beverages with an alcoholic content above 15% volume are defined by law as "spirits". Spirits are the most important business of the group. In this business the company operates today with some key products, such as Campari and CampariSoda, as well as Skyy Vodka, Cynar, Aperol, Glen Grant, Ouzo12, Zedda Piras, Dreher, Old Eight, Drury's and others.

Wines are both sparkling and still wines including aromatized wines such as vermouth. In the wine business the group is present with product brands such as Cinzano, Barbero, Liebfraumilch, Riccadonna, Sella & Mosca, Teruzzi & Puthod and others.

Soft drinks are non-alcoholic beverages. Other products are raw materials, semi-finished and finished products bottled for third parties. In the soft drinks business Campari is present with aperitifs such as Crodino and fruit-based beverages such as Lemonsoda, Oransoda and Pelmosoda.

Table 12.1 Campari sales and brands by business areas in 2013(1)

Business Area	Total sales (€million)	%	Campari brands
Spirits	1116.8	73.3	Campari, Campari Soda, Cynar, Biancosarti, Glenfiddich, Ouzo 12, Skyy Vodka, Cinzano, Aperol, Dreher, Old Eight, Drury's, Gregson's, Zedda Piras, Aperol, Glen Grant, X Rated Fusion, Cabo Wabo, Destiadora San Nicholas, CJSC Odessa, Wild Turkey
Wines	227.5	14.9	Cinzano, Sella & Mosca, Liebfraumilch, Barbero Mondoro and Enrico Serafino, Riccadonna, Teruzzi & Puthod
Soft drinks	88.8	5.8	Lemonsoda, Oransoda, Crodino
Other	91.0	6.0	
Total	1524.5	100	

Note (1): Data of sales by business area were not available for 2014.

Source: Our elaboration of Campari *Annual Report 2013*.

The main product of the Campari rich portfolio is the homonymous Campari, the alcoholic aperitif obtained by the infusion of herbs and fruits in a mix of alcohol and water with a brilliant red ruby colour and an intense aroma; the image of the product is based on concepts of passion and sexuality, two recurrent themes in Campari brand promotions. The market position of Campari is different in the various businesses in which it operates: spirits, wines and soft drinks.

With regard to the spirits business, this is characterized by a significant concentration, that has been favoured by high advertising and promotional expenditure necessary for sustaining brand awareness and image. Also the high investment in distribution networks has favoured concentration, making it convenient to have a large portfolio of brands, with a well known image and reputation, in order to match the needs and preferences of different regional markets. All this has encouraged the most dynamic companies to expand their product lines by buying well affirmed brands and companies, both for entering new markets and consolidating their position in existing markets against incumbent companies and potential entrants. However, in this industry a high number of small firms still operate, focusing on product or market niches.

At present, the most important players in this business are a group of multinational companies such as Diageo, Pernod Ricard, Bacardi, Brown Forman and Fortune Brands. The industry leader is Diageo, a multinational company with £10,813 million in total net sales, after excise duties, and £2,181 million in profits (2014); this company operates in closely diversified businesses, such as spirits, beer, wine and ready-to-drink products. In the premium spirits industry, in 2014 Diageo made $7,100 million net sales with a market share estimated at about 26% of the total world market. The other big competitors in the premium spirits industry are Bacardi with a market share of about 30% and Pernod Ricard with a market share of about 17%; Brown Foreman and Fortune Brands have smaller market shares of about 7% each (*Impact Databank*, 2015). Therefore, on the international rank, the Campari Group has reached the sixth position in terms of sales in the premium spirit market, with a market share of about 2-3%.

With reference to the wine sector, it is highly fragmented with a large number of niche operators, principally located in Italy, Spain, South Africa, Chile and Australia. In this sector large companies also operate. They have implemented strategies similar to those followed in the spirits sector: regional diversification and multi-brand product diversification. In the wine sector Campari is the leading company in Italy, but it is a medium-sized firm in the international wine industry.

Finally, with reference to the soft drinks sector, it is characterized by a few global players, such as *Coca Cola*, *Pepsi Cola* and *Cadbury Schweppes* and by a relevant number of local operating companies. Also in this sector, with the exception of the already mentioned multinational companies, the competitive scenario varies according to the markets and the different segments.

To sum up, Campari is number one in Italy both in the wine and spirits business, but it is still a medium-sized firm with regard to the wine and spirits world markets, even if it is characterized by a high growth rate in the last years.

M&A STRATEGIES: RELATED DIVERSIFICATION AND HORIZONTAL EXPANSION IN SPIRITS AND WINE BUSINESSES

Over time the Campari Group has carried out both a horizontal expansion strategy and a product diversification one. The main objective was to reach adequate size for obtaining economies of scale and product diversification for exploiting economies of scope, so as to successfully compete with the largest international companies.

Campari adopted a related diversification strategy, starting from the original historic Campari product and enlarging its range of products in the spirits, wine and soft drinks sectors. In each business Campari has successfully incremented the portfolio of products and brands, covering different segments of demand and different geographical markets.

The strategies of product diversification and horizontal expansion have been carried out through internal development as well as through external growth by M&As. In effect, the history of the last years points out that the strong growth of the group has been mainly achieved through external growth, primarily with selective acquisitions of well-known trademarks and companies with a solid position in their markets (Table 12.2).

The first important acquisition in the spirits and soft drinks businesses was made in 1995, when the Italian activities of the Holland Bols Wessanen Group, owner of the brands Crodino, Cynar, Lemonsoda, Oransoda, Biancosarti and Crodo, were bought. With this M&A Campari strengthened its position in the spirits business with the trademarks Cynar and Biancosarti, and in the soft drinks business with Crodino, Crodo, Lemonsoda and Oransoda brands. In 1996 the group continued the expansion in the spirits business by buying the distribution rights on the Italian market of some leader brands in the Scotch whisky segment, such as Glenfiddich and Grant's; they joined the production and trading licence in Italy (then extended to Brazil) of Jägermeister. In 1998 the Group accelerated its growth by buying a minority partnership in Skyy Spirits LLC and the world distribution rights (USA excluded) of SKYY Vodka brand, one of the brands with the highest growth rates in the North American market. With this agreement Skyy Spirits LLC became, in turn, the distributor of Campari products in the USA. With this acquisition and strategic alliance Campari strengthened its presence in the spirits business with a leader brand and at the same time strengthened the distribution network of its products in the USA.

Table 12.2 Campari diversified and horizontal acquisitions

Year of acquisition	Spirits	Wines	Soft drinks
1995	Cynar, Biancosarti		Lemonsoda, Oransoda, Codo, Crodino
1996	Glenfiddich, Jagermeister		
1999	Onzo 12, Skyy Vodka, Cinzano, Aperol	Cinzano	
2001	Dreher, All Eight, Drury's, Gregson's		Liebfraumilch
2002	Zedda Piras	Sella & Mosca, Mondoro, Serafino, Riccadonna	
2003	Aperol, Mapo Mapo, Barbieri		
2005		Terruzzi & Puthod	
2006	Glen Grant, Old Smuggler,		
2007	X Rated Fusion		
2008	Sabia, Cabo Wabo, Destiadora S. Nicolas		
2009	CJSC Odessa, Wild Turkey		
2010	T.J.Carolan &Sons Ltd (*Calolans, Frangelico* and *Irish Mist* brands)		
2011	Vasco (CIS) 000; Cazalis and Reserva San Juan (brands); Sagatiba Brasil S.A.		
2012	Lashelles deMercado&C.		
2013	Copack Beverage		
2014	Forty Creek Distillery; Fratelli Averna		

Source: Our elaboration of Campari *Annual Reports 2000–2014*.

In 1999 the Group bought Ouzo 12, an aniseed-based alcoholic Greek beverage, a world leader in this segment and a symbol of Greek lifestyle. In this year Campari also acquired Cinzano, one of the world's leading brands in vermouth and in sparkling wines and one of the most famous worldwide Italian brands.

In 2000 Campari acquired the distribution rights in Switzerland of Henkell Trocken sparkling wine and of Gorbatschow Wodka, from the Group Henkell Söhnlein, leader in sparkling wines. In 2001 Campari formalized the acquisition of the brands Dreher, whisky Old Eight, Drury's, Gregson's and Gold Cup in the spirits business and Liebfraumilch in the wine business. They were leading brands in the Brazilian and Uruguayan markets, all with a strong growth rate. In 2002 Campari acquired the Italian company Zedda Piras, owner of the majority of the Sella & Mosca company. By this M&A Campari strengthened its presence in the spirits business with another leader brand (Zedda Piras) and in the wine business with the Sella & Mosca wines.

In 2003 Campari carried out a further expansion in the wine and spirits businesses buying Riccadonna, a leading brand in sparkling wines in Italy, Australia and New Zeland. At the end of 2003 Campari bought Barbero 1891, an Italian company owner of a large portfolio of brands; among them in the spirits business Aperol, Aperol Soda, Mapo Mapo and Barbieri, and in the wine business Mondoro and Enrico Serafino. With this acquisition Campari expanded its supply in other segments of the wine and spirits businesses. Aperol brand completed the supply in the aperitif segments requiring a moderate alcoholic grade, while the Mondoro brand strengthened the group in the premium sparkling Asti wines segment on international markets. In 2004 and 2005 Campari concluded the acquisition of distribution rights of some important products in the spirits business: Cachaca 51, a famous Brazilian brand, Grand Marnier, the French sweet liqueur, exported all over the world, and the entire portfolio of spirit products of the American Brown-Forman Company, with brands such as Jack Daniel's, Southern Comfort, Woodford Reserve and Finlandia Vodka. In 2005 Campari made a new acquisition in the wine business, buying Teruzzi & Puthod, one of the highest quality wine producers in Tuscany.

In 2006 Campari entered the segment of Scotch whisky, buying from Pernod Ricard the brands of Glen Grant, Old Smuggler and Braemar, in addition to the distillery Rothes in Scotland for the production of Glen Grant, the second leading brand of single malt whisky in the world and leader in the whisky segment in Italy.

In 2007 there were further acquisitions in the spirits business: X-Rated Fusion Liqueur and the super premium vodka Jean-Marc XO. X-Rated Fusion is one of the trendiest liqueurs in the US market with a very high growth rate; this is a unique product for its taste and concept especially directed at the female market. In 2008 Campari entered the Argentinian and Mexican markets, buying the Argentinian company Sabia and the Mexican

Destiadora San Nicolas. This firm operates in Argentina with plants and a distribution structure in the spirits and wine businesses. The second, Destiadora San Nicolas, owns a distillery, tequila brands, like Espolon and San Nicolas, and a distribution network for the Mexican market. In the same year, Campari also purchased Cabo Wabo, an important producer of ultra premium tequila. These acquisitions allowed the Group to directly enter the growing Mexican market, with a consolidated productive and distribution structure.

In 2009 Campari carried out a further expansion in the whisky segment and in the wine business. In May the Campari Group finalized the acquisition from Pernod Ricard of Wild Turkey, one of the leading premium brands of Kentucky bourbon worldwide, strengthening its position among the leaders on the US premium spirits market and on some other important international markets. The acquisition included the American Honey brands, the Wild Turkey distillery in Kentucky (USA) and stocks of product. Wild Turkey is a global brand with sales in more than 60 markets. In 2009 Campari also completed the purchase of the Ukrainian company CJSC Odessa, a company operating in the sparkling wine business. In July 2010, Campari acquired 20% of Cabo Wabo and of Red Fire of Mexico completing the acquisition of this brand. In October 2010 the Group acquired from W.Grant & Sons the company T.J.Carolan & Sons Ltd. owner of the *Calolans*, *Frangelico* and *Irish Mist* brands. The cost of this acquisition, paid in cash, was €128.5 million. With these brands the Group extended its portfolio with three high quality brands, that offer excellent growth prospects, and further expanded its range in the premium spirits market. In particular, the acquisition increased the Group position in some main international markets such as Australia, Russia, Canada, Spain and the UK. As the Campari CEO declared "the acquisition is perfectly consistent with the Group's growth strategy from both a business and financial standpoint, and the risks attached to the integration are very low, as the Group already accounts for 60% of the distribution of the newly-acquired brands in volume terms and produces Frangelico itself' (p. 10 Annual Report, 2010). In particular, *Corolans* is a global brand and leading product in the Irish cream segment, distributed in more than 60 markets, including the USA, the largest market, which accounts for around 60% of total sales. *Frangelico* is a premium Italian liqueur made from hazelnuts, which is highly profitable and sold in more than 90 markets, with the USA accounting for around 50% of total sales. It is a high quality product with distinctive packaging and a strong presence in the on-premise channel. *Irish Mist* is a premium liqueur made from Irish whisky, honey and natural flavours, which is sold in more than 40 markets (the US is also the largest market for this brand). It will enable the Group to capitalize in the growing Irish whisky market, with the opportunities for the development of new products linked to the brand.

In 2011 Campari acquired Vasco (CIS) a wines and spirits import and distribution company based in Moscow. Vasco is a small company, but one with a consolidated presence in the important Russian market. For this reason it forms a solid basis from which the Group can develop a distribution platform in Russia. In May 2011 Campari acquired Cazalis and Reserva San Juan brands in Argentina, from Destilladora International. These brands were already distributed by Campari Argentina S.A. In August Campari also completed the acquisition of Sagatiba Brazil S.A. and its associated assets (a storage facility for finished products) and brands. The purpose was the development of the distribution network in Brazil. In December the acquired company was merged into the Brazilian subsidiary Campari do Brazil Ltda. In 2012 Campari acquired Lashelles de Mercado & C, a company based in Jamaica and listed on the Jamaican stock exchange. It was a very important acquisition: the price paid was €321.6 million and the acquisition was financed by a bank loan. The business perimeter of the acquisition includes the spirit business, as well as the activities relating to the upstream supply chain and a local convenience goods distribution business. The spirit business is represented by a portfolio of rums, including Appleton Estate, a super premium aged rum, and other well-known brands such as Coruba, Wray & Nephew, etc. Upstream supply chain activities, all located in Jamaica, include sugar cane cultivation, two distilleries, a sugar production plant and various warehouses. In 2013 Campari acquired Copack Beverage, an Australian bottling company, specialized in tin and glass bottling that already supplied the Group with packaging for ready-to-drink products. The object of the deal was to strengthen the supply chain structure in the Asia-Pacific region.

In 2014 Campari acquired Forty Creek Distillery Ltd, an independent market leader in the Canadian spirits market. The acquisition included the full brand portfolio, the stocks, distilleries and manufacturing facilities. This transaction enabled the Group to build a critical mass in the key North American market and represented its first move into the important Canadian whisky segment. Moreover it added a high-end premium brand to its current portfolio of brown spirits, a high potential category, especially in the US market. The product portfolio incudes: whisky, volka, brandy, rum and liqueurs. In particular, the Forty Creek Canadian whisky family includes famous brands, well positioned in the Canada and US markets. This was another important M&A with a total transaction price of €132.4 million. In June 2014, Campari completed the acquisition of Fratelli Averna Spa a leading Italian company operating in the spirits market with a portfolio of successful and profitable products, characterized by a premium positioning. The total purchase price of the company was €103.7 million.

In conclusion, from 1995 to 2014 Campari expanded its portfolio of products through the acquisition of a series of brands and companies with the purpose of strengthening its competitive position in different market segments and different geographical markets. In the last years, the focus of the Group's M&A strategy has mainly concentrated on the spirits business, which presents a higher contribution margin than the wine and soft drink businesses (Table 12.3).

Table 12.3 Investments in acquisitions in the period, 2005–2014

Years	Acquisition of companies and trademarks (€mill.)	Total goodwill and trademarks (€mill.)
2005	131	751
2006	179	816
2007	29	812
2008	87	920
2009	441	1,199
2010	115	1,409
2011	26	1,449
2012	321	1,631
2013	14	1,556
2014	236	1,841

Source: Our elaboration of Campari *Annual Reports 2005-2009.*

At present, Campari has a portfolio of products that cover different segments and different countries, both in mature and in emerging markets.

THE ORGANIZATIONAL STRUCTURE FOR IMPLEMENTING M&A STRATEGIES

To implement its M&A strategies the Campari Group developed a holding organizational structure capable of managing differentiated activities and worldwide businesses. The formal structure is based on an operating holding, Davide Campari Milano S.p.A, which controls a number of international subsidiaries, each maintaining its original brand and products (Figure 12.1).

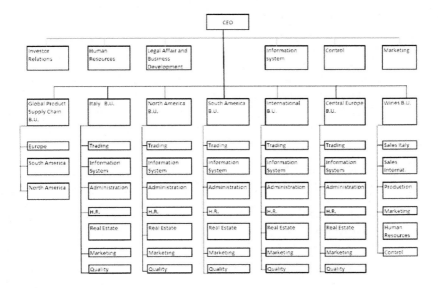

Source: Our elaboration on Campari, "Modello organizzativo, di gestione e controllo" (30 March 2010).

Figure 12.1 Organizational structure of Campari, 2010

Some of these companies are trading companies operating in different markets (for example Campari Austria, Campari Deutschland, Campari Argentina, Campari Australia, Campari International, etc.), other companies are manufacturing and trading companies (such as Zedda Piras, CJSC Odessa, Old Smuggler Whisky Company, etc.), and others are more sub holdings in turn controlling manufacturing and trading companies (such as Glen Grant Ltd a holding controlling Glen Grant Ltd Distillery Company; Sella & Mosca holding, etc.).

The operating structure is characterized by a corporate office with functional staff and seven business units: five geographical business units, one product line business unit (wine) and one manufacturing business unit. Precisely, the business units are the following:

- global product supply chain business unit;
- Italy business unit;
- North America business unit;

- South America business unit;
- international business unit;
- Central Europe business unit;
- wine business unit.

M&As have been implemented through original organizational structure and procedures, that succeeded in integrating different companies, but also maintaining the needed autonomy for exploiting different assets and resources and for meeting different customers demands.

M&A STRATEGIES, GROWTH AND CREATION OF VALUE IN THE PERIOD 2000–2014

In the period 2000-2014, Campari carried out M&A strategies to grow and to create value which were highly demanding in terms of financial resources. The increase in invested capital from 2000 to 2014 reached 487%. The investments made to sustain the growth have been considerable, especially those in acquisitions of companies and brands, as shown by the data reported in Table 12.4.

The effects of the M&A strategy carried out in the period 2000–2014 are shown in Tables 12.3, 12.4 and 12.5. Campari principally invested in the spirits business, obtaining a dramatic increase of 373% in sales, from €236 million in 2000 to €1116 in 2014. The growth in the wine business has also been important: sales increased from €70.7 in 2000 to €227.5 in 2014 (+220%).

The high growth in sales of spirits emphasizes the prominence of this business in the growth strategies of Campari. This is due to the favourable dynamics of demand and higher margins that characterize this sector (Table 12.5).

Through acquisitions Campari diversified and extended its portfolio of products and brands, matching customers' needs and preferences in different countries (Table 12.6).

The growth strategies carried out in the examined period also created a considerable value for shareholders, as Table 12.7 and Table 12.8 show. The growth of sales was accompanied by an increase in *EBITDA* equal to 216% and by an increase in shareholders' equity value equal to 291%. In particular, from 31.12.2001 to 31.12.2014 the price of Campari stock increased in absolute terms by 290% (an average of 11% per year). The company stock gained 282.4% against the FTSE Mib and outperformed the STOXX Europe

600 Food & Beverage index by 117.8% in the period from date of listing to 31.12.2014 (p. 36, Annual Report 2014).

Table 12.4 Sales by business in the period 2000–2013

Sales (in €million)	2000	%	2009	%	2013	%	2013 – 2000	% increase
Spirits	236	54.4	740	73	1,117	73	881	373
Wine	71	16.3	154	15	227	15	156	220
Soft drinks	124	28.6	100	11	89	6	-35	-28
Other sales	3	0.7	14	1	91	6	88	(2)
Total	434	100	1,008	100	1,524	100	1,090	251

Notes: (1) Breakdown of sales by products is not available for 2014.
        (2) Meaningless.

Source: Our elaboration of Campari *Annual Report*.

Table 12.5 Contribution margins by businesses

Businesses	Contribution margins €mill. (2014)	% of Total margins	Contribution margin/ Sales 2013 (%)
Spirits	416.3	82.3	37.2
Wines	49.3	9.7	21.6
Soft drinks	36.8	7.4	41.3
Others	3.1	0.6	(1)
Total	505.5	100	

Note (1) : Meaningless.

Source: Our elaboration on Campari *Annual Report*.

Table 12.6 Sales by geographical markets, 2000–2014

Sales (in €mill.)	2000	%	2009	%	2014	%	*2014-2000*
Italy	249	57.4	388	38.5	412	26.4	163
Europe (rest of)	127	29.3	232	22.9	382	24.5	255
Americas	36	8.4	325	32.3	605	38.8	569
USA			228		305		
Brazil			65		82		
Others			32		218		
Rest of W. & duty free	22	4.9	64	6.3	161	10.3	139
TOTAL	434	100.0	1,008	100.0	1,560	100.0	1,126

Source: Our elaboration of Campari *Annual Reports 2000–2014*.

Table 12.7 Main financial outcomes of Campari from 2000 to 2014

Years	Net sales	Net profit	EBIT	FC flow	Goodwill and marks	Total Assets	Equity
2000	434	53	93	n.a	83	559	404
2001	494	63	100	n.a	153	752	432
2002	661	72	143	60	437	1,025	479
2003	714	53	148	55	552	1,240	548
2004	751	97	185	99	576	1,341	629
2005	810	118	201	82	751	1,601	696
2006	934	117	210	93	816	1,726	798
2007	957	125	220	125	812	1,708	879
2008	942	126	215	123	920	1,790	955
2009	1,008	137	261	184	1,199	2,378	1,046
2010	1,163	156	295	132	1,409	2,651	1,253
2011	1,274	159	326	136	1,449	2,901	1,367
2012	1,340	157	320	126	1,631	3,409	1,433
2013	1,524	150	329	106	1,556	3,302	1,396
2014	1,560	129	294	178	1,841	3,518	1,580

Source: Our elaboration on Campari *Annual Reports 2000–2014*.

Table 12.8 Campari share prices and stock market capitalization 2001–2014

	Share price (€)	Stock market capitalization (€million)
2001	1.32	767
2002	1.50	871
2003	1.93	1,118
2004	2.37	1,374
2005	3.12	1,812
2006	3.76	2,183
2007	3.28	1,904
2008	2.40	1,394
2009	3.65	2,118
2010	4.87	2,828
2011	5.15	2,988
2012	5.80	3,369
2013	6.08	3,531
2014	5.16	2,997

Note: Values at the end of period.

Source: Campari *Annual Report 2014*.

STRATEGIC ASSETS AND RESOURCES FOR SUCCESSFUL M&As

From 2000 to 2014, Campari achieved a 259% increase in sales, mainly obtained by acquisitions of companies and well-known trademarks. This growth has been accompanied by an important creation of value for shareholders, with an increase of equity value around 290%.

The main strategic assets and resources on which Campari has based its successful M&A strategy are the following:

- a strong company brand and image, and a reputation for quality and reliability;
- distinctive competences in marketing management, expecially advertising and communication;
- technological know-how in manufacturing;

- firm reputation, general mangement skill and HR management expertise.

In particular, to create value, Campari made leverage on a strong brand image and superior competence in marketing management. Over the years, Campari sustained and improved its brands and image, with relevant promotional investments. The role of advertising has been very important for communicating unique sensations and emotions, making every Campari product original and attractive. As image is a key factor to success in the beverage business, Campari imposed a very high standard in creating image and sustaining advertising campaigns. The importance for Campari of creating a strong image is proved by the financial means allocated to brands every year. As shown in Table 12.9, advertising and promotion expenditure have constantly represented 17–18% of net sales.

Know-how and advanced technologies in spirits and wines production also explain the success of M&A deals. During its life Campari has always maintained high quality in its products and developed important process innovations, constantly increasing the productivity, especially of labour. Important results in reducing labour costs have been obtained by introducing high precision new technology for bottling sparkling wines. Making leverage on these distinctive resources, it has been possible to create value for shareholders through a series of coherent M&As, carried out in very competitive markets, up until now dominated by large international companies (Figure 12.2).

In particular, through the expansion in new segments of the spirits industry and new geographical markets, Campari has exploited remarkable *economies of scale* and *economies of scope*, particularly in distribution and marketing activities. For example, through the acquisition of Aperol, Campari integrated its offer with a consolidated brand in the medium alcoholic spirits segment which was experiencing a strong growth in Italy and internationally.

Through the acquisition of Skyy Spirits, Campari diversified its product portfolio, acquiring a strong and dynamic brand; the acquisition allowed Campari to strengthen its distribution network in the USA with high cost and revenue synergies for the other brands, also obtaining an important geographical diversification of its sales. More recently, with the acquisition of Corolan & Sons, Campari supplemented its portfolio with three high quality brands in the premium Irish whisky market. With the acquisition of Forty Creek Distillery, Campari has built a *critical sales mass* in the Canadian whisky market. Furthermore, the acquisitions have allowed Campari to have new successful managers at its disposal.

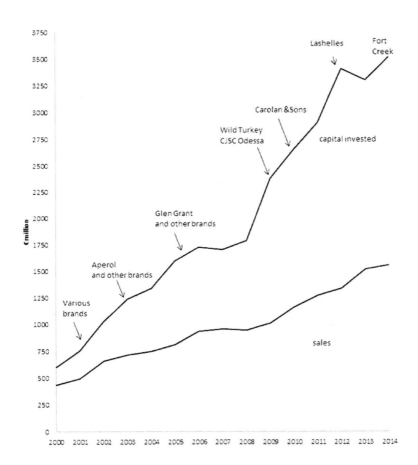

Figure 12.2 Campari sales and invested capital 2000-2014

In the wine business, the Barbero acquisition allowed Campari to acquire the Italian distribution network of Barbero with high cost synergies for other products. The merger also gave Campari increasing bargaining power over wholesalers and large retailers (cost reduction) and allowed it to exploit the know-how and technology of the Barbero firm in wines production.

Merger and acquisition strategies

Table 12.9 Annual advertising and promotional expenditures by Campari

Year	Sales (€million)	Advertising and promo. expenses (€million)	Advertising and promo. expenses/ Net sales (%)
2000	433	80	18.4
2001	498	91	18.5
2002	661	871	19.8
2003	714	131	20.1
2004	751	144	17.5
2005	810	140	17.2
2006	932	163	17.5
2007	957	175	18.2
2008	942	173	18.3
2009	1,008	172	17.2
2010	1,163	203	17.5
2011	1,274	229	18.0
2012	1,341	237	17.7
2013	1,524	249	16.4
2014	1,560	261	16.7

Source: Our elaboration on Campari *Annual Reports*.

At present, Campari has an extensive brand portfolio, well balanced worldwide in terms of products and market areas. Making leverage on its strong image, very distinctive brands and a global distribution network, Campari can aspire to obtain success in international markets and continue to create value for its shareholders through further M&As.

13. The M&A strategies of Luxottica

COMPANY PROFILE

Luxottica is the world leader in the eyewear business, with net sales reaching €7,652 billion in 2014 and 77,734 employees and a strong global presence worldwide. Founded by Leonardo Del Vecchio in 1961, the group is a vertically integrated organization that manufactures prescription glasses and sunglasses with a wide-reaching wholesale distribution network and a direct retail distribution network, mostly in North America, Asia-Pacific and China.

Product design, development and manufacturing take place in six production facilities in Italy, representing 43% of global production output, two wholly-owned factories and one 50% owned joint venture in China with approximately another 43% of total production, two sunglasses production facilities in the USA with 10%, and a facility in Brazil with 4%. Luxottica also has a plant in India, serving the local market.

Luxottica products focus on design and quality and are known all around the world thanks to a strong and well-balanced brand portfolio of house and licensed brands. The group's wholesale distribution, covering 130 countries across five continents, is based on 50 commercial subsidiaries providing direct operations in major markets and 100 independent distributors in other markets. As of 31 December 2014 retail business consisted of 6,471 stores and 613 franchised locations (Luxottica, *Annual Report*, 2014).

Luxottica is a leader also in the prescription glasses business, in North America with its LensCrafters and Pearle Vision chains, and in Asia-Pacific with OPSM, Laubman & Pank and Budget Eyewear chains.

In 2014, Luxottica distributed approximately 20.4 million prescription frames and 38.4 million sunglasses, in approximately 7,000 different styles (Luxottica, *Annual Report 2014*).

The most important Italian competitors of Luxottica are Safilo, Marcolin and De Rigo. Among the foreign competitors the most important are: Essilor International, Marchon, The Cooper Companies and Fielmann.

HORIZONTAL EXPANSION, VERTICAL INTEGRATION AND M&A STRATEGIES

The company's long-term objective has been to expand and to reach a leading position in the global eyewear market by growing in all its businesses, both through internal expansion and through acquisitions. More precisely, the long-term growth of Luxottica has been based on a multi-dimensional strategy characterized by:

- horizontal expansion in different segments and geographical markets through a wide and balanced portfolio of brands;
- vertical integration of production process and retail distribution.

Horizontal expansion and M&A strategies

Until the first half of the 1980s the activity of Luxottica concentrated on producing and selling prescription glasses of high quality with its own brands Luxottica and Steroflex. In the late 1980s Luxottica decided to enter into the sunglasses business. The glasses market was changing from a medical product and instrument to a fashion product, where the non-material characteristics, such as the beauty, style and image become more and more important. Eyeglasses, previously perceived as mere sight-correcting instruments, began to evolve into "eyewear". Also prescription glasses, became a true fashion accessory, a way of expressing a lifestyle, personality and image. In particular, sunglasses became an element of a total look, able to express a personality. The sunglasses market became of increasing importance and the high segment was completely conquered by stylists' brand products.

The management of Luxottica understood that only the introduction of the world's best known fashion brands would determine the radical change in the industry and the success in the market. Therefore, Luxottica decided to increase its presence in the sunglasses business, paying particular attention to the US market that presented high opportunities for growth. This strategy reflected the right understanding of market dynamics: the sunglasses market presented higher profit margins than the prescription market, not only for the existing competitive forces, but also for the possible evolution of medical therapies and optical surgery. Rebalancing the production mix and increasing the share of sunglasses production would increase profits and also reduce the risk of a high presence in the prescription business.

In order to be successful in this new business, style and fashion were of fundamental importance. For this reason in 1988 Luxottica decided to carry out its first collaboration with the fashion industry, by entering into a licensing agreement with Giorgio Armani. Then the company decided to buy some important and well-known brands and to define licensing agreements with other important fashion stylists in order to achieve different market segments.

The segmentation was developed to meet specific needs and demands of different targets, even through an increase of advertising pressure. The advertising leverage became more and more important, so that the communication expenditure came to represent 12–13% of sales for sunglasses and 8% for prescription glasses.

An M&A strategy was carried out to develop these markets, rapidly and in depth. In 1990 the brand portfolio was increased by the acquisition of Fidia, a company licensee of the Valentino brand, and of Florence Line, a trading company owner of the brand Vogue Lunettes. In the same year the licence of the Yves Saint Laurent brand was signed. In 1995 Luxottica acquired Persol, an Italian firm, specializing in sunglasses and well known for its quality, innovation and fashion products. It was positioned in the high segment of the international sunglasses business. Through this acquisition Luxottica enforced its position in the high segment of the market, acquiring a very prestigious and famous brand, well known among the Hollywood stars.

In 1999 Luxottica acquired the optical division of Bausch & Lomb, producer of the famous sunglasses Ray-Ban. This was one of the world's best-known sunglasses brands. Bausch & Lomb was the leader in the American market, in particular in the medium–high segment, with a share of about 36–40%, due to the Ray-Ban brand.

Through this acquisition, Luxottica also obtained crystal sunglass lens technology and the associated manufacturing capacity and upgraded its portfolio with brands like Arnette, REVO and Killer Loop. The acquisition of Ray-Ban represented for Luxottica the opportunity to balance its portfolio of products, reinforcing its position in the medium–high segment of the sunglasses market through a leading brand affirmed and known worldwide. The acquisition also allowed Luxottica to balance the ratio between sales carried out with house brands and sales with licensed brands. Then, this acquisition allowed Luxottica to increase the critical mass of production with a consequent reduction in unit cost, due to the economies of scale. Finally, the Ray-Ban brand also offered new opportunities for growth in North America and in the original markets of Luxottica, in addition to the opportunities offered by the acquisition of know-how owned by Bausch & Lomb on sun lenses. Thanks to this acquisition Luxottica extended its portfolio to the Ray-Ban, Killer Loop, Rēvo, Porsche Design, Arnette and Suncluod lines. In addition Luxottica also acquired all Ray-Ban factories in Texas, Ireland, Hong Kong and Italy.

In the following years Luxottica continued to pursue a horizontal expansion strategy, extending its product line by acquiring new brands and signing new licensing agreements with famous stylists and fashion companies. Enlarging the range of products and the brand portfolio,

Luxottica exploited great synergies in costs and revenues. From 1995 to 2009 a number of brands were included in the Luxottica portfolio: Anne Klein, Bulgari (1996), Chanel (1999) and Salvatore Ferragamo (1998). In 2003 other licensing agreements were signed for the brands Emporio Armani, Sergio Tacchini, Brooks Brothers, in 2004 for Versace and Prada, in 2005 for Donna Karan and Burberry, in 2006 for Dolce and Gabbana, in 2007 for Polo, Ralph Lauren, in 2008 for Tiffany and in 2009 for Stella McCartney and Tory Burch.

In 2007 Luxottica carried out another important M&A: the acquisition of California-based Oakley, a leading sport and performance glasses brand. To acquire this firm, Luxottica paid $2.1 billion. The stock of resources and strategic assets was extraordinary: Oakley, a brand known and appreciated worldwide, owned the Oliver Peoples brand and had a licence to manufacture and distribute the Paul Smith brand; furthermore it owned a retail network of over 160 direct stores.

In 2012 Luxottica acquired *Tecnol*, so entering the Brazilian market. Tecnol, with its manufacturing facility in Campinas produces both plastic and metal frames for the Brazilian market.

In 2013 Luxottica acquired Alain Mikli Int., a French luxury and contemporary eyewear company, owner of the Alain Mikli brand and the Starck Eyes licence. As a result of the acquisition, Luxottica strengthened both its luxury brand portfolio and prescription offering.

The Luxottica strategy in the sunglasses business has clearly been successful; the increase in sales has been relevant and since 2002 sunglasses have become the most important business (Table 13.1).

Table 13.1 The evolution of Luxottica businesses from 1990 to 2014

Sales in units by use (%)	1990	1994	1998	2002	2009	2014
Sunglasses	10	24	35	59	64	65
Prescription glasses	90	76	65	41	36	35
Total	100	100	100	100	100	100

Source: Our elaboration of Luxottica *Annual Reports*.

Table 13.2 shows, in chronological order, the main acquisitions made by Luxottica for penetrating the medium–high segments of the sunglasses business.

Table 13.2 Important Luxottica acquisitions in the sunglasses business

Year of acquisition	Company acquired	Brands
1990	Florence Line	Vogue
1995	Persol	Persol
1999	Bausch & Lomb	Ray-Ban, Arnette, Rēvo, Killer L.
2007	Oakley	Oakley, Oliver People, Paul Smith
2013	Alain Mikli	Alain Mikli, Starck Eyes

Source: Our elaboration of Luxottica *Annual Reports*.

In the last years Luxottica has further extended its brand portfolio, currently owning 28 brands of which eight are house brands and 20 licensed brands. The long-term objectives have remained the same: focusing on leading brands, balancing house and licensed brands and avoiding brand dilution. Therefore, the Luxottica portfolio is a continuous evolution, through the acquisition of new brands, the stipulation of new licensing agreements and the renewal of existing ones and the withdrawal of brands no longer deemed strategic.

Today, Luxottica's brand portfolio is formed with major global brands backed by leading brands at a regional level and in particular segments and niche markets. It is balanced between house and licensed brands, combining the stability and volumes of the former with the prestige and high margins of the latter. Consider that in 2002 designer lines represented only 39.5% of total sales, with respect to 60.5% of house brands. Through house brands Luxottica develops approximately 500 distinct styles, of which 300 are in optical and 200 are in sunglasses. Each style is typically produced in two sizes and five colours. The different house brands are positioned to cover different market segments on the basis of characteristics of each brand. In particular, the presence of Ray-Ban, one of the world's best-selling brands of sun and prescription eyewear, and Oakley, a leader in the sport and performance category, gives the portfolio a strong base on the medium–high market segment, complemented by Persol and Oliver Peoples in the high-end of the market, the Arnette and REVO brands in the sports market, and Vogue in the fashion market.

Alongside the house brands, the Luxottica portfolio today has 20 license brands, including some well-known and prestigious names in the global fashion and luxury industries. With its manufacturing know-how, capillary distribution and direct retail operations, supported by targeted advertising and experience in international markets, Luxottica is the ideal partner for fashion houses and stylists seeking to translate their style and values into successful premium quality eyewear collections. Luxottica differentiates each designer's offering as much as possible, to produce a broad range of models capable of satisfying the most diverse tastes and tendencies and of responding to the demands and characteristics of widely differing customers. Table 13.3 shows the most important licensed brands of major fashion houses. Designer lines are produced and distributed through licensing agreements. The operating profile of the licensing agreements is characterized by a ten-year average duration and the payment to the fashion houses and stylists of a royalty of 8–11% on net sales and the sustaining of advertising costs of about 5% on sales. Designer collections are developed through the collaborative efforts of Luxottica's in-house design staff and brand designers.

Since the 1970s Luxottica has also developed a horizontal expansion entering foreign markets through M&As, the opening of commercial branches and agreements or joint ventures with local partners, often wholesalers. Luxottica expanded in Germany, Spain, the UK, France and Sweden, while still continuing to grow in North America.

Table 13.3 Luxottica house and licensed brands in 2014

Type of brand	Brands
House brands	Luxottica, Sferoflex, Persol, REVO, Vogue, Olivier People, Ray-Ban, K&L, Mosley Tribes, Eye Safety Systems, Oakley, Alain Mikli, Arnette.
Licensed brands	Brooks Brothers, Paul Smith, Bvlgari, Chanel, Anne Klein, Prada, Burberry, Dolce & Gabbana, D&G, Donna Karan, DKNY, Fox, Miu Miu, Chaps, Ralph Lauren, Ralph, Salvatore Ferragamo, Stella McCartney, Tiffany & Co., Club Monaco, Polo, Ralph Lauren Purple Label, Tory Burch, Versace, Versus, Giorgio Armani, Coach.

Source: Our elaboration of Luxottica *Annual Report 2014*.

The breakdown of sales by geographical areas, shown in Table 13.4, demonstrates the success of the international expansion strategy.

Table 13.4 Luxottica net sales by geographical area in 2005, 2009
and 2014

Sales (€mill)	2005	%	2009	%	2014	%
North America	3,060	70	3,056	60	4,285	56
Rest of the World	874	20	1,379	27	2,372	[1] 31
Asia, Pacific	437	10	662	13	995	13
Total	4,371	100	5,094	100	7,652	100

Note (1) Rest of the World 31%, of which: Europe 20%; Latin America 7% and Rest of World 4%.

Source: Our elaboration of Luxottica *Annual Report*.

Horizontal expansion allowed Luxottica to exploit the opportunities emerging in different market segments and in different geographical markets, diversifying risks and activating learning processes at an international level, transferring technical solutions, products and marketing knowledge and value from one country to another. This allowed Luxottica to become a cost leader in the industry by exploiting economies of scale in production (through a higher specialization and a larger plant size) and in marketing activities and by exploiting learning economies through a larger cumulative production of components, parts and products. It has also allowed Luxottica to exploit economies of scope in production, marketing and distribution.

Vertical integration in wholesale and retail distribution and M&A strategies

International expansion in wholesale distribution began in the 1980s with the acquisition of independent distributors, the opening of branches and the forming of joint ventures in key international markets. Having started with the opening of the first commercial subsidiary in Germany in 1981, the company's international wholesale development continued with the acquisition of Avant-Garde Optics Inc., a wholesale distributor in the US market, in the mid-1980s.

After having used the consolidated wholesale channel in the beginning, like all companies in the eyewear industry, Luxottica decided to use a direct selling channel for both a stronger control of distribution and a direct relationship with customers. This strategy has represented another constant line in the development of Luxottica until recent years. In this way Luxottica gradually entered the rich retail glasses business that is characterized by higher markup and profit margins, especially in the luxury sunglasses segment.

The vertical integration of retail activities was mainly obtained through some important acquisitions. The first acquisition was Avant-Garde Optics Inc. (1982), one of the largest commercial companies in the world operating in the optical industry and based in Long Island (New York). The strategy was reinforced in 1995 by the acquisition of US Shoe and, within this group, of LensCrafters, the largest retail optical chain operating in the US market with 600 stores. The American market was the most important market for Luxottica, where the company already exported 39% of its production, and it presented great opportunities for growth. The acquisition of LensCrafters allowed Luxottica to exploit important synergies in product distribution, due to the commercial and marketing strength of the American chain stores and increasing penetration of its products through LensCrafters stores.

In 2001 the Luxottica Group further enforced its leadership with the acquisition of Sunglass Hut International, the largest world retail chain for sunglasses. Sunglass Hut focused on a high segment of the sunglasses market in North America and in Europe and was a leader in retail distribution with 1,962 stores, distributed throughout the USA, Australia, New Zealand and Singapore. The acquisition permitted Luxottica to have a preeminent position on the entire market of glasses distribution in North America, unifying the distribution chain leader in prescription glasses (LensCrafters) with the largest sunglasses distribution chain.

Making leverage on the successful brands in its portfolio, such as Ray-Ban, Rēvo, Persol, Killer Loop, Vogue, Arnette and Sunglass Hut, Luxottica largely increased sales in its retailing stores, thus obtaining considerable synergies in costs and revenues.

Moreover, in 2003 Luxottica acquired the retail chain OPSM, operating in Australia, New Zealand, Hong Kong, Singapore and Malaysia, reaching an important market share in this area. OPSM Group was the leader in the retail market in Australia (with 481 stores and three brands), New Zealand (34 stores) and south-east Pacific, in particular Hong Kong with 80 stores and Singapore and Malaysia with 12 each. OPSM Group had three chains: OPSM, Laubman & Pank and Budget Eyewear, each of them operating in a well defined market segment. This acquisition allowed Luxottica to reinforce its presence in a market area that was not yet covered. The strategy of segmentation and rationalization of OPSM Group brands made the original brands well distinguished: Laubman & Pank for sight care; OPSM for fashion demand; Budget Eyewear for more price sensitive customers.

Soon after, at the beginning of 2004 Luxottica bought the American Cole National, with its chain of 2,100 shops with brands Pearle Vision, Sears Optical, Target Optical and BJ's Optical. Cole National was the second player in the US market, owner of the historical brands Pearle Vision and of a large net of stores as well as of an optical department managed by licensed brands such as Sears Optical, Target Optical and BJ's Optical.

Among these brands the most important was Pearle Vision, present in the US market for more than 40 years with stores specializing in eyesight care and glasses of high quality, elegance and proverbial refinement. At the end of 2004, 1,300 stores were located in diversified department stores such as Sears, Target and BJ's Wholesale Club, each of them with a specific position on the retail market.

In addition to the retail chain, the acquisition of Cole National gave Luxottica the property of seven central laboratories which, together with those of LensCrafters, make Luxottica one of the largest networks in the USA. Finally, the integration of Cole National Managed Vision Care in EyeMed Vision Care, made Luxottica the second manager of agreements concerning companies, public administration and insurance companies.

In 2007, Luxottica acquired the California-based Oakley, a leading sport and performance brand. Oakley, a brand which is known and appreciated worldwide, owned a retail network of over 160 stores.

In 2011 Luxottica started its optical retail expansion in Latin America by completing the acquisition of Multioticas International, a leading reatailer in Chile, Peru, Ecuador and Columbia. Moreover, in 2011 it completed the acquisition of GMO (started in 2009), a leading retailer in Chile, Peru, Equador and Columbia.

Table 13.5 lists in chronological order the main acquisitions of distribution chains by Luxottica.

The entry through M&As into the retail business has been a winning strategy for Luxottica, as the dynamics of sales confirms (Table 13.6). It allowed the company to stay in touch with its end users and understand their tastes and tendencies, directly communicating design and quality and avoiding the price competition of wholesalers. Direct distribution is also perceived as a strength by the stylists and fashion houses, because it allows Luxottica to have access to global and widespread markets and maximize the image and visibility of brands.

Table 13.5 Luxottica vertical integration strategy in retail distribution: the main acquisitions

Year	Company	Distribution retail chains
1982	Avant Garde Optics	
1995	US Shoe	LensCrafters
2001	Sunglass Hut International	Sunglass Hut
2003	OPSM Group	Laubman & Pank, OPSM, Budget Eyewear
2004	Cole National	Pearle Vision, Sears Optical, Target Optical*, BJ's Optical*
2007	Oakley	Oakley "O" and Vault, Oliver Peoples
2011	Multiopticas International	Multiopticas
2011	GMO	GMO

Note: * Licensed brands.

Source: Our elaboration of Luxottica *Annual Reports*.

Furthermore, the group's experience in the direct operation of stores in some of its more important countries gives it a unique understanding of the world's eyewear markets. All this makes it possible, among other things, to achieve tight control and strategic optimization of brand diffusion, both house and licensed brands. As of 31 December 2014, Luxottica's retail business consisted of 6,471 stores, 613 of which were in franchising. The extraordinary evolution of the number of direct stores from 2,000 to 2,014 is shown in Table 13.7.

Also in the retail distribution business Luxottica developed a horizontal strategy to reach different demand segments, also offering customers a variety of differentiated sales points, including the latest in designer and high-performance sun frames, advanced lens options, advanced eye care, everyday value and high-quality vision care health benefits.

Table 13.6 Dynamics of net sales by distribution channel

Sales (€million)	1995	%	2000	%	2009	%	2014	%
Retail	869	77	1,352	61	3,158	62	4438	58
Wholesale	266	23	873	39	1,936	38	3214	42
Total	1,135	100	2,225	100	5,094	100	7652	100

Source: Our elaboration on Luxottica *Annual Reports.*

In particular, with regard to optical retail, Luxottica's operations are anchored by leading brands such as LensCrafters and Pearle Vision in North America, and OPSM, Laubman & Pank and Budget Eyewear, which are active throughout Australia and New Zealand. The group also has a major retail presence in China, where it operates in the premium eyewear market with LensCrafters. LensCrafters stores offer a wide selection of prescription frames and sunglasses, mostly made by Luxottica, but also a wide range of lenses and optical products made by other suppliers. Points of sale are normally in high-traffic commercial malls and shopping centres and have an on-site optometrist (sometimes a Luxottica employee), so that customers can have immediate eye examinations. Most LensCrafters stores in North America also include a lens finishing laboratory, which improves the customer service level.

Pearle Vision stores focus on the factors that made the brand a success: customers' trust in the doctor's experience and the quality of service they receive. Pearle Vision stores are mostly located in strip malls instead of the conventional malls where most LensCrafters and Sunglass Hut stores are located. OPSM, the largest of the three optical chains Luxottica operates in Australia and in New Zealand, is a leading eyewear retail brand for luxury and fashion-conscious customers. Laubman & Pank is well known for its high quality assortment and services. Its target segment is for the optical shopper looking for quality eye-care and services.

Differently, Budget Eyewear focuses on the price-conscious shopper and offers an easy selection process for frames and lens packages in a bright and modern store environment.

Table 13.7 Evolution of number of stores from 2000 to 2014

Business areas and brands	2014	2009	2004	2000
North America	4,618	4,723	4,642	864
EU	437	159	110	0
Central and South America	714	10	0	0
Africa and India	46	34	0	0
South Africa	131	80	0	0
Asia Pacific	831	963	683	0
China	274	248	74	0
Atelier	33	10	0	0
Total	7,084	6,217	5,509	864

Source: Our elaboration on Luxottica *Annual Report 2014.*

Finally, Luxottica also operates through a network of retail locations under the brand names of their respective host American department stores. These "licensed brands" are Sears Optical and Target Optical. These points of sale offer consumers the convenience of taking care of their optical needs while shopping at these department stores. Both brands have a precise market positioning that Luxottica has reinforced by improving service levels while strengthening their fashion reputation offering brands such as Ray-Ban and Vogue. As of December 31, 2014 Luxottica operates 638 Sears Optical and 346 Target Optical locations throughout North America.

With regard to the sunglass retail business, Luxottica operates through leading retailer brands such as Sunglass Hut, ILORI, The Optical Shop of Aspen, Bright Eyes and Oakley, each of them specialized in different retail segments. For example, Sunglass Hut has focused increasingly on selling premium sunglasses. In 2007 Luxottica developed an exclusive new store concept, which is now being extended to all prime Sunglass Hut locations around the world. This repositioning was made possible by substantial changes to the product mix allowing the chain to focus more on fashion and luxury brands, especially for women, while maintaining a varied selection of lifestyle, sport and performance sunglasses.

ILORI addresses a different, more exclusive clientele than Sunglass Hut, offering a richer purchasing experience in prestige locations, featuring sophisticated luxury collections, exclusive niche brands and a highly personalized service. The Optical Shop of Aspen is known in the optical industry for its luxury brands for both prescription glasses and sunglasses and its first class customer service in some of the most upscale and exclusive locations throughout the United States.

Oliver Peoples operates in luxury retail stores only offering Oliver Peoples, Mosley Tribes and Paul Smith branded optical products.

David Clulow is a premium optical retailer operating in the United Kingdom and in Ireland, predominantly in London and the South East of the United Kingdom. With 50 years of experience, the brand emphasizes service, quality and fashion; its marketing is targeted to reinforcing these brand values and to building long-term relationships with customers. In addition to operating optical stores, David Clulow operates a number of sunglass concessions in upmarket department stores, further reinforcing its position as a premium brand in the United Kingdom. Bright Eyes, one of Australia's largest and fastest-growing sunglass chains, operated 55 corporate store locations and 84 franchise locations, mostly in tourist resorts and high-traffic areas. Oakley Stores and Vaults offer a full range of Oakley products including sunglasses, apparel, footwear and accessories in stores designed and merchandised to immerse consumers in the Oakley brand through innovative use of product presentation, graphics and original audio and visual elements. In the United States, Oakley "O" Stores can be found in major shopping centres.

To sum up, the vertical integration strategy, carried out through M&As, produced significant competitive advantages for Luxottica. They can be summarized as follows:

- a reduction in the bargaining power and opportunistic behaviour of clients (wholesalers and retailers);
- price control in different markets;
- direct information on market trends and stability in orders and delivery of products;
- guarantees in service levels and post selling services;
- a larger capability in differentiating products and brands;
- an increase of entry barriers to the industry.

ORGANIZATIONAL STRUCTURE FOR IMPLEMENTING M&As

Luxottica is quoted on the Milan stock exchange and New York stock exchange. The major shareholders are Delfin S.r.l. (Del Vecchio family) with 67.7% and Giorgio Armani with 4.9%.

Luxottica is an operating holding that controls more than 50 commercial subsidiaries worldwide. As of December 2014, Luxottica Group had 77,734 employees, with 61.2% dedicated to the retail business, 13.3% dedicated to the wholesale business and 24.9% dedicated to production and distribution activities (operations). Corporate central services, based in Milan, represent 0.6% of the total Group's workforce.

The organizational structure at the end of 2009 is shown in Figure 13.1. It is characterized by three organizational areas, reporting directly to the CEO:

1. central service functions,
2. operating processes departments and
3. business units.

The central service functions are the following:

- Information Technology,
- Business Development,
- Administration, Finance & Control,
- Communications,
- Investor Relations,
- Human Resources.

These form a system of services that support the CEO and the managers of divisional units. They also guarantee the framework of governance within which these managers are authorized to operate.

The operating processes departments are the following:

- Marketing, Style & Product;
- Operations Department;
- Quality Department.

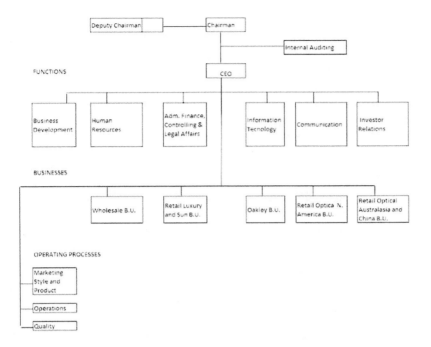

Figure 13.1 Luxottica's organizational structure at February 2010

The Marketing, Style & Product Department is responsible for marketing and developing collections. The department has teams in all the main markets to track new styles and trends. The Operations Department, based in Agordo (Italy), is responsible for planning, engineering and product manufacturing and distribution. The Quality Department, also based in Agordo, is responsible for quality and product quality control processes in all of the group's production sites.

This functional organizational structure is integrated by five divisions or "business units". They are the following:

- Wholesale;
- Retail, luxury and sun;
- Oakley;
- Retail Optical North America;
- Retail Optical Australasia and Greater China.

In effect, the so-called "business units" are not business units specializing in product lines, but organizational structures to manage some important sales channels and markets. The retail and wholesale divisions are responsible for establishing commercial presence on the world's markets and developing profitable businesses. They have local sales organizations in their various markets and use centralized structures for providing support services.

Luxottica substantially adopts a hybrid structure, with a functional organization for managing traditional activities of manufacturing companies and a divisional structure for managing retail activities. The maintaining of a functional base structure is due to limited differences in value chain activities of the two main lines of products: prescription glasses and sunglasses. The divisional structure is due to the large number of retail stores to manage worldwide and the different markets. This structure has allowed the company to benefit from advantages of M&As with the integration of production and marketing activities, as well as of support activities. At the same time, through the four retail business units, a balanced autonomy has been maintained, thereby benefitting from a larger capability in differentiating the product being offered in different markets. In 2009 Luxottica adopted a new performance valuation system which considers the company operating in two main businesses: a) manufacturing and wholesale distribution; b) retail distribution. For the manufacturing and wholesale distribution business, net sales include third-party customers only, while inter-company sales to the retail segment are not included. For the retail distribution business, net sales to the retail customers are included and the costs of acquired goods are estimated at manufacturing cost; therefore the sales of this segment include the so-called "manufacturing profit". The use of this methodology indicates the interest of the group in monitoring the performance of the manufacturing business unit and the retail distribution unit separately, perhaps preparing a future change in the organizational structure.

The Luxottica Group's governance system is based on a traditional management and control system with shareholders who vote in ordinary and extraordinary meetings and a board of directors. Amongst its members, it appoints an Internal Control Committee, which also assists the board in its internal control functions, and a Human Resources Committee, which provides consultation and recommendations on compensation for top management positions and incentive plans and the composition of management structures for the main subsidiaries. A board of statutory auditors is responsible for, among other things, overseeing compliance with the law and with the company by-laws, its principles of governance and organizational model. The board of auditors also acts as an audit committee under the Sarbanes-Oxley Act. The company's accounts are audited by a firm of accountants registered with Consob and appointed at the shareholders' meeting.

M&A STRATEGIES, GROWTH AND CREATION OF VALUE IN THE PERIOD 1994–2014

The analysis of economic and financial data allows us to evaluate the strong growth and value created by Luxottica through M&As from 1994 to 2014 (Table 13.8). In particular, the great growth achieved from 1994 to 1996 is due to the acquisition of Persol in 1995 and of US Shoe, whose optical division LensCrafters represented the largest premium optical retail brand in the US market. The period registered an extraordinary increase of sales from €419 to €1,225 million and an increase of 66% in net income. From 1996 to 1999, the growth of Luxottica continued constantly at an average annual rate of 16% both in net sales and industrial gross margin, while the operating income registered an increase of 9% and the net income of 14%. We observe that in 1999 Luxottica bought the optical division of Bausch & Lomb and with that the brand Ray-Ban. The success of this acquisition is proved by the outcomes obtained in 2000: an increase in sales of 30% in 2000, an increase in gross profit of 13%, in operating income of 73% and in net income of 68%. The growth of Luxottica continued in 2001 and 2002, due to the acquisition of Sunglass Hut, the world's leading premium specialty sun retailer. In 2003 Luxottica registered a contraction of sales due to three adverse conditions: the fall of the dollar, the adverse economic situation and the negative effect of the non-renewal of the Armani licence. In 2004 Luxottica returned to growth by the acquisition at the end of 2003 of OPSM, the leading optical store chain operator in Asia-Pacific. New brands compensated for the loss of the Armani licence: Donna Karan and Dolce & Gabbana. In 2004 Luxottica also acquired Cole National, the second-largest optical store chain operator in North America, with retail brands including Pearle Vision, Sears Optical and Target Optical. In 2005 Luxottica entered the Chinese optical retail market through the acquisition of two retail chains; the group became a leading player in China's premium optical market segment, with stores in Beijing, Guangdong and Hong Kong. In 2005 sales exceeded €4 billion with an increase of 34% with respect to the previous year and the net income increased by 19%, mainly due to the acquisition of Cole National. In 2006 the Group expanded its distribution in North America and China through acquisitions in Canada, the Midwest United States and Shanghai; it entered into an agreement to open Sunglass Hut stores in the Middle East.

Table 13.8. Main financial outcomes of Luxottica from 1994 to 2014

Years	Net sales	Total assets	Operating income	Net income	Shareholders equity	Earning x share (€) (1)
1994	419	n.a	118	64	n.a	0.14
1995	954	n.a	153	83	n.a	0.19
1996	1,225	n.a	179	106	n.a	0.24
1997	1,430	n.a	223	129	n.a	0.29
1998	1,538	n.a	226	133	n.a	0.30
1999	1,874	2,568	238	152	n.a	0.34
2000	2,439	2,968	412	255	n.a	0.57
2001	3,105	3,948	510	316	n.a	0.70
2002	3,201	3,586	601	372	n.a	0.82
2003	2,852	3,913	431	267	1,374	0.60
2004	3,180	4,456	479	286	1,495	0.64
2005	4,134	4,973	581	342	1,954	0.76
2006	4,676	4,969	756	424	2,216	0.95
2007	4,966	7,157	833	492	2,495	1.08
2008	5,202	7,305	732	390	2,554	0.83
2009	5,094	7,136	571	299	2,860	0.65
2010	5,798	7,999	712	402	3,269	0.88
2011	6,222	8,374	807	452	3,625	0.99
2012	7,086	8,442	982	542	3,933	1.22
2013	7,313	8,083	1,056	549	4,150	1.15
2014	7,652	9,594	1,158	646	4,929	1.35

Notes: Data from 1994 to 2001 have been converted from Italian lira to Euro (Lire 1,936.27 = €1.00); all data in US dollars have been converted at the average change of the reference period. (1) Attributable to Luxottica Group shareholders.

Source: Our elaboration on Luxottica, *Annual Reports 2000–2014* (Consolidated financial statements).

The acquisition of Oakley in 2007 provided the group with exceptional potential, due not only to the force and name recognition of the Oakley brand, but, in addition, to its portfolio of seven brands and four distribution chains. The effect of the M&A was remarkable: in 2008 sales exceeded €5 billion. The growth of the company was accompanied by a considerable increase in shareholders' equity and in earnings per share. In particular, operating income increased by €118 million in 1994 to €238 million in 1999 and to €833 million in 2007 (the last year before the recent great recession of 2008–2009); net income increased from €64 million in 1994 to €152 million in 1999 and to €492 million in 2007.

In 2008 and 2009 net income reduced to €390 and €299, and earning per share decreased to 0.83 and 0.65, due to the great recession,.

Finally, from 2010 to 2014 the acquisition of GMO allowed Luxottica to expand its distribution to Central and South America. The Group obtained in this period a total increase in sales equal to 32% and an increase in net income equal to 60.7%. In the same period the total invested capital increased from €7,999 million in 2010 to €9,594 million in 2014 (Fig. 13.2). The shareholder equity increased from €3,269 million to €4,929 million in the same period and the earnings per share increased from €0.88 in 2010 to €1.35 in 2014.

The extraordinary growth of the company and the strong creation of value obtained in this period is clear evidence of the success of the M&A strategies.

STRATEGIC ASSETS AND RESOURCES FOR SUCCESSFUL M&As

The main strategic assets and resources on which Luxottica has based its success in M&A strategies can be summarized as follows:

- distinctive competence in product manufacture and innovation;
- reputation for quality and reliability;
- firm reputation, general mangement skill and HR management expertise.

Luxottica has been capable of exploiting its strategic assets and resources, but, over all, it has been capable of accumulating new strategic assets and resources from its acquisitions; these enforced its original stock of resources and capabilities, making it possible to continue a virtuous process of improving and enlarging this franchise.

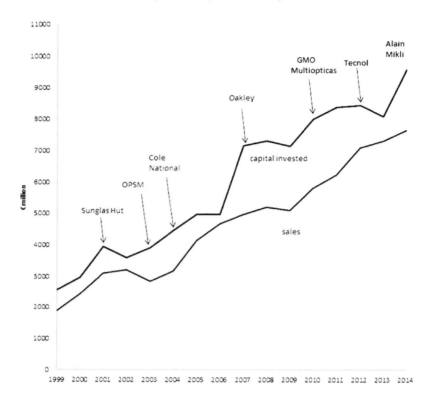

Source: Our elaboration of Luxottica *Annual Reports* data.

Figure 13.2 Luxottica acquisitions, invested capital and sales

In particular, Luxottica has made leverage on its distinctive know-how in glasses manufacturing, product quality and efficiency. It continuously invested in research and development activities related to its manufacturing processes. It owns factories with advanced technologies and new plants, and continues to improve efficiency and product quality. These resources have been transferred to the acquired firms operating in different countries.

For reducing product costs, all facilities have been specialized by product technology. Three main manufacturing technologies are involved: metal, acetate slabs and plastic (injection moulding). Plastic frames are made in the Agordo, Sedico, Pederobba and Lauriano plants, while metal frames are produced in Agordo, Rovereto and Cencenighe plants (all in North Italy). The Lauriano plant also makes crystal and polycarbonate lenses for sunglasses. The Dongguan plants, in China's Guangdong province, make both plastic and metal frames. In 2009, approximately 46% of the frames manufactured by Luxottica were metal-based, and the remaining were plastic. In 2014 only 32% of frames were in metal, 35% in plastic injection and 33% in acetate.

The vertical integration of production, that characterizes Luxottica, has represented a fundamental and critical factor in its success, because it enabled the firm to maintain leadership in costs, together with high quality products.

In short, the vertical integration strategy in manufacturing permitted Luxottica to obtain:

- economies in transaction costs;
- scope economies in joint production operations;
- scale economies in production, control, coordination and R&D activities.

This strategy also allowed Luxottica to raise barriers to enter the glasses industry and to obtain stronger bargaining power in respect to suppliers and clients, with remarkable effects on margins.

Distinctive capabilities on product innovation and continuous development of new styles have been the other strategic assets and resources of Luxottica. It is capable of adding, every year, approximately 2,300 new types to its eyewear collections. Each collection, each pair of glasses, is the result of an ongoing process of research and development, the aim of which is to anticipate and interpret the needs, desires and aspirations of consumers all over the world.

Furthermore, the "culture of quality" has been central to the whole organization, assuming a role of strategic resource. This culture of quality is the underlying principle applied in every process involved in creating eyewear and is the drive behind the continual improvement of products and processes. This characteristic feature also covers the entire organization: quality is applied to product development, procurement, the distribution network, analysis of processes and uniform and measurable performance management in the plants. To achieve this Luxottica continually improves quality in every phase of the production process (and also distribution). That has been the reason for undertaking the full vertical integration of every production phase. Most of the manufacturing equipment used is specially designed and adapted for the manufacturing processes; this helps the company to respond more quickly to customer demand and to adhere to strict quality-control standards.

The achievement of high standards of quality reflects the group's strong technical and manufacturing know-how, the result of 50 years of experience, and its constant commitment to technological innovation, style and design, the study of changing lifestyles and interpretation of fashion trends.

Quality and customer satisfaction also characterize the wholesale and retail distribution networks. Furthermore these structures are organized to offer a high quality after-sales service that is consistent but not standardized, being specially tailored to specific local needs. This explains why in two decades Luxottica has reached world leadership in the high and luxury segments of the eyewear business.

The company now presents a solid competitive advantage over competitors and a sustainable value principally based on:

- a wide and balanced portfolio of brands;
- high quality, flexibility and productivity of the production and distribution processes;
- a very large wholesale and retail distribution network, capable of efficiently serving the world market;
- a high level of customer service.

This is the result of a combination of successful growth strategies: closely related diversification, horizontal expansion and vertical integration strategies both in manufacturing and in retailing. These have been constantly pursued in the last 20 years through both internal development and acquisitions. In particular, the strategy of acquisitions not only allowed the Group to exploit its strategic assets and resources, but it provided the Group with exceptional potential due to new brands, distribution chains and human resources.

References

Abell D.F. (1993), *Managing with Dual Strategies. Mastering the Present, Preempting the Future*, New York: The Free Press.

Abell D.F. and J.S. Hammond (1979), *Strategic Market Planning*, Englewood Cliffs, NJ: Prentice Hall.

Adler P.S. and K.B. Clark (1991), "Behind the Learning Curve: A Sketch of the Learning Process", *Management Science*, vol. 37, n. 3, March, pp. 267-280.

Agrawal A. and J. Jaffe (2000), "The Post Merger Performance Puzzle", *Advance in Mergers and Acquisitions*, vol. 1, n. 4, pp. 119-156.

Agrawal A., J. Jaffe and G. Mandelker (1992), "The Post Merger Performance of Acquiring Firms: A Re-examination of an Anomaly", *The Journal of Finance*, vol. 47, n. 4, pp. 1605-1621.

Ahuja G. and R. Katila (2001), "Technological Acquisitions and the Innovation Performance of Acquiring Firms: a Longitudinal Study", *Strategic Management Journal*, vol. 22, n. 3, pp. 197-220.

Alchian A. (1963), "Reliability of Progress Curves in Airframe Production", *Econometrica*, vol. 31, pp. 679-693.

Ambrosini V., C. Bowman and N. Collier (2009), "Dynamic Capabilities: An Exploration of How Firm Renew their Resource Base", *British Journal of Management*, vol. 20, pp. 9-24.

Amram M. and N. Kulatilaka (1999), *Real Option*, Boston: Harvard Business School Press.

Andrade G., M. Mitchell and E. Stafford, (2001), "New Evidence and Perspective in Mergers", *Journal of Economic Perspectives*, vol. 15, n. 2, Spring, pp. 103-120.

Ansoff H.I. (1968), *Corporate Strategy: An Analytical Approach to Business Policy for Growth and Expansion*, New York: McGraw-Hill.

Ansoff H.I. (1988), *New Corporate Strategy*, New York: J. Wiley.

Appelbaum S.H., J. Gande, B.T. Shapiro, P. Belisle and E. Hoeven (2000), "Anatomy of a Merger: Behavior of Organizational Factors and Processes throughout the Pre-During-Post-Stage" (part 1), *Management Decision*, vol. 38, n. 10, pp. 674-684.

Appelbaum S.H., J. Robert and B.T. Shapiro (2009), "Cultural Strategies in M&As: Investigating Ten Case Studies", *Journal of Executive Education*, vol. 8, n. 1, pp. 33-35.

Arrow K.J. (1974), *The Limit of Organization*, New York: Norton.

Asquith P. (1983), "Merger Bids, Uncertainty, and Stockholder Returns", *Journal of Financial Economics*, vol. 11, n. 1, pp. 51-83.

Baden Fuller C. (1983), "The Implications of the Learning Curve from Strategy and Public Policy", *Applied Economics*, vol. 15, pp. 541-551.

Baden Fuller C. and J. Stopford (1992), *Rejuvenating the Mature Business*, London: Routledge.

Bain J. (1956), *Barriers to New Competition*, Cambridge, MA: Harvard University Press.

Baldwin J. (1995), *The Dynamics of the Competitive Process*, Cambridge: Cambridge University Press.

Baloff N. (1971), "Extension of the Learning Curve: Some Empirical Results", *Operational Research Quarterly*, vol. 22, n. 4, pp. 329-340.

Banal-Estañol A. and J. Seldeslachts (2011), "Merger failures", *Journal of Economics & Management Strategy*, vol. 20, n. 2, pp. 589-624.

Barney J.B. (1988), "Return to Bidding Firms in Mergers and Acquisitions. Reconsidering the Relatedness Hypothesis", *Strategic Management Journal*, vol. 9, pp. 71-78.

Barney J.B. (1991), "Firm Resources and Sustained Competitive Advantage", *Journal of Management*, vol. 17, pp. 99-120.

Barney J.B. (1996), *Gaining and Sustaining Competitive Advantage*, Upper Saddle River: Pearson/Prentice Hall.

Barney J.B. (2001), "Is the Resource-Based View a Useful Perspective for Strategic Management Research? Yes", *Academy of Management Review*, vol. 26, n. 1, pp. 41-56.

Bekier M.A., A.J. Bogardus and T. Oldham (2001), "Why Mergers Fail", *The McKinsey Quarterly*, n. 4, pp. 6-9.

Bellandi M. (1995), *Economie di Scala e Organizzazione industriale*, Milano: Franco Angeli.

Berger P.G. and E. Ofek (1995), "Diversification's Effect on Firm Value", *Journal of Financial Economics*, vol. 37, pp. 39-65.

Berry C.H. (1975), *Corporate Growth and Diversification*, Princeton, NJ: Princeton University Press.

Besanko D., D. Dranove and M. Shanley (1996), *Economics of Strategy*, New York: Wiley.

Blasko M., J.N. Netter and J.F. Sinkey (2000), "Value Creation and Challenges of an International Transaction. The DaimlerChrysler merger", *International Review of Financial Analysis*, vol. 9, n. 1, pp. 77-102.

Bohn R.E. (1995), "Noise and Learning in Semiconductor Manufacturing", *Management Science*, vol. 41, n. 1, pp. 31-42.

Boston Consulting Group (1972), *Perspective on Experience*, BCG.

Bower J.L. (2001), "Not All M&As Are Alike and That Matters", *Harvard Business Review*, vol. 79, n. 3, pp. 92-101.

Bradley M., A. Desai and E.H. Kim (1988), "Synergistic Gain from Corporate Acquisitions and their Division between the Stockholders of Target and Acquiring Firms", *Journal of Financial Economics*, vol. 21, pp. 3-40.

Bragado J.F. (1992), "Setting the Correct Speed for Postmerger Integration", *M&A Europe*, vol. 5, pp. 24-31.

Brealey R.A. and S.C. Myers (1996), *Principles of Corporate Finance*, New York: McGraw-Hill.

Bruner R. (2004), *Applied Mergers and Acquisitions*, Hoboken: John Wiley and Sons.

Campari (2000–2014), *Annual Report*.

Campbell A. and K. Sommers Luchs (eds) (1998), *Strategic Synergy*, London: International Thomson Business Press.

Capron L. and N. Pistre (2002), "When do Acquirers Earn Abnormal Returns?", *Strategic Management Journal*, vol. 23, pp. 781-794.

Capron L. and J.C. Shen (2007), "Acquisitions of Private vs. Public Firms: Private Information, Target Selection, and Acquirer Returns", *Strategic Management Journal*, vol. 28, pp. 891-911.

Capron L., W. Mitchell and A. Swaminathan (2001), *Strategic Management Journal*, vol. 22, pp. 817-844.

Carow K., R. Heron and T. Saxton (2004), "Do Early Birds Get the Returns? An Empirical Investigation of Early-Mover Advantages in Acquisitions", *Strategic Management Journal*, vol. 25, n. 6, pp. 563-585.

Carr R., G. Elton, S. Rovit and T. Vestring (2005), "Merging on the Miraculous: Mastering Merger Integration", *Business Strategy Review*, vol. 16, n. 2, pp. 25-29.

Cartwright S. and C.L. Cooper (1992), *Mergers and Acquisitions: the Human Factor*, Oxford: Butterworth Heinemann.

Cartwright S. and C. Cary (1995), *Managing Mergers, Acquisitions and Strategic Alliances*, Oxford: Butterworth-Heinemann.

Cartwright S. (1998), "International merger and acquisitions: the issues and challenges". In M.C. Gersten, A.M. Sodemberg and J.E. Torpo (eds), *Cultural Dimension of International Merger and Acquisitions*, New York: Walter de Gruiter.

Cartwright S. and S. McCarthy (2005), "Developing a framework for cultural due diligence in merger and acquisition: issues and ideas". In G.K. Stahl and M.E. Mendenhall (eds), *Mergers and Acquisitions*, Stanford, CA: Stanford University Press. pp. 253-267.

Cartwright S. and R. Schoenberg (2006), "Thirty Years of Mergers and Acquisitions Research: Recent Advances and Future Opportunities", *British Journal of Management*, vol. 17, n.1, pp. S1-S5.

Ceccanti G. (1996), *Corso di Tecnica imprenditoriale*, Padova: Cedam.

Chakrabarti A., J. Hauschildt and C. Suverkrup (1994), "Does it Pay to Acquire Technological Firms?", *R&D Management*, vol. 24, n. 2, pp. 47-56.

Chandler A.D. (1962), *Strategy and Structure. Chapters in the History of the American Industrial Enterprise*, Cambridge, MA: The MIT Press.

Chandler A.D. (1977), *The Visible Hand: The Managerial Revolution in American Business*, Cambridge, MA: Harvard University Press.

Chandler A.D. (1990), *Scale and Scope. The Dynamics of Industrial Capitalism*, Cambridge, MA: Harvard University Press.

Chatterjee S. (1986), "Types of Synergy and Economic Value: The Impact of Acquisition on Merging and Rival Firms", *Strategic Management Journal*, vol. 7, n. 5, pp. 119-139.

Chatterjee S. (2007), "Why is synergy so difficult in merger of related business", *Strategy and Leadership*, vol. 35, n. 2, pp. 46-52.

Chatterjee S., M. Lubatkin, D.M. Schweiger and Y. Weber (1992), "Cultural Differences and Shareholders Value in Related Merger: Linking Equity and Human Capital", *Strategic Management Journal*, vol. 13, n. 5, pp. 319-334.

Christensen H.K. and C.A. Montgomery (1981), "Corporate Economic Performance: Diversification Strategy versus Market Structure", *Strategic Management Journal*, vol. 2, pp. 327-343.

Collis D.J. and C.A. Montgomery (2005), *Corporate Strategy. Resources and Scope of the Firm*, New York: McGraw-Hill (2nd ed.).

Conn R., A. Cosh, P. Guest and A. Hughes (2005), "The Impact on UK Acquirers of Domestic, Cross-border, Public and Private Acquisition", *Journal of Business Finance & Accounting*, vol. 32, n. 5-6, pp. 815-870.

Copeland T. and J.F. Weston (1988), *Financial Theory and Corporate Policy*, New York: Addison Wesley.

Copeland T., T. Koller and J. Murrin (1995), *Valuation. Measuring and Managing the Value of Companies,* New York: Wiley.

Cosh A., A. Hughes and A. Singh, (1980), "The causes and effects of takeovers in the United Kingdom: an empirical investigation for the late 1960s at the microeconomic level". In D.C. Mueller, *The Determinants and Effects of Mergers: An International Comparison*, Cambridge and Oelgeschlager: Gunn & Hain, pp. 227-270.

Cosh, A. and P. Guest (2001), *The Long-run Performance of Hostile Takeovers: UK Evidence*, ESRC Centre for Business Research Working Paper No. 215, Centre for Business Research, University of Cambridge.

Daft R.L. (2001), *Organization Theory and Design*, London: South-Western College Publishing.

Damodaran A. (1994), *Damodaran on Valuation*, New York: J. Wiley & Sons.

Damodaran, A. (2005), "The Value of Control", *Working Paper*, www.damodaran.com.

Damodaran A. (2006), *Damodaran on Valuation: Security Analysis for Investment and Corporate Finance*, 2nd edition, New York: Wiley Finance.

Datta D.K. and J.H. Grant (1990), "Relationships Between Type of Acquisitions, the Authonomy Given to Acquired Firms and the Acquisition Success. An Empirical Analysis", *Journal of Management*, vol. 16, pp. 29-44.

Datta D.K. (1991), "Organizational Fit and Acquisition Performance: Effects of Post Acquisition Integration", *Strategic Management Journal*, vol. 12 n. 4, pp. 281-297.

Datta D.K. and G. Puia (1995) "Cross-Border Acquisitions: An Examination of the Influence of Relatedness and Cultural Fit on Shareholder Value Creation in U.S. Acquiring Firms", *Management International Review*, vol. 35, n. 4, pp. 337-359.

Day G.S. (1990), *Market Driven Strategy. Processes for Creating Value*, New York: The Free Press.

Dealogic, *World Merger Deals*, 2013.

Diageo (2014), *Annual Report*.

Dierickx I. and K. Cool (1989), "Asset Stock Accumulation and Sustainability of Competitive Advantage", *Management Science*, vol. 35, n. 12, December, pp. 1504-1514.

Dixit A.K. (1995), "The Option Approach to Capital Investment", Boston: *Harvard Business Review*, May–June, pp. 105-115.

Dixit A.K. and R.S. Pyndick (1994), *Investment Under Uncertainty*, Princeton, NJ: Princeton University Press.

Dringoli A. (1995), *Struttura e Sviluppo dell'Impresa Industriale*, Milano: McGraw-Hill.

Dringoli A. (2000), *Economia e Gestione delle Imprese. Modelli e Tecniche per la Gestione*, Padova: Cedam.

Dringoli A. (2006), *La Gestione dell'Impresa*, Padova: Cedam.

Dringoli A. (2009), *Creating Value through Innovation*, Cheltenham, UK and Northampton, MA, USA: Edward Elgar.

Dringoli A. (2011), *Corporate Strategy and Firm's Growth*, Cheltenham, UK and Northampton, MA, USA: Edward Elgar.

Dunning J.H. (1981), *International Production and the Multinational Enterprise*, London: Allen & Unwin.

Dunning J.H. (2001), "The Eclectic (OLI) Paradigm of International Production", *Economics of Business: Past, Present and Future*, vol. 8, n. 2, pp. 173-190.

Easterby-Smith M., M.A. Lyles and M.A. Peteraf (2009), "Dynamic Capabilities: Current Debates and Future Directions", *British Journal of Management*, vol. 20, pp. 1-8.

Edwards J., I. Kay and C. Meyer (1987), *The Economic Analysis of Accounting Profitability*, Oxford: Oxford University Press.

Eisenhardt K.M. and J.A. Martin (2000), "Dynamic Capabilities: What are They?", *Strategic Management Journal*, vol. 21, pp. 1105-1121.

Fama E.F. (1968), "Risk, Return and Equilibrium: Some Clarifying Comments", *Journal of Finance*, vol. 23, pp. 29-40.

Finkelstein S. (2002), *The DaimlerChrysler Merger*, Tuck School of Business at Dartmouth, working paper n. 1-0071.

Forrester J.W. (1961), *Industrial Dynamics*, Cambridge, MA: The MIT Press.

Franks J.R., R.S. Harris and S. Titman (1991), "The Post-Merger Share Price Performance of Acquiring Firms", *Journal of Financial Economics*, 29 March, pp. 81-96.

Galbraith J.R. (1977), *Organizational Design*, Reading, MA: Addison-Wesley.

Gary M.S. (2005), "Implementation Strategy and Performance Outcomes in Related Diversification", *Strategic Management Journal*, vol. 26, n. 4, July, pp. 643-664.

Gerloff E.A. (1985), *Organizational Theory and Design*, New York: McGraw-Hill.

Gertsen M.C., A.M. Soderberg and E.T. Jens (1998), *Cultural Dimensions of International Merger Acquisition*, Berlin: De Gruyter.

Ghemawat P. (1985), "Building Strategy on the Experience Curve", *Harvard Business Review*, March–April, pp. 143-149.

Ghemawat P. (1991), *Commitment. The Dynamic of Strategy*, New York: The Free Press.

Gomes E., D.N. Amgwin, Y. Weber and S.Y. Tarba (2013), "Critical Success Factors through the Mergers and Acquisitions Process: Revealing Pre- and Post-M&A Connections for Improved Performance", *Thunderbird International Business Review*, vol. 55, n. 1, pp. 14-34.

Gort M. (1962), *Diversification and Integration in American Industry*, Princeton, NJ: Princeton University Press.

Guillart F.J and J. Kelly (1995), *Transforming the Organization*, New York: McGraw-Hill.

Grant R.M. (1991), "The Resource-Based Theory of Competitive Advantage. Implications for Strategy Formulation", *California Management Review*, Spring, pp. 119-135.

Grant R.M. (1998), *Contemporary Strategy Analysis*, Malden, MA: Blackwell.

Grant R.M., A.P. Jammine and H. Thomas (1988), "Diversity, Diversification and Profitability among British Manufacturing Companies", *Academy of Management Journal*, vol. 31, n. 4, pp. 771-801.

Gregory A. (1997), "An Examination of the Long Run Performance of UK Acquiring Firms", *Journal of Business, Finance & Accounting*, vol. 24, n. 7-8, pp. 971-1002.

Grocer S. (2007), "A Holiday Toast Biggest Year in M&A History", *The Wall Street Journal*, 21 December.

Gruber H. (1992), "The Learning Curve in the Production of Semiconductor Memory Chips", *Applied Economics*, vol. 24, pp. 885-894.

Gugler K., D.C. Mueller, B.B. Yurtoglu and C. Zulehner (2003), "The Effects of Mergers: an International Comparison", *International Journal of Industrial Organization*, vol. 21, pp. 625–653.

Gunter K.S., G. Stahl and M.E. Mendenhall (2005), *Mergers and Acquisition: Managing Culture and Human Resources*, Stanford: Stanford University Press.

Habeck M.M., F. Köger and M.R. Träm (2000), *After the Merger*, London: Person Education, Financial Times Prentice Hall.

Hamel G. and A. Heene (1994), *Competence Based Competition*, New York: Wiley.

Hamel G. and C.K. Prahalad (1994), *Competing for the Future*, Boston: Harvard Business School Press.

Harding, D. and T. Rouse (2007), "Human Due Diligence", *Harvard Business Review*, vol. 85, n. 4, pp. 124-131.

Harrigan K.R. (1986), *Managing for Joint Venture Success*, Lexington: Lexington Books.

Harrison J.S., M.A. Hitt and R.D. Ireland (1991), "Synergies and post-acquisition performance: Difference versus similarities in resource allocation", *Journal of Management*, vol. 17, n. 1, pp. 173-190.

Haspeslagh P.C. and D.B. Jemison (1987), "Acquisition: Myth and Reality", *Sloan Management Review*, vol. 28, n. 2, pp. 53-58.

Haspeslagh P.C. and D.B. Jemison (1991), *Managing Acquisition: Creating Value Through Corporate Renewal*, New York: Simon & Schuster.

Hatch N.W. and D.C. Mowery (1998), "Process Innovation and Learning by Doing in Semiconductor Manufacturing", *Management Science*, vol. 44, n. 11, pp. 1461-1477.

Hatch N.W. and J.H. Dyer (2004), "Human Capital and Learning as a Source of Sustainable Competitive Advantage", *Strategic Management Journal*, vol. 25, pp. 1155-1178.

Hax A.C. and N.S. Majluf (1984), *Strategic Management*, Englewood Cliffs, NJ: Prentice Hall.

Hay D.A. and D.J. Morris (1979), *Industrial Economics. Theory and Evidence*, Oxford: Oxford University Press.

Hayward M. (2002), "When do firms learn from their acquisition experience? Evidence from 1990-1995", *Strategic Management Journal*, vol. 23, pp. 21-39.

Healey P.M., K.G. Palepu and R.S. Kuback (1992), "Does Corporate Performance Improve after Mergers?", *Journal of Financial Economics*, vol. 31, n. 1, pp. 135-175.

Helfat C.E. and K.M. Eisenhardt (2004), "Inter-Temporal Economies of Scope, Organizational Modularity, and the Dynamics of Diversification", *Strategic Management Journal*, vol. 25, pp. 1217-1232.

Helfat C.E. and M.A. Peteraf (2003), "The Dynamic Resource-Based View: Capability Lifecycles", *Strategic Management Journal*, vol. 24, pp. 997-1010.

Helfat C.E., S. Filkestein, W. Mitchell, M. Peterlaf, H. Singh, D. Teece and S. Winter (2007), *Dynamic Capabilities: Understanding Strategies Change in Organizations*. Oxford: Blackwell.

Hietala P., S.N. Kaplan and D.T. Robinson (2003), "What is the Price of Hubris? Using Takeover Battles to Infer Overpayments and Synergies", *AFA 2001 New Orleans Meetings*.

Hill C.W. and R.E. Hoskisson (1987), "Strategy and Structure in the Multiproduct Firm", *Academy of Management Review*, n. 12, pp. 331-341.

Hill C.W., M.A. Hitt and R.E. Hoskisson (1992), "Cooperative versus Competitive Structures in Related. and Unrelated Diversified Firms", *Organization Science*, vol. 3, n. 4, pp. 501-521.

Hitt M.A., J.S. Harrison, R.D. Ireland and A. Best (1998), "Attributes of Succesful and Unsuccessful Acquisition of U.S. Firms", *British Journal of Management*, vol. 9, n. 2, pp. 91-144.

Hitt M.A., R.D. Ireland and R.E. Hoskisson (1997), *Strategic Management*, St Paul, Minneapolis: West Publishing Company.

Hitt M.A., J.S. Harrison and R.D. Ireland (2001), *Merger and Acquisition. A Guide to Creating Value for Stakeholders*, New York: Oxford University Press.

Hofer C.W. and D. Schendel (1978), *Strategy Formulation: Analytical Concepts*, St Paul, Minneapolis: West Publishing Co.

Homburg C. and M. Bucerius (2006), "Is Speed of Integration Really a Success Factor of Mergers and Acquisitions? An Analysis of the Role of Internal and External Relatedness", *Strategic Management Journal*, vol. 27, pp. 347-367.

Hubbard N. (1999), *Acquisition Strategy and Implementation*, Basingstoke, UK: McMillan Business.

Hughes A. (1989) "The impact of merger: a survey of empirical evidence for the UK". In J. Fairburn and K. John (eds.), *Mergers and Merger Policy*, Oxford: Oxford University Press, pp. 30-98.

Hull J. (1997), *Options, Futures and Other Derivatives Securities*, Englewood Cliffs, NJ: Prentice Hall.

Hunt J.W. (1990), "Changing Pattern of Acquisition Behavior in Takeovers and the Consequences for Acquisition Processes", *Strategic Management Journal*, vol. 11, n. 1, pp. 69-77.

Ikeda, K. and N. Doi (1983), "The Performance of Merging Firms in Japanese Manufacturing Industry: 1964–75", *Journal of Industrial Economics*, vol. 31, pp. 257-266.

Impact Databank, Top 100 Premium Spirits, February 2015.

Inkpen A.C., A.K. Sundaram and K. Rockwood (2000), "Cross-Border Acquisitions of U.S. Technology Assets", *California Management Review*, vol. 42, pp. 50-71.

Jemison D.B., A. Pablo and S. Sitkin (1996), "Acquisition Decision-Making Process: the Centre Role of Risk", *Journal of Management*, vol. 22, n. 5, pp. 723-746.

Jensen M. (1988), "Takeovers: Their Causes and Consequences", *Journal of Economic Perspectives*, n. 2, pp. 21-48.

Jensen M.C. and W.H. Meckling (1976), "Theory of the Firm: Managerial Behavior, Agency Cost and Ownership Structure", *Journal of Financial Economics*, vol. 3, n. 4, Oct., pp. 305-360.

Jensen M.C. (1986), "Agency Costs of Free Cash Flow, Corporate Finance and Takeovers", *American Economic Review*, vol. 76, pp. 323-329.

Jensen M.C. and K.L. Murphy (1990), "Performance Pay and Top Management Incentives", *Journal of Political Economy*, vol. 98, pp. 225-264.

Johnson G. and K. Scholes (2002), *Exploring Corporate Strategy*, Harlow: Prentice-Hall, 6th edition.

Johnson P. (2006), Strategy and valuation. In D.O. Faulkner and A. Campbell (eds), *The Oxford Handbook of Strategy*, Oxford: Oxford University Press.

Johnson R.A., R.E. Hoskisson and M.A. Hitt (1993), "Board of Director Involvement in Restructuring: the Effects of Board versus Managerial Controls and Characteristics", *Strategic Management Journal*, vol. 14, pp. 33-50.

Kaplan and Weisbach (1992), "The success of Acquisitions: Evidence from disinvestures", *Journal of Finance*, vol. 47, n. 1, pp. 107-138.

Karim S. and W. Mitchell (2000), "Reconfiguring Business Resources Following Acquisitions in the US Medical Sector 1978–1995", *Strategic Management Journal*, vol. 21, n. 10–11, pp. 1062-1081.

Kind D.R., D.R. Dalton, C.M. Daily and J.G. Covin (2004), "Meta-Analyses of Post-Acquisition Performance: Indication of Unidentified Moderators", *Strategic Management Journal*, vol. 25, n. 2, pp. 187-200.

Kitching J. (1974) "Winning and Losing with European Acquisitions", *Harvard University Review*, n. 52, pp. 124-136.

Klein B., R.A. Crawford and A.A. Alchian (1978), "Vertical Integration, Appropriable Rents and the Competitive Contracting Process", *Journal of Law and Economics*, vol. 21, October, pp. 297-326.

Kogut B. and N. Kulatilaka (2006), "Strategy, heuristic and real option", *The Oxford Handbook of Strategy*, Oxford: Oxford University Press.

Koller T., M. Goedhart and D. Wessel (2010), *Valuation. Measuring and Managing the Value of Companies*, McKinsey & Company: Hoboken (NJ): J. Wiley & Sons.

Kumar S., C. Massie and M.D. Dumonceaux (2006), "Comparative Innovative Business Strategies of Major Players in the Cosmetics Industry", *Industrial Management & Data Systems*, vol. 106, n. 3, pp. 285-306.

Kummer C. and U. Steger (2008), "Why Merger and Acquisition Waves Reoccur: The Vicious Circle from Pressure to Failure", *Strategic Management Review*, vol. 2, n. 1, pp. 44-63.

L'Oreal (2000–2014), *Annual Report*.

L'Oreal International (2008), Home page, www.loreal.com.

L'Oreal Italia (2008), Home page, www.loreal.it.

Larsson R. and S. Finkelstein (1999), "Integrating Strategic, Organizational and Human Resource Perspectives on Merger and Acquisitions: a Case Survey of Synergy Realization", *Organization Science*, vol. 10, n. 1, pp. 1-26.

Leiblein L.M.J. and D.J. Miller (2003), "An Empirical Examination of Transaction and Firm-Level Influences on the Vertical Boundaries of the Firm", *Strategic Management Journal*, vol. 24, pp. 839-859.

Levy H. and M. Sarnat (1986), *Capital Investment and Financial Decisions*, Englewood Cliffs, NJ: Prentice Hall.

Lieberman M. (1984), "The Learning Curve and Pricing in the Chemical Processing Industries", *Rand Journal of Economics*, vol. 15, Summer, pp. 213–228.

Lins K. and H. Servaes (1999), "International Evidence on the Value of Corporate Diversification", *Journal of Finance*, vol. 54, pp. 2215-2239.

Lintner J. (1965), "The Valuation of Risk Assets and the Selection of Risky Investments in Stock Portfolios and Capital Budgets", *The Review of Economics and Statistics*, vol. 47, n. 1, pp. 13-37.

Lintner J. (1965), "Security Prices, Risk and Maximal Gains from Diversification", *Journal of Finance*, vol. XX, n. 4, pp. 587-615.

Lorenzoni G. (1990), *L'Architettura di Sviluppo delle Imprese Minori*, Bologna: Il Mulino.

Lorenzoni G. (ed.) (1992), *Accordi, Reti e Vantaggio Competitivo*, Milano: EtasLibri.

Lubatkin M. (1987), "Merger Strategies and Stockholder Value", *Strategic Management Journal*, vol. 8, pp. 39-53.

Luffman G.A. and R. Reed (1984), *The Strategy and Performance of British Industry 1970–1980*, London: MacMillan.

Luxottica (2000–2014), *Annual Report*.

Markides C.C. (1995) "Diversification, Restructuring and Economic Performance", *Strategic Management Journal*, vol. 16, pp. 101-118.

Markowitz J. (2003), "Daimler, Chrysler Merger a Failure", *Pittsburgh Tribune-Review*, 2 October.

Marks M.L. and P.H. Mirvis (2001), "Making Mergers and Acquisition Work: Strategic and Psicological Preparation", *Academy of Management Executive*, vol. 15, n. 2, pp. 80-94.

Marks M.L. and P.H. Mirvis (2012), "A research agenda to increase merger and acquisition success", in Y. Weber (ed.), *Handbook of Research on Mergers and Acquisitions*, Cheltenham, UK and Northampton, MA, USA: Edward Elgar.

Marris R. (1964), *The Economic Theory of Managerial Capitalism*, London: Macmillan.

Marris R. and A. Wood (eds) (1972), *The Corporate Economy. Growth, Competition and Innovative Potential*, London: Macmillan.

Martynova M. and L. Renneboog (2011), "The Performance of the European Market for Corporate Control: Evidence from the Fifth Takeover Waves", *European Financial Management*, vol. 17, n. 2, pp. 208-259.

McDonald J., M. Coulthard and P. De Lange (2006), "Planning for a Successful Merger or Acquisition: Lessons from an Australian Study", *Journal of Global Business and Technology*, vol. 1, n. 2, pp. 1-11.

McKinsey & Co. (1990), "Creating Shareholder Value through Merger and/or Acquisitions". A McKinsey & Company perspective. An internal 1987 memorandum cited in Copeland Koller T. and Murrin J., *Valuation: Measuring and Managing the Value of Companies*, New York: John Wiley & Sons.

Meek G. (1977), *Disappointing Marriage: A case Study of the Gains from Mergers*, Cambridge: Cambridge University Press.

Mellen C.M. and F.C. Evans (2010), *Valuation for M&A. Building Value in Private Companies*, Hoboken, NJ: J. Wiley & Sons.

Michel A. and I. Shaked (1984), "Does Business Diversification Affect Performance?", *Financial Management*, vol. 13, n. 4, pp. 18-24.

Milgrom P. and J. Roberts (1992), *Economics, Organization and Management*, Englewood Cliffs, NJ: Prentice Hall.

Miller D.J. (2004) "Firm's Technological Resources and the Performance Effects of Diversification: a Longitudinal Study", *Strategic Management Journal*, vol. 25, pp. 1097-1119.

Miller R. (2000), "How Culture Affects Mergers and Acquisitions", *Industrial Management*, vol, 42, n. 5, pp. 22-26.

Mintzberg H. (1983), *Structure in Five: Designing Effective Organizations*, Englewood Cliffs, NJ: Prentice Hall.

Modigliani F. (1958), "New Developments on the Oligopoly Front", *Journal of Political Economy*, vol. 66, June, pp. 215-232.

Moeller S.B., F.P. Schlingemann and R. Stulz (2004), "Firm Size and the Gains from Acquisitions", *Journal of Financial Economics,* vol. 73, n. 2, pp. 201-228.

Moeller S.B. and F.P. Schlingermann (2004), "Are Cross-border Acquisition Different from Domestic Acquisition? Evidence from Stock and Operating Performance of US Acquirers", working paper SSRN.

Moeller S.B., F.P. Schlingermann and R. Stulz (2005), "Wealth Destructive on Massive Scale? A Study of Acquiring-Firm Returns in the Recent Merger Wave", *Journal of Finance*, vol. 60, n. 2, pp. 757-782.

Monteverde K. and D.J. Teece (1982), "Supplier Switching Costs and Vertical Integration in the Automobile Industry", *Bell Journal of Economics*, vol. 13, pp. 206-213, reprinted in J. Birkinshaw (ed.) (2004),

Strategic Management, vol. 1, Cheltenham, UK and Northampton, MA: Edward Elgar Publishing.

Montgomery C.A. (1985), "Product-Market Diversification and Market Power", *Academy of Management Journal*, vol. 28, n. 4, pp. 789-798.

Moomaw R.L. (1974), "Vertical Integration and Monopoly: A Resolution of the Controversy", *Rivista Internazionale di Scienze Economiche e Commerciali*, Milano, vol. 47, n. 1, pp. 267-293.

Mueller, D.C. (1997), "Merger Policy in the United States: a Reconsideration", *Review of Industrial Organization*, vol. 12, pp. 655–685.

Muller D.C. (1997), "The finance literature in mergers: a critical survey". In *Competition, Monopoly, and Corporate Governance* (2003) Cheltenham: Edward Edgar, new edition.

Nelson R. (1994), "Why Firms Do Differ and How Does it Matter?" In Rumelt P., D. Schendel and D.J. Teece (eds), *Fundamental Issues in Strategy*, Boston, MA: Harvard University Press.

Nelson R. (1995), "Recent Evolutionary Theorizing About Economic Change", *Journal of Economic Literature*, vol. 33, n. 1, pp. 87-112.

Nelson R. and S. Winter (1982), *An Evolutionary Theory of Economic Change*, Cambridge, MA: Harvard University Press.

Nerlove M. and K.J. Arrow (1962), "Optimal Advertising Policy under Dynamic Conditions", *Economica*, May, pp. 129-142.

Nguyen H.T. and M. Kleiner (2003), "The Effective Management of Mergers", *Leadership & Organization Development Journal*, vol. 24, n. 8, pp. 447-454.

Nguyen H.T., M. Kleiner and Q. Sun (2012), "Motives for Mergers and Acquisitions: Ex-Post Market Evidence from the US", *Journal of Business Finance & Accounting*, vol. 39, n. 9-10, pp. 1357-1375.

Norman G. (1979), "Economies of Scale in the Cement Industry", *The Journal of Industrial Economics*, June, pp. 317-337.

Norman, R. (1977), *Management for Growth*, New York: J. Wiley & Sons.

Ollinger M. (1994), "The Limits of Growth of the Multidivisional Firm: A Case Study of the U.S. Oil Industry from 1930-90", *Strategic Management Journal*, vol. 15, pp. 503-520.

Pablo A.L. (1994), "Determinants of Acquisition Integration Level: a Decision Making Perspective", *Academy of Management Journal*, vol. 37, n. 4, pp. 803-836.

Pammolli F. (1996), *Innovazione, Concorrenza e Strategie di Sviluppo nell'Industria Farmaceutica*, Milano: Guerrini Scientifica.

Panzar J. and R. Willig (1979), "Economies of Scope", *American Economic Review*, Conference supplement.

Papadakis V. (2007), "Growth Mergers and Acquisition: How it Won't Be a Loser Game", *Business Strategy Series*, vol. 8, pp. 43-50.

Paulter P.A. (2003), *The Effects of Mergers and Post Merger Integration: A Review of Business Consulting Literature*, Washington, DC: Federal Trade Commission.

Penrose, E.T. (1959), *The Theory of the Growth of the Firm*, Oxford: Oxford University Press.

Perry M.K. (1980), "Forward Integration by Alcoa: 1888–1930", *Journal of Industrial Economics*, n. 29, pp. 37-53.

Peteraf M.A. (1993), "The Cornerstones of Competitive Advantages: A Resource Based View", *Strategic Management Journal*, vol. 14, pp. 179–191.

Peters T. and R. Waterman (1982), *In Search of Excellence*, New York: Harper & Row.

Petitt B.S. and K.R. Ferris (2013), *Valuation for Mergers and Acquisitions*, Upper Saddle River, NJ.: FT Pearson Education.

Pisano G.P., W. Shan and T. Teece (1988), "Joint ventures and collaboration in the biotechnology industry". In D.C. Mowery (ed.), *International Collaborative Ventures in US Manufacturing*, Cambridge, MA: Ballinger.

Pisano G.P. (1994), "Knowledge, Integration and the Locus of Learning: an Empirical Analysis of Process Development", *Strategic Management Journal*, Winter, Special Issue, vol. 15, pp. 85-100.

Porter M.E. (1980), *Competitive Strategy*, New York: Free Press.

Porter M.E. (1985), *Competitive Advantage*, New York: Free Press.

Porter M.E. (1987), "From Competitive Advantage to Corporate Strategy", *Harvard Business Review*, vol. 65, n. 3, pp. 43-59.

Prahalad C.K. and Y.L. Doz (1986), *The Multinational Mission: Balancing Local Demands and Global Vision*, New York: The Free Press.

Prahalad C.K. and Y.L. Doz (1998), "Evaluating interdependences across businesses". In A. Campbell and K. Somers Luchs (eds), *Strategic Synergy*, London: International Thomson Business Press.

Pratten C.F. (1971), *Economies of Scale in the Manufacturing Industry*, Cambridge: Cambridge University Press.

Prichett P., D. Robinson and R. Clarkson (2007), *After the Acquisition: the Authoritative Guide for Integration Success*, London: McGraw Hill.

Rajan R., H. Servaes and L. Zingales (2000), "The Cost of Diversity: the Diversification Discount and Inefficient Investment", *Journal of Finance*, vol. 55, pp. 35-80.

Rappaport A. (1986), *Creating Shareholder Value. The New Standard for Business Performance*, New York: The Free Press.

Ravenscraft D.J. and F.M. Scherer (1987), *Mergers, Sell-offs and Economic Efficiency*, Washington, DC: Brookings Institute.

Reed-Lajoux A. and J.F. Weston (1999), *The Art of M&A. Financing and Refinancing, Sources and Instruments for Growth*, NY: McGraw-Hill.

Rehm W. and C.B. Silverstsen (2010) "A Strong Foundation for M&A in 2010", *McKinsey on Finance*, n. 34, Winter.

Risberg A. and O. Meglio (2010), "Merger and acquisition outcomes– is it meaningful to talk about high failure rates?" In Y. Weber (ed.), *Handbook of Research on Merger and Acquisition*, Cheltenham, UK and Northampton, MA, USA: Edward Elgar.

Rispoli, M. (1998), *Sviluppo dell'Impresa e Analisi Strategica*, Bologna: Il Mulino.

Roberts E.B. (1999), *Managerial Application of System Dynamics*, Portland, Oregon: Productivity Press.

Roll R. (1986), "The Hubris Hypothesis of Corporate Takeover", *The Journal of Business*, vol. 59, n. 2, pp. 197-216.

Ross S.A., R.W. Westerfield and J. Jaffe (1999), *Corporate Finance*, Boston: McGraw-Hill.

Rumelt R.P. (1974), *Strategy, Structure and Economic Performance*, Boston, MA: Harvard Business School Press.

Rumelt, R.P. (1982), "Diversification, Strategy and Profitability", *Strategic Management Journal*, n. 3, pp. 359-369.

Ryden B. and J.O. Edberg (1980), "Large mergers in Sweden, 1962–1976". In D.C. Mueller (ed.), *The Determinants and Effects of Mergers: An International Comparison*, Oelgeschlager, Cambridge, MA: Gunn & Hain, pp. 193-226.

Saloner, G., A. Shepard and J. Podolny (2001), *Strategic Management*, New York: John Wiley.

Scherer R.M. and D. Ross (1980), *Industrial Market Structure and Economic Performance*, Boston: Houghton and Mifflin.

Scherer R.M., A. Beckenstein, E. Kaufer and R.D. Murphy (1975), *The Economics of Multi-Plant Operation: An International Comparisons Study*, Cambridge, MA: Harvard University Press.

Schnitzer M. (1996), "Hostile versus Friendly Takeovers", *Economica*, vol. 63, n. 249, pp. 37-55.

Schweiger D.M. and P. Very (2003), "Creating Value through Merger and Acquisition Integration", *Advances in Mergers and Acquisitions*, vol. 2, pp. 1-26,

Schweiger D.M., E. Csiszar and N.K. Napier (1993), "Implementing International Mergers and Acquisitions", *Human Resource Planning*, vol. 16, pp. 53-70.

Seth A. (1990), "Value Creation in Acquisition: a Re-examination of Performance Issues", *Strategic Mangement Journal*, vol. 11, n. 2, pp. 99-115.

Seth A., K.P. Song and R.R. Pettit (2000), "Synergy, Materialism or Hubris? An Empirical Examination of Motives for Foreing Acquisitions of US Firms", *Journal of International Business Studies*, vol. 31, pp. 387-405.

Seth A., K.P. Song and R.R. Pettit, (2002), "Value Creation and Destruction in Cross-border Acquisition: an Empirical Analysis of Foreign Acquisitions of U.S. Firms", *Strategic Management Journal*, vol. 23, pp. 921-940.

Shanley M.T. and M.E. Correa (1992), "The agreement between top management teams and expectations for post acquisition performance", *Strategic Management Journal*, vol. 13, pp. 245-266.

Sharpe W.F. (1964), "Capital Asset Prices: A Theory of Market Equilibrium under Conditions of Risk", *Journal of Finance*, vol. 19, n. 3, pp. 425-442.

Shleifer A. and R.W. Vishny (1994), "Takeovers in the 1960s and 1980s. Evidence and implications". In R.P. Rumelt, D.E. Shendel and D.J. Teece (eds), *Fundamental Issues in Strategy*, Boston, MA: Harvard Business School Press.

Shrivastava P. (1986), "Postmerger Integration", *Journal of Business Strategy*, vol. 7, n. 1, pp. 65-76.

Simon, H. (1981), *The Sciences of the Artificial*, Cambridge, MA: The MIT Press.

Sirower M. (1997), *The Synergy Trap: How Companies Lose the Acquision Game*, New York: Free Press.

Sloan A.P. (1963), *My Years with General Motors*, New York: Doubleday and Co.

Spence A.M. (1981), "The Learning Curve and Competition", *Bell Journal of Economics*, vol. 12, n. 1, Spring, pp. 49-70.

Stellmann S., (2010), *The Impact of Cultural Differences on the Daimler Chrysler Merger*, Northumbria University, Newcastle upon Tyne, UK: Grin Verlag.

Stigler G.J. (1951), "The Division of Labour is Limited by the Extent of the Market", *Journal of Political Economy*, vol. 59, n. 3, June, pp. 185-193.

Sudarsanam P.S. (1995), *The Essence of M&A*, Englewood Cliffs: Prentice Hall.

Sudarsanam S. and A. Mahate (2006), "Are Friendly Acquisitions Too Bad for Shareholders and Managers? Long-term Value Creation and Top Management Turnover in Hostile and Friendly Acquiers", *British Journal of Management*, vol. 17, n. S1, pp. S7-S30.

Sudarsanam S. (2010), *Creating Value from Mergers and Acquisitions*, Edinburgh Gate: FT Pearson Education.

Sylos Labini P. (1964), *Oligopolio e Progresso Tecnico*, Torino: Einaudi.

Teece D.J. (1980), "Economies of Scope and the Scope of the Enterprise", *Journal of Economic Behaviour and Organization*, vol. 1, n. 3, pp. 223-247.

Teece D.J. (ed.) (1987), *The Competitive Challenge. Strategies for Industrial Innovation and Renewal*, Cambridge, MA: Ballinger.

Teece D.J. (2007), "Explicating Dynamic Capabilities: the Nature and Microfoundations of (Sustainable) Enterprise Performance", *Strategic Management Journal*, vol. 28, n. 13, pp. 1319-1350.

Teece D.J., G. Pisano and A. Shuen (1997), "Dynamic Capabilities and Strategic Management", *Strategic Management Journal*, vol. 18, n. 7, August, pp. 509-533.

Teerikangas S. and P. Very (2006), "The Culture Performance Relationship in M&A: from Yes/No", *British Journal of Management*, vol. 17, pp. 31-48.

Telser L. (1962), "Advertising and Cigarettes", *The Journal of Political Economy*, vol. 70, pp. 471-499.

Thompson A.A. and A.J. Strickland (1998), *Strategic Management Concepts and Cases*, Boston, MA: McGraw Hill.

Tosi H.L., S. Werner and J.P. Katz (2000), "Analysis of CEO Pay Studies", *Journal of Management*, vol. 26, pp. 301-339.

Utton, M.A. (1979), *Diversification and Competition*, Cambridge: Cambridge University Press.

Vaccà S. (1986), "L'Economia delle Relazioni tra Imprese: dall' Espansione Dimensionale allo Sviluppo per Reti Esterne", *Economia e Politica Industriale*, n. 51.

Vancil R.F. (1979), *Decentralizationj: Managerial Ambiguity by Design*. Homewood, IL: Dow Jones Irwin.

Vermeulen F. and H. Barkema (2001), "Learning through Acquisitions", *Academy of Management Journal*, vol. 44, n. 3, pp. 457-476.

Very P. (1999), "Ce Que Ne Disent Pas Les Chiffres", *L'expansion Management Review*, 93, pp. 70-74.

Vlasic B. and S. Bradley (2001), *Taken for a Ride: How Daimler-Benz Drove off with Chrysler*, New York: Harper Collins.

Walsh J.P. and J.W. Ellwood (1991), "Merger, Acquisitions and the Pruning of Managerial Deadwood", *Strategic Management Journal*, vol. 12, n. 3, pp. 201-217.

Weber R.A. and C.F. Camerer (2003), "Cultural Conflict and Merger Failure: An Experimental Approach", *Management Science*, vol. 49, n. 4, pp. 400-415.

Weber Y. (ed) (2010), *Handbook of Research on Mergers and Acquisitions*, Chelteham, UK and Northampton, MA, USA: Edward Elgar.

Weber Y., S.Y. Tarba, G.K. Stahl and Z. Bachar-Rozen, (2010), "Integration in International Merger and Acquisitions: Test of a New Paradigm". In Y. Weber (ed.), *Handbook of Research on Mergers and Acquisitions*, Chelteham, UK and Northampton, MA, USA: Edward Elgar.

Wernerfelt B. (1984), "A Resource-Based View of the Firm", *Strategic Management Journal*, vol. 5, n. 2, April–June, pp. 171-180.

Weston J.F. (1994), "Divestiture: mistakes or learning"? In P.A. Gaughan (ed.), *Reading in Merger and Acquisitions*, Oxford: Blackwell.

Weston J.F. and K.S. Chung and S.E. Hoang (1990), *Mergers, Restructuring and Corporate Control*, Englewood Cliffs: Prentice Hall.

Weston J.F., M.L. Mitchell and J.H. Mulherin (2004, 2014), *Takeovers, Restructuring and Corporate Governance*, Englewood Cliffs: Pearson-Prentice-Hall.

Williamson O.E. (1975), *Markets and Hierarchies: Analysis and Antitrust Implication*, New York: The Free Press.

Williamson O.E. (1981), "The Economics of Organization: the Transaction Cost Approach", *American Journal of Sociology*, vol. 87, n. 3, pp. 548-577.

Williamson O.E. (1986a), *The Economic Institutions of Capitalism: Firms, Markets, Relational Contracting*, New York: The Free Press.

Williamson O.E. (1986b), "Vertical integration and related variations on a transaction-cost theme". In J.E. Stiglitz and F. Mathewson (eds), *New Developments in the Analysis of Market Structure*, Proceedings of a conference held by the International Economic Association in Ottawa, Houndmills, Canada: MacMillan Press.

Winter S.G. (1987), "Knowledge and competence as strategic assets". In D.J. Teece (ed.), *The Competitive Challenge. Strategies for Industrial Innovation and Renewal*, Cambridge, MA: Bollinger.

Winter S.G. (2003), "Understanding Dynamic Capabilities", *Strategic Management Journal*, vol. 24, pp. 991-995.

Wolf T. (2007), *The DaimlerChrysler Merger- One Company, Two Cultures*, Northeastern University of Boston, Boston, MA: GRIN Verlag.

Wright P., M. Kroll, A. Lado and B. Van Ness (2002), "The Structure of Ownership and Corporate Acquisition Strategies", *Strategic Management Journal*, vol. 23, n. 1 pp. 41-53.

Young J.B. (1981), "A conclusive investigation into the causative elements of failure in acquisition margers". In S.J. Lee and R.D. Colman, *Handbook of Mergers, Acquisitions and Buyouts*, Englewood Cliffs: Prentice Hall.

Zaheer A., X. Castañer and D. Souder (2013), "Synergy Sources, Target Autonomy, and Integration in Acquisitions", *Journal of Management*, vol. 39, n. 3, pp. 604-632.

Zollo M. and S.G. Winter, (2002), "Deliberate Learning and the Evolution of Dynamic Capabilities", *Organization Science*, vol. 13, pp. 339-351.

Index